anglistik & englischunterricht
Twenty-First Century Fiction

Twenty-First Century Fiction

Verantwortlicher Herausgeber
für den thematischen Teil des Bandes:
Christoph Ribbat

UNIVERSITÄTSVERLAG WINTER
HEIDELBERG

Gabriele Linke · Erwin Otto
Gerd Stratmann · Merle Tönnies (Hg.)

anglistik & englischunterricht

Band 66

Twenty-First Century Fiction

Readings, Essays, Conversations

UNIVERSITÄTSVERLAG WINTER
HEIDELBERG

Bibliografische Information Der Deutschen Bibliothek
Die Deutsche Bibliothek verzeichnet diese Publikation
in der Deutschen Nationalbibliografie;
detaillierte bibliografische Daten sind im Internet
über *http://dnb.ddb.de* abrufbar.

Herausgeber:
Prof. Dr. Gabriele Linke
Dr. Erwin Otto · Prof. Dr. Gerd Stratmann
PD Dr. Merle Tönnies

ISBN 3-8253-5029-0
ISSN 0344-8266

Anschrift der Redaktion:
Ruhr-Universität Bochum, Englisches Seminar
Universitätsstraße 150, 44801 Bochum

Dieses Werk einschließlich aller seiner Teile ist urheberrechtlich geschützt.
Jede Verwertung außerhalb der engen Grenzen des Urheberrechtsgesetzes ist ohne Zustimmung
des Verlages unzulässig und strafbar. Das gilt insbesondere für Vervielfältigungen, Übersetzungen,
Mikroverfilmungen und die Einspeicherung und Verarbeitung in elektronischen Systemen.
© 2005. Universitätsverlag Winter GmbH Heidelberg
Imprimé en Allemagne · Printed in Germany
Gesamtherstellung: Memminger Medienzentrum AG, 87700 Memmingen
Gedruckt auf umweltfreundlichem, chlorfrei gebleichtem und alterungsbeständigem Papier
Den Verlag erreichen Sie im Internet unter: www.winter-verlag-hd.de

Contents

Christoph Ribbat:
The Windshield and the Rear-View Mirror.
An Introduction to Twenty-First Century Writers, Books,
and Readers 7

Fiona Mills:
Living 'in between'.
The Identification of Afro-Latino/a Literature 33

Merle Tönnies:
A New Self-Conscious Turn at the Turn of the Century?
Postmodernist Metafiction in Recent Works by 'Established' British Writers 57

Christoph Ribbat:
The Washcloth at the Bottom of the Pile.
A Conversation with Jonathan Franzen 83

Astrid Böger:
Making the Best of It.
New American Short Stories after 9/11 93

Nicole Schröder:
'Love Across a Distance'. Friendships and Family Relations in Twenty-First Century American Short Stories .. 109

Christoph Ribbat:
Reading Novels for the *Boston Globe*.
A Conversation with Gail Caldwell 129

Greta Olson:
Introducing Alice Sebold's *The Lovely Bones* 137

Claus-Ulrich Viol:
Golden Years or Dark Ages? Cultural Memories of the
1970s in Recent British Fiction 149

Ralph J. Poole:
"I am the worst thing since Elvis Presley". J T LeRoy,
Eminem, and the Art of Hate Speech 171

Christoph Ribbat:
  Nomadic with the Truth.
  Holocaust Representations in Michael Chabon, James
  McBride, and Jonathan Safran Foer 199

Contributors' Addresses 219

Christoph Ribbat, Bonn

The Windshield and the Rear-View Mirror.
An Introduction to Twenty-First Century Writers, Books, and Readers

> It is undeniable that the world has never seen so many zeros and ones, so many bits and bytes of information – but by the same token, it has never been so easy to ignore them altogether.
> Steven Johnson, *Interface Culture* (1997)[1]

"What is it that you need from these books?", the terrorist asks the hostage, who has just begged for a book, any book, to read in his tiny cell somewhere in Lebanon, where he is being held in complete isolation. "What can you learn from them?", the captor inquires. The hostage, a young American who teaches English in Beirut, ponders these questions for a while. Then he answers. "I can learn from them", he says, "how not to be me."[2]

The episode appears in Richard Powers's novel *Plowing the Dark* (2000), a most fitting starting point for a survey of twenty-first century fiction. It is fitting for several reasons. Most obviously, the novel could almost be read as a prophetic narrative of pre- and post-9/11 political, military, and cultural clashes between the US and Britain on the one hand and central factions of the Islamic world on the other. To the literary critic, though, or to any person interested in the future of fiction and the survival of the book, a peculiar subtext of Powers's novel is just as fascinating. Taken as a whole, *Plowing the Dark*, in all its richness and complexity, reads like an advertisement for the old-fashioned art of fiction, for the novel, paper-based storytelling, the book. In a narrative strand intertwined with the hostage story, Powers describes a collective of artists, scientists, and computer programmers, at work on developing a wholly new concept of Virtual Reality in a research lab in Washington State. And yet: what readers of *Plowing the Dark* might remember as the most powerful moments of the novel will not have anything to do with state-of-the-art computer technology. Much more memorable – and much more grippingly rendered – are the events described in those passages that conjure up the active, vibrant, chaotic imagination of the hostage and his almost desperate yearning for a book. For any book. Simply, as the young man says, "to hear someone else thinking."[3]

Powers's belief in the power of the novel, of literature as such, was extremely influential in shaping the idea for this collection of essays: a tentative overview of twenty-first century American and British fiction. *Plowing the Dark* has also influenced the approach taken by this introduction, which focuses less on literary history than on contemporary debates about transformations of the media and thus of the literary world itself. If this essay's subtitle somewhat awkwardly evades using the term 'literature', it does so for a reason. It might be a little early, this editor believes, to tie the novelists and short fiction writers discussed in this volume into a tight, solid narrative of literary history (as critic Alan Cheuse points out, the critical reception of *Moby-Dick* "ruined Melville's career as a contemporary writer"[4] – there's something dangerous about the quick response). Instead of attempting to invent neat categories and new or old -isms for contemporary fiction, this introduction asks questions related directly to the possible fate of books as objects in the hands of readers and writers.

In a programmatic essay, cultural historian Robert Darnton has argued for a closer affiliation of reader-response oriented literary criticism and the history of books. Darnton proclaims that greater attention should be paid by both historians and literary critics to the "physical organization" of texts.[5] Reflections of Darnton's perceptive comments certainly appear in these introductory remarks. Without being lured too much by a hardware-oriented approach that examines only paper and screens, attempts will be made here to sketch some of the more basic and more physical features of books, reading, and writing in the twenty-first century. Clearly, this approach is also informed to a great extent by the narrative strands of *Plowing the Dark*. Powers's novel, after all, feeds a booklover's paranoia like few other narratives: for every lonely reader immersed in a book, there is a whole collective of computer wizards shaping the future of Virtual Reality.

1. The Future of the Book

The observation that the future of the book seems precarious has become a pet phrase of cyberenthusiasts and bibliophiles alike. As Steven Johnson has noted, the dogmatic conflicts seem so entrenched that it might be much more useful to celebrate the coexistence of the virtual and the paper-based, the "commingling of traditional culture and its digital descendants".[6] Some of the more recent debates should be sketched here nevertheless.

As the "paperless society"[7] looms (at least for some), teaching literature and writing literary criticism have long become ambiguously pleasurable enterprises for low-tech humanists. The 'remembrance of things past', the cultural archive of Western civilization, Jerome McGann proclaims, will surely be taken over by modern information technology. "That event", he states, "is neither a possibility nor a likelihood; it is a certainty."[8] Even those notoriously unaffected by the rhetoric of such technology visionaries will not be able to deny that the visual and digital rivals of what now seems the old-fashioned medium of literature have changed the entire context of storytelling. Apparently, all things related to literature are shrinking: from the space reserved for literary reviews or essays on newspaper and magazine pages to the attention span especially of younger readers. In an essay on the relationship between words and images, Nancy Allen cites a film editor who comments on the current preference for fast cuts and narrative condensation with the phrase: "The war is over. The kids have won."[9]

Indeed: heavy usage of electronic media has changed the very process of reading. Our eyes move differently now when confronted with text.[10] As Armando Petrucci has observed, twenty-first century individuals are "accustomed to reading messages in movement". Reading on pages made of paper is no longer the first "instrument of acculturation". In contrast to the linear and progressive narratives of paper-based literature, Petrucci argues, television zapping and electronic messaging favors a "transverse, desultory, interrupted" reading style.[11] More than that: the very rhythms of our daily life run counter to the slow, meditative experience of reading. And yet: is this a recent development? We "tend to think and act in terms of energy translated into tense and often fevered motion", the literary critic John Livingston Lowes noted in a commencement address at Radcliffe College, a speech later published in a small pamphlet titled *Of Reading Books*. The year was 1929: Lowes had just excitedly travelled on a train going "fifty miles an hour" and tried to convince his audience to read in spite of the fact that "the human dynamo is fast becoming our ideal".[12]

This is one advantage fate has granted to twenty-first century literature: Lowes was giving a speech in a time when the reading of paper-based narrative was still sandwiched between two groups of enemies instead of just one. The first is familiar: almost eighty years ago, the fast-moving, image-dominated media of popular culture (magazines, talkies, records) were encroaching on literature's territory in similarly threatening ways as they do now. The second group of enemies, however, was a remnant of the eighteenth and nineteenth centuries and has long disappeared: it was formed by critics who argued that excessive reading was dangerous for your health.[13] In a speech given at the University of Dayton, Ohio, also in 1929, Theodore Wesley Koch warned that "over-indulgence" in reading was certainly a "menace to character building". Girls reading sentimental stories and boys consuming tales of adventure, Koch warned, were "running the risk of an unhealthy and warped growth".[14] While Koch's argument reflects early twenty-first century admonitions concerning teenage 'addiction' to computer games, Lowes's passionate advocacy of reading seems much more in tune with today's advocates of the book – Richard Powers among them. "[A]s we read", Lowes states, "our spirit is enriched and grows, and we *become* something".[15]

The speaker at Radcliffe's 1929 commencement ceremony was worried about his contemporaries' lack of reading time. In contrast, writers of the late twentieth and early twenty-first century claim to be facing the ultimate challenge: the possible extinction of the book from the media ecosystems of our planet. In a 2002 essay collection ironically subtitled *Job Opportunities in Contemporary Poetry*, Thomas M. Disch envisions two imminent developments: first the extinction of the library, then the decay of literature as a lively, contemporary expression. With the perfection of computer-based reading technology, the printed book, according to Dish, will eventually share the same fate as the 78-rpm-record. Most books, he predicts, "will become landfill on the shores of an ocean of free-flowing data".[16] Literature then might be transformed into a "curatorial venue".[17] Like ballet, classical music, and sculpture, Disch argues, serious and complex literature would be kept alive merely as a cultural expression of the past and lose its vitality as a contemporary idiom. Alan Cheuse strikes a similar note as he muses about the future of reading. In his analysis, the past enemy of literature – television – will be replaced by the very medium Powers's collective is working on in the rainy Washington of *Plowing the Dark*: Virtual Reality. As VR will become "the distraction of choice" for school kids, Cheuse fears that "reading will be denoted even further down the line [...], somewhere between violin lessons and learning a foreign language". The fact that Cheuse's essays and reviews frequently emphasize the democratic and populist vibrancy of literary works adds further urgency to his warning that reading might become an activity only pursued by the "few and elite".[18]

The worries expressed by these early twenty-first century critics are not particularly new. As early as 1984, the US Library of Congress undertook a research project titled *Books in Our Future*, investigating the perspectives of paper-based literature in an era threatened by "the twin menaces of illiteracy and alliteracy" (i.e. the unwillingness, rather than the inability, to read). The project asked two central questions: "What is the future of the traditional book in the electronic age?" and: "How are the new technologies and other influences affecting books, reading, and learning [...]?"[19] In response, some of the expert contributors expressed their optimism and identified themselves as firm believers in the power of the book as a bound volume. Daniel J. Boorstin, the Librarian of Congress, enthusiastically observed that contemporary Americans were able to "reap the harvest of a half-millennium of the printed word". He called for an "American renaissance of the culture of the book".[20] Almost all scholars involved recognized, however, that the world of book lovers was about to change fundamentally in the last decades of the twentieth century. Some simply did not believe in the book's future. Few, though, were as outspoken about the issue as F. Wilfrid Lancaster, whose bold announcements should be looked at in detail:

> As far as I have been able to tell [...], rejection of electronic publishing is more often than not based on the rather vague feeling that the printed book is an indispensable element in our society and that it has been with us too long to be easily displaced.
>
> This argument, of course, is complete nonsense. The printed book has lasted for only 500 years, which is a mere dot in the history of human communication, and many of its most common manifestations – the novel and the science journal, for example – have been around for a much shorter time. Some reasons given me for the preservation of the book have been nothing less than amazing. For example, "I like to read on the beach." How long have people been reading on beaches? I would suspect less than a hundred years. Or, "I like to read in the bathroom." How long have we had bathrooms [...]?[21]

Today, twenty years later, Lancaster's comments seem somewhat short-sighted. People are still reading printed books. Many of them read on beaches. Many – though this is less easily verifiable – in bathrooms. While the territory of paper-based storytelling, of serious literature, is perceived as shrinking in ever so many ways, it is especially the contemporary novel that appears to be prospering in spite of its plug-and-play rivals. One of the most prevalent fears – that literature might soon only cater to a small, elite group of readers – proves especially unfounded. A good number of twenty-first century novels elegantly accomplished the difficult feat of pleasing both reviewers, academic readers and the reading public, both the elite and the mass audience, thus demonstrating powerfully the continuing function of the novel as a truly democratic genre.[22] Alice Sebold's *The Lovely Bones* (2002), Jonathan Franzen's *The Corrections* (2001), Jeffrey Eugenides's *Middlesex* (2002), and Jhumpa Lahiri's *The Namesake* (2003) are examples from the American context. In British fiction, Ian McEwan's *Atonement* (2001) and Zadie Smith's *White Teeth* (2000) and *The Autograph Man* (2002) located themselves in a comfortable position at once outside and inside the cultural mainstream. From Tasmania, a literary territory not too frequently mapped, Richard Flanagan's *Gould's Book of Fish. A Novel in Twelve Fish* (2003) testified powerfully to the continuing relevance of the playful, though reader-friendly postmodernist fictional deconstruction of the colonial discourse (and, of course, to the relevance of fish).

The list could go on and on, of course – and it will go on as the contributors to this volume investigate works of contemporary fiction they find particularly fascinating and meaningful in the cultural and political context of our time. To talk about the early twenty-first century as an era of the 'renaissance of English-language fiction' might not be much more than an unformed idea of an overly excited reader better expressed in small talk than in an introduction to a volume of scholarly essays. Suffice it to say then that, again, the most radical predictions of the visionaries of a 'paperless' (and, thus, in many ways, 'novel-less') society right now seems wide off the mark. It is still entirely possible, to once more quote Theodore Wesley Koch, to run the risk of an "unhealthy and warped growth"[23] by reading too many exciting books.

2. Clutching a Page. The Technology of Representation

A certain enthusiasm for the new can be found in the following pages. Nevertheless, this volume does not claim that the literary scene changed profoundly when 31 December 1999 turned into 1 January 2000.[24] Nor do the critics whose work is collected here attempt to construct a literary generation of twenty-first century writers (an attempt made, for instance, by Zadie Smith in her recent introduction to a collection of contemporary short stories).[25] One aim this collection does hope to achieve, however, is to trace the continuing power of literature on the contemporary cultural scene, in spite of the fact that novels and short stories are sometimes treated as the old-fashioned, paper-based, poor relations of raspberry-colored laptops and search engines retrieving 44,600 results in 0.44 seconds.[26] By exploring twenty-first century novels and short stories in close readings, by discussing their themes, ideas, and strategies as well as their negotiations with history, popular culture, and identity politics, this collection hopes to sketch a usable map of contemporary fiction from Britain and the US, however tentative and in many ways limited it might be.

One of the most conspicuous limitations of this volume is the absence of critical discussions of hypertext fiction. It was not much more than a notion that informed this decision. After a period of great enthusiasm, digital narrative seems to have lost some of its edge – at least to the uninitiated observer. In *Design and Debris*, his study of contemporary

American fiction, Joseph M. Conte makes the claim that the pioneers of hypertext have "yet to match for sheer fictive power and inventive genius" the most innovative figures in paper-based postmodernism. While Don DeLillo is frequently referred to as a key figure in twenty-first century debates on media and narrative, Conte cites the fact that the author of novels such as *White Noise* and *Underworld* feels unable to compose fiction without hearing the "clack" of a typewriter's keys hitting paper.[27]

In the absence of breathtaking cyberliterature it is the search engine google.com – and certainly not some paper-based masterpiece by a postpostmodern Tolstoy, Balzac or Eliot – which to believers in an online future reflects the contemporary moment best. Authorless, anonymous google, after all, is what the novel used to be to readers three centuries ago: we use it to find things out, we depend on it to make sense of the world, we're not quite sure where the facts end and fiction begins.[28] This form of technoenthusiasm, however, sours quickly once we remind ourselves that behind google's conceit of anonymity, people work, think, and make decisions that control the accessibility of 'real' people's voices (the manipulative novelist, in contrast, merely tampers with the expressions of fictional protagonists). Search engines do not save us from the limiting organization procedures of conventional narrative: they simply introduce new forms of such procedures. The same is true for digital fiction. As Rasmus Blok points out, the reader of a digital novel will find him- or herself in a much tighter "grasp" than the reader of a conventional work of fiction. Digital literature might seem digressive and might seem all about making choices. As Blok argues, however, "choices are often tied to previously made choices, and the earlier read passages can seldom be read again".[29]

Perhaps because of a certain *ennui* with online euphoria, this collection is more interested in the printed page than in the virtual web. Contributors have gone offline to scrutinize the works explored in this collection. The volume intends to supply a forum to what some might call literary works in a 'traditional' media format. Again, it is helpful to turn to Richard Powers in this matter. In an essay on the technology of representation, Powers has made a case for the book not in spite of its technological "disadvantages," but because of them:

> But the beauty of a book lies in its ability to unmake us, to interrupt our imaginary continuities and put us head to head with a maker who is not us. Story is a denuding, laying the reader bare, and the force of that denuding lies not in our entering into a perfect representation, but in our coming back out. It lies in that moment, palpable even before we head into the final pages, when we come to remember how

finely narrated is the life outside this constructed frame, a story needing only some other mind's pale analogies to resensitize us to everything in it that we've grown habituated to.[30]

In their low-tech nature, then, the true power of books can be found. If we follow Powers, books allow the reader to feel the difference between immersion and outside life. They simply do this better than the digital media – which, for one thing, have no "final pages" for the reader to head into. In a similar vein, Sven Birkerts has talked about the novel as "a kind of slow-motion replay of materials that we have not been able to absorb properly".[31] Using metaphors of the automotive century (possibly because the same historical moment gave birth to the car and to the modernist novel), Birkerts calls the novel "a windshield through which to face what is in front of us" and also a "rear-view mirror that allows us to see where we have been".[32] It is not accidental that the essayist uses objects associated with security and everyday omnipresence to metaphorically describe literature. A much more far-reaching cultural observation can me made here: as we spend more and more time staring at screens, the book as a physical entity seems to matter more and more. The ending of Toni Morrison's 1992 novel *Jazz* sets the tone: "Look where your hands are. Now", a voice calls out on the last page.[33] It is, in fact, the voice of the book itself, reminding its readers, as the narrative closes, of the actual reading process (and, in a novel focusing on intimacy and estrangement, of the intimate relationship between the reader and the object he or she holds).

This emphasis on bodily intimacy might reflect a development in what could be called the physical history of reading. Based on his observations at American universities, Armando Petrucci makes the point that the rules of reading behavior have changed radically for young readers, and that the major transformation of the reading process concerns the body. Petrucci describes the new "*modus legendi*" in detail as he watches young people read:

> First of all, the body takes totally free positions determined by individual preferences: a reader can stretch out on the floor, lean against a wall, sit under (yes, under) a reading room table, sit with his or her feet up on a table […] and so on. Second, the 'new readers' either almost totally reject the normal supports for the operation of reading – the table, the reading stand, the desk – or else they use them in inappropriate (that is, unintended) ways. Rather than as places to put an open book, such supports tend to be used as places to rest the reader's body, legs or arms in an infinite series of variations on physical positions for reading. Finally, the new *modus legendi* also includes a physical relationship with the book that is much more intense and

direct than in traditional modes of reading. The book is constantly manipulated, crumpled, bent, forced in various directions and carried on the body. One might say that readers make it their own by an intensive, prolonged and violent use more typical of a relationship of consumption than of reading and learning.[34]

There is something almost erotic in this description of loose, young American readers by a narrator playing the role of an Old World intellectual. Petrucci almost inadvertently uses the term "inappropriate" in his depiction. Clearly, it is his amazement at the bodily creativity of the students that has led him to note in detail the manifold ways in which these individuals interact with the printed page. Petrucci indeed interprets the new bodily intimacy between readers and books as something damaging not only to books as objects but to the very culture of learnedness. The fundamentally important process of rereading, he states, will be made impossible by such forms of consumption. According to Petrucci, the idea of the book as a "text to be meditated on, learned, respected and remembered",[35] will disappear if contemporary readers continue to destroy their books as they force their bodies on them.

It might be possible to find another, to bibliophiles more hope-inspiring way of making sense of this new culture of reading. After all, the students described by Petrucci would not handle their laptops in quite the same fashion. (This, in fact, might be the safest prophecy to make in this essay on the future of reading and writing – laptops will always be much too expensive for cuddling). Nor would too many websites – found, briefly looked at, and left – motivate readers to come as close and to move as languorously as the printed page would (pornography might be seen as an exception). Petrucci's readers turn books into parts of themselves. One side effect of the way they crumple and bend them is that these books become more human. Precisely because it will soon show wear and tear, the printed page resembles the skin of men and women so much more than the sleek plastic surfaces of IT equipment can. Geoffrey Nunberg has diagnosed both bibliophiles and technology enthusiasts as fetishists so in love with objects (whether made of plastic or leather-bound) that they cannot believe in the coexistence of the computer and the book – a doctrine of media supersession that has its basis in Marshall McLuhan's work and frames its idea in a form of millennial postmodernism.[36] Instead of fetishizing the book, though, the young readers Petrucci describes simply and comfortably seem to make love to it. Hence, their reading positions could be expressions of a new pragmatism of contemporary media users: the less physical the experience of gathering information online, the more physical the relationship to the old, trusted book. Here, a model could be found for the peaceful coexistence of screen and print in our everyday lives.[37]

A good ten years after the publication of Toni Morrison's *Jazz*, American author Jhumpa Lahiri designs her first novel *The Namesake* to symbolically link the power of literature to the book as a physical object. And it is precisely the mangled book that is immensely charged in her narrative. In her 2003 debut (following her Pulitzer Prize-winning story collection *Interpreter of Maladies*), the life of a young man in 1960s India is saved because he, a survivor of a train wreck, calls attention to himself with a torn Gogol story collection. ("He was still clutching a single page of 'The Overcoat'", Lahiri writes, "crumpled tightly in his fist, and when he raised his hand the wad of paper dropped from his fingers. 'Wait!' he heard a voice cry out. 'The fellow by that book. I saw him move.'"[38]) Decades later, the man's adult son starts reading an edition of these stories in a Boston suburb: for him, too, the very act of touching the book provides an option for coming back to life.[39] Twice, then, in key moments of the narrative, the book as a physical object has the power to save lives, once truly, once figuratively. The episodes relate to a notion often expressed in contemporary discourses on reading. While electronic writing, as Carol Maso argues, will make readers understand the "instability" of texts and worlds, print writing will remind them of their "love for the physical, for the sensual world".[40]

Some critics, of course, are less in love with the printed page than others. In light of the fact that praising the book and praying for its survival has become one of the most frequent rituals performed by Western intellectuals, James J. O'Donnell reminds readers to keep in mind "the oddity of textuality" and the strangeness of institutions like libraries, publishing houses, universities, and schools. "Is it not strange?", O'Donnell asks, "that we take the spoken word, the most insubstantial of human creations, and try through textuality to freeze it forever?" To him, books are merely "secondary bearers of culture".[41] The transformations of civilization, he observes, are not dependent on these objects. Similarly, Janet H. Murray has argued against clear-cut boundaries between the high-tech media of the late twentieth century and the old-fashioned, paper-based narrative medium. In *Hamlet on the Holodeck* (the title refers to the *Star Trek* television series), Murray, a former software developer, assures her readers that the computer is not the book's natural foe. The computer, she points out, "is the child of print culture, a result of the five centuries of organized, collective inquiry and invention that the printing press made possible".[42] Murray envisions cybernarratives as kaleidoscopic forms of story-telling, helping individuals in a globalized, computerized era "to sort things out". "We fear the computer", the literary critic states, "as a distorting fun house mirror of the human brain." Murray envisions an age, however, in which the computer, with a little help from the "narrative imagination", might turn into "a cathedral in which to celebrate human consciousness as a function of our neurology". She envisions a "James Joyce of the electronic age", a "Dickens [...] of chatterbots", and, finally, a "cyberbard".[43]

Again: in the early years of the twenty-first century, such figures apparently have not arrived yet. If James Joyce, as Steven Johnson put it, "wrote software for hardware originally conjured up by Gutenberg",[44] no-one has yet followed in his footsteps to greet the era of new machines with a state-of-the-art masterpiece. At least one attempt has been made to imagine such a cutting-edge author: Joseph M. Conte imagines a digitally raised writer making full use of the capabilities of the multimedia text, who would thus accomplish the difficult feat of making hypertext fiction "both compelling and natural". Only such a "masterly" author, Conte emphasizes, would make the transition from the age of print to the age of electronic texts complete (and, one might add, would theoretically turn 'print order' novelists such as Powers and Pynchon into anachronistic figures in spite of their cutting-edge negotiations with information flow and postmodern communication).[45]

Instead of Conte's imagined computer lit wunderkind, however, the creatures of J.R.R. Tolkien's and J.K. Rowling's imagination have captured our attention recently, turned into global superstars by twenty-first century multimedia marketing machinery that appropriates literature if it seems worth appropriating (and of course only then). This extreme and almost unprecedented global visibility of literary products might also be taken as an indication for the renaissance of the book. After all, the written word is still what is behind these pop culture phenomena. The text is their reason for being, the book precedes all visual and digital versions, and these versions might actually, possibly, turn consumers and users into readers. Extreme optimists could thus be led to believe that children and teenagers, usually the first to be thought about in apocalyptic terms as individuals growing up without books or reading skills, are absolutely ready for the slow, anachronistic task of reading if only the right book comes along. The book, enthusiasts might say, might make a comeback as the true PlayStation of the twenty-first century – as long as authors manage to connect to popular culture instead of analyzing it too closely, as long as they please their readers instead of challenging them too much.

3. A Shrinking Community. Writers and Readers

What to do, though, with 'difficult' books – those novels and short stories which cannot be digested by the gigantic stomach of the visual media? Ten years ago, American critic Sven Birkerts published his starkly pessimistic *Gutenberg Elegies* and seemed to know exactly what was going to happen to complex literature. As "electronic communications assert dominance", Birkerts assumed that both the printed book and the activities of writing and reading would be altered forever.[46] From his perspective, the Internet indeed ranks as the natural enemy of serious fiction, quite simply because being "on-line", he argued, "and having the subjective experience of depth, of existential coherence, are mutually exclusive situations".[47] According to the essayist, "the old act of slowly reading a serious book" would thus turn into an "elegiac exercise".[48] Peter Dimock, a former book editor at Random House, has depicted literature in similar terms as an endangered species, urging his contemporaries to teach and understand reading as a "meditative tradition"[49] which, unless protected by institutions, will not be able to "compete" with the "permanent, discontinuous, wired attention" produced by contemporary media.[50]

More recently, American novelist Jonathan Franzen has added a slightly more optimistic twist to literature's situation in an age when 'difficult' all too quickly is taken to mean 'unreadable'. In a 2002 essay on the notoriously difficult William Gaddis, Franzen invents two categories for literary fiction: 'status' books and 'contract' books. The status model, as Franzen outlines "invites a discourse of genius and art-historical importance". The people who "manage to write them", Franzen semi-ironically states, "deserve extraordinary credit, and if the average reader rejects the work it's because the average reader is a philistine". In contrast to that, the "contract model" defines the novel as a "compact between the writer and the reader". Franzen explains:

> Writing [...] entails a balancing of self-expression and communication within a group, whether the group consists of *Finnegan's Wake* enthusiasts or fans of Barbara Cartland. Every writer is first a member of a community of readers, and the deepest purpose of reading and writing fiction is to sustain a sense of connectedness, to resist existential loneliness; and so a novel deserves a reader's attention only as long as the author sustains the reader's trust. This is the Contract model. The discourse here is one of pleasure and connection. My mother would have liked it.[51]

It is important to note that Franzen does not make a clear-cut distinction here between 'high' and 'low', the 'elite' and the 'popular'. Rather, the novelist speaks about reading habits – and about the ambivalence of all kinds of literature, both the simple and gripping and the challenging and complex. Early on in his essay, Franzen calls himself a "Contract kind of person".[52] The purpose of his essay, however, is, again, to praise the highly sophisticated and not at all crowd-pleasing work of American novelist William Gaddis. Even the "Contract model", Franzen states, "sometimes calls for work". A story like Gaddis's *The Recognitions*, "where the difficulty is the difficulty of life itself", is, according to Franzen, "what a novel is for".[53] The difference to "Status", though, is the interest in connection: in the literary community that consists of writers *and* readers. Here, Franzen's ideas are similar to Birkerts's when the author of *The Gutenberg Elegies* is at his most optimistic. At one point in his book, Birkerts outlines a possible "resurgence" of the arts, especially of literature. Then, he imagines, the book would be seen "as a haven, as a way of going [...] into a space sanctified by subjectivity".[54]

As writers perceive the literary world as shrinking, challenged territory, their firm belief in subjectivity frequently gives way to an emphasis on the connections between writers and readers. In the case of Franzen and Birkerts, these perceptions are informed by somewhat melancholy notions of the author's loss of voice and stature in the contemporary marketplace. In Zadie Smith's case, the liaison of readers and writers is treated with considerably more optimism. In her introduction to the anthology *The Best American Nonrequired Reading 2003*, the young British author emphasizes issues of craft to sketch both the writer's utter dependency on knowing how reading works and the necessary move away from that knowledge:

> When I write, the kind of exactitude that most concerns me is a bit tricky to explain. I'll try, quickly. So you know the rhythm and speed of reading. Okay, keep that in mind. Now remember the rhythm and speed of writing – the jaggedy, retentive, tortured, unnatural lack of flow. Okay. Now to me, the mystery of that exactitude lies in finding the perfect fit between *what you know it is to write* and *what you know it is to read*. If you are writing, and have forgotten the rhythm and speed and, actually, the texture, of what it is to read, you're in trouble. But *at the same time*, to keep the idea of reading in mind too strongly while you're writing is to grow fearful at the keyboard, dreading all that you might write that would be complex, awkward, resistant (to the ear, to the brain), intimate, and seemingly unshareable.[55]

Authors of Smith's age and generation seem to engage in much less troubled relationships with popular culture and its audiences than their predecessors (note Smith's conversational tone). Nevertheless, the passage quoted here shows how the ambiguity of both playing to the audience and retaining one's own complexity obviously remains central to the writing process – in spite or because of Smith's global celebrity status, in spite or because of her youth and her audaciousness. There is something almost old-fashioned about Smith's discussion of craft and the ambiguities of the creative process. What might be new to the literary world of the twenty-first century, however, is the extent to which such notions are shared.

Almost twenty years ago, Dan Lacy, an expert contributing to the aforementioned study by the Library of Congress, blamed the shrinking significance of serious literature in some part on the authors and artists themselves. Many of "the most expressive creators of our time", Lacy argued with reference to, among others, Thomas Pynchon, "to some degree fail in broad communication with a large and comprehending audience".[56] It would be difficult to make the same observation today. As fewer and fewer readers can be counted on (and as twentieth-century avant-garde concepts are increasingly being called into question), writers seem to become more and more interested in reaching out to their audience. And their audience reaches out to them. Even more than they used to, many readers probably think of themselves as aspiring writers and will be all too willing to hear about the secrets of the trade from those who have 'made it'. This might create problems of its own (and stacks of unsolicited manuscripts piling up in the mail rooms of publishing houses and literary agents' offices), yet it might also help form a more intimate literary community engaged in more complex debates on craft, aesthetics, themes. This community, one might imagine, might also be more open to the cultural discourses surrounding it than the larger, more established and more hierarchically organized literary world that dominated much of the second half of the twentieth century. If books, as Jay David Bolter states, will "lose their status as a defining symbolic communication",[57] it might be precisely their marginality that will enable the readers and writers of literature to engage in meaningful discourses on this strange, yet extremely significant craft.

4. The Contexts of Fiction

Sven Birkerts describes the space of literature's survival as an isolated area that resembles a wildlife reservation removed from the predatory culture surrounding it. In contrast, most essays collected in this volume investigate the contexts of contemporary fiction, its cultural and social functions, and the workings of literature's communities. Also, some of the authors collected here pay precise attention to the literary marketplace. No close readings of 'airport novels' (a genre Edith Wharton, in a different era of mass transportation, called "railway novels")[58] can be found in this volume. However, a significant portion of this issue is devoted to the complex relationship between literature, its audiences, and its distribution systems. All great novels once were contemporary novels, critic Alan Cheuse reminds us. Some had mixed reviews, some were highly praised and all too soon forgotten. Novels, Cheuse succinctly states, "are made by generations of readers".[59] This collection, then, is an attempt to assemble the explorations of those belonging to a first generation of readers for a highly diverse group of works of long and short fiction. It is less the desire to discover a classic 'now!' that motivates this volume than a curiosity to find out about contemporary acts of reading, writing, and reviewing that shape our thinking about works of fiction.

Astrid Böger's essay on contemporary American short story collections is one characteristic example. Böger reads both the literary texts as such and the conventions and rituals that shape today's canons – and then connects her findings to the precise historical moment of the post 9/11 United States. Greta Olson's approach is similarly two-fold. Her contribution investigates Alice Sebold's novel *The Lovely Bones* (2002), exploring its cultural context as well as seemingly timeless issues of form (one connection Olson makes is between Sebold's novel and Lawrence Sterne's *Tristram Shandy*). Ralph Poole reads an extremely young American author – 'child prodigy' J T LeRoy – whose position between popular culture and literature seems somewhat uncertain (perhaps even more so than Sebold's). Poole turns that ambivalence into productive ambiguity and connects LeRoy with two ends of the cultural spectrum which, like all extremes, are much closer to each other than we think: the ancient art of rhetoric and the Hip Hop lyrics of Eminem. The politics and aesthetics of the present, as the studies by Böger, Olson, and Poole point out, are just as significant for our understanding of contemporary literature as literary history and the cultural traditions that inform reading and writing.

The interactions of history and popular culture play a similarly important role in the articles by Claus-Ulrich Viol and this editor. Their explorations investigate the representations of history – the 1970s and the Holocaust, respectively – in contemporary British and American novels. Both pieces stress how fictional reworkings of the past become relevant in political debates of the present. Also, they accentuate the significance of pop culture narratives to these literary working-throughs of the past. And a similar terrain – from daytime television to poststructuralist theory – is sketched in a writer's interview conducted specifically for this issue of *anglistik & englischunterricht*. Jonathan Franzen, author of the novels *The Twenty-Seventh City* (1988), *Strong Motion*

(1992), *The Corrections* (2001) and the essay collection *How To Be Alone* (2002), comments on his career as an ambivalent wandering between 'high' and popular culture. The conversation with Franzen spans cultural territory from Derridean and Lacanian theory to the intricacies of dealing with US-American talk show host Oprah Winfrey.

Literature's engagement with popular culture, however, should not divert our attention from the richness and diversity of the literary scene itself. The essays by Fiona Mills and Merle Tönnies represent two complimentary investigations of twenty-first century English-language fiction. Whereas Mills outlines the complex, rich relations between ethnicity, identity, and literary expression in the United States, Tönnies studies the first years of the twenty-first century as the beginning of another postmodernist decade for (white) British novelists. The articles could be taken as depictions of two different worlds: the one Mills describes has identity politics at its center, describing both its fluidity and its categorizations, the one depicted by Tönnies focuses on the self-reflexivity of literary expression. The most important issue, however, is the same in both pieces: the problematic positioning of the author. His or her cultural 'location', these studies argue, is just as determined by him- or herself as it is assigned by other voices in contemporary cultures, voices that are increasingly self-conscious both about ethnic identity and about artistic and aesthetic strategies. In spite of the myth of the lonely genius that informs so much thinking and writing about literature – and in spite of Jonathan Franzen's credo that reading and writing might teach us "how to be alone":[60] the literary scene is, obviously, organized in groups, tribes, cliques, families. Thus, the significance of friendship and family relationships, a theme Nicole Schröder sensitively maps in her close readings of contemporary short stories from the multicultural US, cannot be ignored, neither as a subject in the works themselves nor in our explorations of the literary landscape. Just as relevant in this context is this volume's documentation of a conversation with *Boston Globe* chief book critic Gail Caldwell. One thing the Pulitzer-Prize winning reviewer reveals is that no experience and no intellectual tradition was as important in introducing her to fiction as growing up, as she puts it, in a Texas family of "oddballs" – a biographical context and background that to Caldwell made reading fiction seem like both the easiest and the most pleasing thing to do.

5. Reading in Groups

"So long as there is a natural inclination toward independent selfhood", Sven Birkerts states, "so long will literature be able to prove the reports of its death exaggerated."[61] That may well be true. However, as much as writers and readers are interested in the concept of independent selfhood, and as much as it is the driving force behind storytelling, the main reason why people either tell or read stories are the ties that bind individuals together. The ethnography of reading teaches important lessons in this respect. Once we change our perspective, it turns out that the tropes of independence, selfhood, and being alone are less natural to the world of literature than we think. Sociologist Elizabeth Long, for instance, has challenged the "ideology of the solitary reader". Long has studied nineteenth-century paintings mostly showing men reading as intellectuals and women reading for pleasure. These conventional images of lonely booklovers, she argues, serve to hide what she calls the "infrastructure of literacy". Most importantly, Long states, the myth has made "invisible" the "groups of readers and their modes of textual appropriation".[62]

In her own ethnographic work of reading groups in the Houston area, Long has described the collectives, their decision-making processes, their hierarchies, and their attitudes toward literature and literary criticism. These circles are not utopian collectives: the groups "operate within a commonly recognized hierarchy of taste". Long does emphasize, however, that the mere cultural presence of a multitude of reading collectives in the United States challenges notions of "trickle down" cultural models. The vibrant culture of reading groups, Long notes, can show us that people are both: "products and producers of culture".[63] In addition, Long's analysis describes a world of women readers. As *Washington Post* columnist Jonathan Yardley puts it, the world of American literature is "a woman's world now".[64] How this changes the cultures of reading would have to be explored in much more detail – clearly, though, the myth of the solitary reader has been exposed as a fiction all too frequently instrumentalized by male writers and critics to reinforce existing gender hierarchies.

There is one reading group, however, in which the gendered and social encoding of reading usually remains invisible to outside observers. In families, books might play completely different roles than in the public arena. These might be roles that transcend gender categorizations. Since the ways families treat books is a subject area quite invisible to sociologists of reading, we depend on novelists to invent such 'case studies' for us. One such place to look is, again, Jhumpa Lahiri's first novel, the story of a man named Gogol who, after his father's death, starts reading the Russian author. His whole life, Gogol has looked at his name as a freakish aberration, a curious, strange manifestation of literariness in a world where books play marginal roles at best. At this turning point, though, the book as object matters. "In a few minutes he will go downstairs, join the party, his family", the last passage of the novel informs us. The recently divorced architect, a man in his mid-thirties, sits down on the bed of what used to be the room of his boyhood, opening a book of short stories he has not touched in decades. "[F]or now", the novel then ends, "his mother is distracted, laughing at a story a friend is telling her, unaware of her son's absence. For now, he starts to read."[65]

6. Epilogue. Thursdays in Tehran

To conclude this introduction, let us return briefly to Richard Powers's *Plowing the Dark*. The novel has been read here as an elaborate and sophisticated, yet altogether enthusiastic love song for the written word, especially for book-based literary fiction. With some ill will, though, another reading could be applied to the text – a reading one might label as Orientalist. The contrast between the bookish, freedom-loving Westerner and his simple-minded, brutal Arabic-speaking captors might seem overly clean-cut to some readers of the novel, especially since the early summer of 2004, when globally distributed photographs from Iraq made the Westerner as brutal captor just as much an icon of the world media. In spite of its high-tech sophistication, or perhaps even because of it, Powers's narrative could be taken as another simplistic dichotomy of the Westerns lands of reason and the Orient as an irrational, potentially threatening space that only comes alive if narrated by a Western voice.

Such a reading would not do justice to Richard Powers's novel. It suggests a perspective, though, that should not be missing from a contemporary discussion on the territory of Western literary fiction in our contemporary moment. The question raised here has not always been central to the debates on the canon, on multiculturalism, and on the relationship between ethnic identity and literary idioms: how are books being read around the world? We know much more now than we did three decades ago about the literary production of non-white, non-Western authors (though many will say we do not know enough). However: what are the ways in which people read – especially people outside of the territory that might be called the 'Amazon.com Belt' of this planet? The shrinking territory of literature in Western countries has by now become a much-lamented fact – chain bookstores, Internet chat rooms, and cable Television are the usual suspects blamed when novelists and critics discover that their audience gets smaller and smaller no matter how much genius they invest in their essays, stories, and books. What about countries, though, in which most individuals still spend most of their days offline and off-cable? What about political contexts which make it difficult for people to read, study, or talk about modernist and postmodernist literature in all its beauty, complexity, and provocative power? What happens to literature when the imaginary capabilities of twenty-first century readers have not been 'damaged' by 'reality' TV?

Ethnographers have described the interpretative practices of Koran readers in Indonesian villages and the interactions of literacy, orality, and rituals by indigenous farmers in highland Colombia.[66] While these studies present rich and detailed descriptions of the communities, institutions, social and cultural codes that inform reading and writing, readers more interested in the private, inner worlds of 'non-Western reading' might have to turn to a more personal and more literary work to imagine for them those moments in which the writing and reading of literature takes place precisely in that delicate balance between togetherness and being alone.

When Azar Nafisi published her memoir *Reading Lolita in Tehran* in 2003, she certainly did not intend to answer all of the questions posed here – if she intended to answer questions at all. Nevertheless, her work is extremely relevant in this context. The subject of Nafisi's account is relatively simple: the literature professor, after being expelled from the University of Tehran for refusing to wear the veil, taught secret literature classes to seven of her best woman students and chronicled these conversations on such forbidden key authors of the Western canon as Jane Austen, Henry James, F. Scott Fitzgerald, and Vladimir Nabokov. Here, to quote Powers again, works of fiction indeed helped both teacher and students to "hear someone else thinking". The women Nafisi's narrative describes overcome the isolation imposed on them in post-revolutionary Iran. They take off their veils when in their professor's apartment – a symbolic gesture that mirrors the mind-opening power of fiction. With reference to Nabokov's *Invitation to a Beheading*, the scholar argues that an "atmosphere of perpetual dread" pervaded the Islamic Republic. Thus, art and literature became "essential to our lives", she explains, a "necessity", not a "luxury".[67] Nafisi remains ambivalent, though. On the one hand, reading and discussing what they read represents not much more than just the "minutest opening" in a totalitarian society. On the other hand, she ascribes to it a lasting, liberating effect for the women in the course. "We felt when we were together", Nafisi writes, "that we were almost absolutely free." (28)

Nafisi's account encompasses much more than the clandestine Thursday classes and the biographies of her students (though these depictions do supply the narrative backbone). The "memoir in books" (Nafisi's subtitle) in many ways mirrors what Nafisi observes about Jane

Austen's *Pride and Prejudice*. "One of the most wonderful things" about this nineteenth-century novel, Nafisi states, "is the variety of voices it embodies". (268) Multivocality is also employed as the central narrative strategy of *Reading Lolita*. The memoir not only attempts to capture as many voices as possible. Also, as most of these voices talk about reading experiences, Nafisi's memoir creates a panorama of reader's responses: from the Islamic to Leftist revolutionaries and their simplistically political readings which always seem to take fiction at face value, she moves on to her own, professional, yet enthusiastic interpretive approaches, and to the highly personal ways in which her students tie their readings to their experiences in the Islamic Republic. Frequently, Nafisi comments on the democratic qualities of the novel. In fact, her book extends the democraticizing effect of narrative and constructs a democracy of readers as a hidden, almost imaginary network.

Perhaps as a consequence of this approach, some of the most deeply entrenched rituals of Western academic literary criticism are either ignored, subverted or ridiculed by Nafisi. "Everyone has gone postmodern", an Iranian Henry James scholar (and friend of the author) comments in the memoir. "They can't even read the text in the original – they're so dependent on some pseudo-philosopher to tell them what it says." (236) Nafisi consoles her friend, telling her "not to worry" and to read unfashionableness as "a sign that we must be doing something right". (*ibid.*) In a similar vein, Nafisi quotes an Islamic student who informs her that Jane Austen had to be ranked not only as "anti-Islamic" but also "a colonial writer". (289) A while later, Nafisi realizes the origin of this student's ideas: Edward Said's *Culture and Imperialism*. "It was ironic", Nafisi concludes tersely, "that the most reactionary elements in Iran had come to identify with and co-opt the work and theories of those considered revolutionary in the West." (290)

Reading Lolita in Tehran puts an optimistic twist on Sven Birkerts's pessimistic vision of literature's bleak future in our media age. If literature can survive in the face of a totalitarian regime, as it does in the world Nafisi describes, why should it not be able to deal with and easily challenge banal computer games and trivial chat rooms, mere rivals on the marketplace, however powerful, however attractive they might seem? Nafisi describes an approach to literature that is remarkably similar to the one proposed by Birkerts: The narrator and her protagonist create a secure space for books (and, as books are lacking, for photocopies). In turn, the novels they read create a secure, imaginary, albeit temporary space for these Iranian women. As in Birkerts' metaphoric phrase of the windshield and the rear-view mirror, books serve to reflect what lies behind them and to face what's in front. The specific images might be confusing, however: Nafisi constantly emphasizes that fiction to her is neither window nor mirror. In fact: to discount the imaginary and to read novels and stories as transparent representations of the moral and political is one of the central cultural strategies of the totalitarian regime. Nafisi and her group, in contrast, preserve the power of literature precisely by emphasizing its imaginary quality, its other-worldliness. They do so with an amount of force and energy that not only transforms their own lives but might also be able to raise the spirits of the melancholic book lovers of the West.

Contrary to Western expectations, this book-loving network of passionate, serious, dedicated interpreters of literature forms not in the absence of rivaling media, but in spite of their attractiveness. Satellite television – illegal, yet present in almost every household – connects the people of Tehran to the global flow of images. Nafisi quotes David Hasselhoff, star of *Baywatch*, bragging about the fact that his bikini epic was taken to be the most popular show with the Ayatollah's subjects (67). Are such things beneath the narrator – Professor Nafisi, the tireless fighter for literature's power and independence? Not necessarily. One day, the door bell rings: two members of the feared Revolutionary Committee enter her house. They are not there to raid the reading group, nor to confiscate books. Nevertheless, their visit's effect is so depressing that a period of "semi-mourning" ensues in the family. "They were there", Nafisi relates, "to take our satellite dish away." (67)

Notes

1 Johnson (1997: 237). The guest editor wishes to thank the editors of *anglistik & englischunterricht* for commissioning this volume. Many thanks to Gail Caldwell and Jonathan Franzen and, most importantly, to this volume's contributors for their original ideas and essays. Work on this volume was completed during a research year as a Humboldt Foundation / Feodor Lynen Fellow at Boston University and the Massachusetts Institute of Technology. The author wishes to thank the institutions and individuals involved, especially John-Paul Riquelme, William Uricchio, and the Lynen Program staff. Special thanks, however, are due to Greta Olson for her advice and her generous help at a crucial moment. Apologies go out to those readers who find US fiction grossly over-represented in this collection. The imbalance implies no value judgment. It only reflects this Americanist's shortsightedness.
2 Powers (2000b: 292). See also: Reinfandt (2002).
3 Powers (2000b: 292).
4 Cheuse (2001: 251).
5 Darnton (2001: 174-175).
6 Johnson (1997:8).
7 See Lancaster (1980).

8 McGann (2001: 18). For an early overview of projects and analyses in the context of hypermedia and literary studies see Delany and Landow (1991).
9 Allen (2002: 3). Allen also argues, however, that to see words and images as "opposing forces" lacks historical accuracy (39).
10 See also Johnson, who describes the transformation of his own writing by word-processing and cites as the main reason that word processors "eliminated the penalty that revisions normally exacted" (1987: 144).
11 Petrucci (1999: 362).
12 Lowes (1929: 4-5).
13 See, with regard to German literary history, Schön's explorations of late eighteenth-century discussions of *Lesesucht* (Schön 1987: 46-49).
14 Koch (1929: 12).
15 Lowes (1929: 33, his emphasis).
16 Disch (2002: 11).
17 *Ibid.*, 9.
18 Cheuse (2001: 28). Like Richard Powers's protagonist (though much less concisely), Cheuse supplies his reasons for writing, his apologia for the book: "To know another mind. To know another life. To feel oneself in the heart of another age, in the heart of another human being. [...] To move out of ourselves, lifted into another scene, another action, another destiny, so that we might gain a better sense of our own." (28).
19 Cole (1987: ix-x).
20 Boorstin (1987: 373-4).
21 Lancaster (1987: 215).
22 See Yehoshua (1999).
23 See endnote 3.
24 In spite of what logic dictates, this collection treats all novels and stories published after that latter date as twenty-first century fiction.
25 Smith introduces a collection of short stories by such American writers as David Foster Wallace, Jeffrey Eugenides, Aimee Bender, Dave Eggers, and Jonathan Safran Foer. "It seemed to me," Smith states, "that the writers were offering their readers an America quite different in spirit from the generation that preceded them. Set apart from the exuberant possibilities of Bellow's America, the masculine raging of Roth's, the lyricism of Morrison's. The America of these stories is more muted, the characters less hysterical in their trajectory, at odds with themselves, uncertain. Sad." (2003a: xv)
26 Results for the words 'Zadie Smith' on google.com.
27 Conte (2002: 198). The critic cites Michael Joyce, Stuart Moulthrop, and Jane Yellowlees Douglas as the "most promising pioneers" of a hypertext literary environment (*ibid.*, 198).
28 For an early analysis of the precarious relations of fact and fiction in the English novel see Davis (1996).
29 Blok (2002: 176-177).
30 Powers (2000a).
31 Birkerts (1996: 12).
32 *Ibid.*, 9.
33 Morrison (1992: 229).
34 Petrucci (1999: 364).

35 *Ibid.*, 365.
36 Nunberg (1996: 10).
37 Cf. Erich Schön's analysis of discourses around 1800 when reading was newly defined as a practice which made individuals 'lose' their bodies as they read. As the body of the reader was more and more seen as immobilised, studying texts was seen as an aphysical "reading dream" (*"Lektüretraum"*) (1987: 96).
38 Lahiri (2003: 18).
39 *Ibid.*, 291.
40 Maso (1996: 63).
41 O'Donnell (1996: 54).
42 Murray (1997: 8).
43 *Ibid.*, 281-284.
44 Johnson (1997: 3).
45 Conte (2002: 198-189).
46 Birkerts (1994: 6). In a 1996 piece for the *Review of Contemporary Fiction*, Birkerts, without altering the "original premise" of his work, adds a more enthusiastic note about the novel's future as the "ideal antidote for the timesickness" contemporary media users are "beginning to experience" (1996: 12).
47 Birkerts (1994: 219).
48 *Ibid.*, 6.
49 Dimock (2000b).
50 Dimock (2000a).
51 Franzen (2002b: 100).
52 *Ibid.*
53 *Ibid.*, 111.
54 Birkerts (1994: 197).
55 Smith (2003b: xxxiii, her emphasis).
56 Lacy (1987: 255).
57 Bolter makes the case that the book's loss of relevance in the physical and social sciences, in business and government, will turn print into a "secondary or special medium" associated with qualities such as "stability and authority", whereas the computer will represent "flexibility" and "interactivity" (1996: 254).
58 Wharton (1997: 58).
59 Cheuse (2001: 251).
60 See the title of Franzen's collection of non-fiction, a book concerned with, as the author states in his preface, "the problem of preserving individuality and complexity in a noisy and distracting mass culture: the question of how to be alone" (2002a: 6).
61 Birkerts (1994: 197).
62 Long (1993: 193).
63 *Ibid.*, 203-205.
64 Yardley (1990: 10).
65 Lahiri (2003: 291).
66 See Baker (1993) and Digges & Rappaport (1993), whose studies mainly focus on the everyday intersections of orality and literacy.

67 Nafisi (2003: 23). Further references to this edition will be included in the text.

Bibliography

Allen, Nancy: "Relationships between Words and Images. An Overview". – In N.A. (Ed.): *Working with Words and Images. New Steps in an Old Dance*, Westport, 2002, pp. 1-22.
Baker, James N.: "The Presence of the Name. Reading Scripture in an Indonesian Village". – In John Boyarin (Ed.): *The Ethnography of Reading*, Berkeley, 1993, pp. 98-138.
Birkerts, Sven: *The Gutenberg Elegies. The Fate of Reading in an Electronic Age*, Boston, 1994.
–: "Second Thoughts", *Review of Contemporary Fiction* 16, no.1, 1996, 9-12.
Blok, Rasmus: "A Sense of Closure. The State of Narration in Digital Literature". – In Hans Ballind & Anders Klinkby Madsen (Eds.): *From Homer to Hypertext. Studies in Narrative, Literature, and Media*, Odense, 2002, pp. 167-180.
Bolter, Jay David: "Ekphrasis, Virtual Reality, and the Future of Writing". – In Geoffrey Nunberg (Ed.): *The Future of the Book*, Berkeley, 1996, pp. 253-272.
Boorstin, Daniel J.: "Books in Our Future". – In John Y. Cole (Ed.): *Books in Our Future. Perspectives and Proposals*, Washington, 1987. pp. 359-374.
Boyarin, John (Ed.): *The Ethnography of Reading*, Berkeley, 1993.
Cheuse, Alan: *Listening to the Page. Adventures in Reading and Writing*, New York, 2001.
Cole, John Y.: *Books in our Future. Perspectives and Proposals*, Washington, 1987.
Conte, Joseph M. *Design and Debris. A Chaotics of Postmodern American Fiction*, Tuscaloosa, 2002.
Darnton, Robert: "First Steps toward a History of Reading". – In James L. Machor & Philip Goldstein (Eds.): *Reception Study. From Literary Theory to Cultural Studies*, New York, 2001, pp. 160-179.
Davis, Lennard J.: *Factual Fictions. The Origins of the English Novel*, Philadelphia, 1996.
Delany, Paul and George P. Landow: *Hypermedia and Literary Studies*, Cambridge, 1991.
Digges, Diana and Joanna Rappaport: "Literacy, Orality, and Ritual Practice in Highland Colombia." – In John Boyarin (Ed.): *The Ethnography of Reading*, Berkeley, 1993, pp. 139-155.
Dimock, Peter: "The Presence of Reading", *Context. A Forum for Literary Arts and Culture* 2, 2000a, http://www.centerforbookculture.org/context/no2/dimock.html (accessed 20 July 2004).
–: "The Presence of Reading, Part II", *Context. A Forum for Literary Arts and Culture* 2, 2000b, http://www.centerforbookculture.org/context/no7/dimock.html (accessed 20 July 2004).

Disch, Thomas M.: *The Castle of Perseverance. Job Opportunities in Contemporary Poetry*, Ann Arbor, 2002.
Franzen, Jonathan: *How To Be Alone*, New York, 2002.
–: "Mr. Difficult", *The New Yorker*, 30 September 2002, 100-110.
Johnson, Stephen: *Interface Culture. How New Technology Transforms the Way We Create and Communicate*, San Francisco, 1997.
Koch, Theodore Wesley: *Reading. A Vice or a Virtue?*, Dayton, 1929.
Lacy, Dan: "The Book and Literature in the 1980s". – In John Y. Cole (Ed.): *Books in our Future. Perspectives and Proposals*, Washington, 1987. pp. 250-256.
Lahiri, Jhumpa: *The Namesake*, Boston, 2003.
Lancaster, F. Wilfrid: *The Impact of a Paperless Society on the Research Library of the Future*, Springfield, 1980.
–: "The Paperless Society Revisited". – In John Y. Cole (Ed.): *Books in Our Future. Perspectives and Proposals*, Washington, 1987. pp. 232-239.
Long, Elizabeth: "Textual Interpretation as Collective Action". – In John Boyarin (Ed.): *The Ethnography of Reading*, Berkeley, 1993, pp.180-211.
Lowes, John Livingston: *Of Reading Books*, Cambridge, Mass., 1929.
McGann, Jerome: *Radiant Textuality. Literature after the World Wide Web*, New York, 2001.
Maso, Carole: "Rupture, Verge and Precipice. Precipice, Verge, and Hurt Not", *Review of Contemporary Fiction* 16, no.1, 1996, 54-74.
Morrison, Toni: *Jazz*, New York, 1992.
Murray, Janet H.: *Hamlet on the Holodeck. The Future of Narrative in Cyberspace*, New York, 1997.
Nafisi, Azar: *Reading Lolita in Tehran. A Memoir in Books*, New York, 2003.
Nunberg, Geoffrey: "Introduction". – In G.N. (Ed.): *The Future of the Book*, Berkeley, 1996. pp. 9-20.
O'Donnell, James J.: "The Pragmatics of the New. Trithemius, McLuhan, Cassiodorus" – In Geoffrey Nunberg (Ed.): *The Future of the Book*, Berkeley, 1996. pp. 37-62.
Petrucci, Armando: "Reading to Read. A Future for Reading". – In Gugliemo Cavallo & Roger Chartier (Eds.): *A History of Reading in the West*, Amherst, 1999, pp. 344-367.
Powers, Richard: "Being and Seeming. The Technology of Representation", *Context. A Forum for Literary Arts and Culture* 3, 2000, http://www.centerforbookculture.org/context/no3/powers.html (accessed 20 July 2004).
–: *Plowing the Dark*, New York, 2000.
Reinfandt, Christoph: "Literatur im digitalen Zeitalter. Zur Gegenwartsdiagnose in Richard Powers' Roman *Plowing the Dark*", *Literatur in Wissenschaft und Unterricht* 35, no. 4, 359-379.
Schön, Erich: *Der Verlust der Sinnlichkeit, oder Die Verwandlungen des Lesers. Mentalitätswandel um 1800*, Stuttgart, 1987.
Smith, Zadie: "Introduction". – In Dave Eggers (Ed.): *The Burned Children of America*, London, 2003, pp. xi-xxii.
Smith, Zadie: "Introduction. Dead Men Talking". – In Dave Eggers (Ed.): *The Best American Nonrequired Reading 2003*, Boston, 2003, pp. xxiv-xxxiv.
Wharton, Edith: *The Writing of Fiction*, New York, 1977.

Yardley, Jonathan: "Foreword". – In Nicholas Zill & Marianne Winglee (Eds.): *Who Reads Literature. The Future of the United States as a Nation of Readers*, Cabin John, 1990, pp. vii-x.

Yehoshua, A.B.: "Modern Democracy and the Novel". – In Arthur M. Melzer *et al.* (Eds.): *Democracy and the Arts*, Ithaca, 1999, pp. 42-55.

Living 'in between'.
The Identification of Afro-Latino/a Literature

> I'd like to be able to deal with the whole American continent in my fiction – the whole Americas – and to write imaginatively of blacks anywhere/everywhere.
>
> Gayl Jones[1]
>
> Ethnicity is thus constantly being invented anew in contemporary America
>
> Werner Sollors[2]

1. Introduction. Crossing Cultures, Crossing Boundaries

A few years back, I attended the College Language Association Conference during which I joined a roundtable discussion entitled "Teaching Afro-Hispanic Literature at Historically Black Colleges". While the participants in this discussion were all very knowledgeable about their subject matter and pedagogical issues in general, their dialogue centered solely on teaching Afro-Hispanic literature; namely texts written in Spanish that implicitly or explicitly depicted the experiences of blacks.[3] Although that was the title of the roundtable, and hence I should not have been disappointed by their conversation, something really puzzled me – namely, the absence of any consideration for Anglophone texts written by US-based authors that presented cross-cultural exchanges between African Americans and Latino/as. When I broached this subject, no-one seemed to know what to say as they had given little if no consideration to the existence of what I termed 'Afro-Latino/a' literature. One professor was willing to concede the sociological usefulness of this term given the existence of persons who identify themselves as in between the traditionally disparate ethnoracial[4] categories of African American and Hispanic or Latino/a; for example, as 'Afro-Dominicano' or 'Afro-Caribbean'. When I pushed the subject matter a little farther, I was quickly dismissed as suggesting an insubstantial area of study. I mention this anecdote not as an attempt to criticize those panel members who were resistant to my inquiry; rather, this experience exemplifies the kind of palpable resistance I have encountered all too often while attempting to bring this area of research to light. This resistance, I believe, literally signifies the efforts of those within and without the academy to keep the disciplines of African American and Latino/a literature separate, whether consciously or unconsciously. It is within this context that my project has emerged: borne of a desire to transgress these traditional boundaries in an effort to open up spaces of cross-cultural exchange within the field of multi-ethnic American literary study.

Until recently, most scholars of African American and Latino/a literature have insisted on keeping African American and Latino/a literary traditions distinct. However, many authors, including Gayl Jones, Ntozake Shange, and Miguel Algarín, have resisted such separation and routinely lay claim to a more complex 'Afro-Latino/a' heritage[5] – one that is neither singularly African American nor Latino/a, but both. Several important literary theorists, including William Luis, Antonia Darder, and Rodolfo Torres, have similarly argued for the breakdown of false barriers between literary and cultural groups in order to better understand the complex relationships among ethnic groups within the United States. My study of the cross-cultural exchanges in Afro-Latino/a literature examines interactions between writers from African American, African, Latin American and American diasporic communities. The underlying concerns of these writers include a critique of US foreign policy and interaction with their island communities (a kind of neo-colonialism), an emphasis on more fluid conceptions of identity, and fusion of African and Latin American peoples and heritages based on shared experiences of discrimination and displacement. A major unifying element of this literature is its emphasis on social change – these authors use their work to protest the oppression of persons of color in the Americas and issue calls for change. Specifically, they argue against oppressive racist, sexist, and classist American ideologies.

I am proposing a new way to read, understand, and interpret African American and Latino/a literature under the rubric of 'Afro-Latino/a Literature' through the examination of the complicated exchanges between these two literary traditions. Recent re-conceptualizations of diaspora have opened up a space in which an examination of the exchanges between African American and Latino/a literatures can occur. Within this diasporic context, various critics contend that ethnoracial identities are naturally fluid and shape-shifting. Thus, it is within the diaspora that new categories of identity emerge as a result of interracial political coalitions between previously disparate groups of people. The term 'Afro-Latino/a' privileges the hybrid nature of these texts and emphasizes the similarities in the ways in which authors from these two groups grapple with issues of nationality and ethnicity. These authors refigure the map of the Americas in order to tell a very different tale about the relationships between persons of color within the United States. Specifically, such authors reveal as yet unheard of histories about the relationships between African American and Latino/a peoples. They, in effect, broaden popular conceptions about these distinctive cultural groups. By using the term 'Afro-Latino/a' rather than 'African American' or 'Latino/a', one can better distinguish the location of such work as in-between traditionally defined African American and Latino/a categories of literature. Consequently, the foregrounding of such interchanges broadens our understanding of both of these categories of literature and the experiences of ethnic persons in the United States. My study, centered on twentieth-century authors of the United States, brings these connections to the foreground through its development of a new understanding and interpretation of African American and Latino/a literature under the classification of 'Afro-Latino/a'. This approach breaks down rigidly constructed borders between both traditions by emphasizing alliances between these American ethnic groups. Accordingly, my study is informed by a concept of culture that does not insist on the purity of tradition but instead emphasizes the similarity of experience, shared suffering, shared need, and shared political mission. Given that this particular categorization of literature has yet to be formally determined, part of the aim of this study is to define this nascent literary discipline and make a case for the importance of its incorporation into the study of American literature.

Both African American and Latino/a authors grapple with the task of establishing identity and claiming citizenship within the United States in their writing. These texts often focus on the hardship of attempting to forge identity in the face of oppression and injustice. This common effort links African American and Latino/a literature since authors from one particular cultural background invoke those from the other as rhetorical figures. For example, many Chicana and Latina authors make specific references to radical and political African American women writers, including Audre Lorde and Angela Davis, in their works. Writers such as Cherríe Moraga and Gloria Anzaldúa credit these writers as 'paving the way' for them as radical women writers of color. Additionally, US-based Latino/a writers, including Piri Thomas, Rosario Morales and Victor Hernández Cruz, have increasingly laid claim to an African heritage in order to define themselves in opposition to Anglo-Americans. Similarly, African American writers, including Langston Hughes, Gayl Jones and Ntozake Shange, have declared ties to Latin America in their work. Both groups of writers collectively articulate a much more complex understanding of identity and citizenship within the United States than most critical and popular ideologies have allowed for. They argue, implicitly and explicitly, for the breakdown of barriers between these American ethnic groups. My project explores the basis for this argument and examines the attempts of both African American and Latino/a writers to forge successful alliances between these ostensibly disparate groups. Given the importance of such connections, my project ultimately argues for the recognition and establishment of Afro-Latino/a literature within the academy. Since the writers have explicitly politicized Afro-Latino/a literature, the teaching of that literature is inherently politicized. Consequently, if we teach African American and Latino/a literatures as two distinctly separate literary traditions, then our politics are interfering with those of the writers.

2. New Notions of Diaspora. Movement, Geography and the Creation of Transracial Identifications

Since the 1980s, new understandings of diaspora have begun to emerge – ones that move beyond established perceptions of the African diaspora to encompass the experiences of Latino/a and Afro-Latino/a peoples displaced from their island homelands and living abroad in the United States. New visions of diaspora that move beyond traditional conceptions of African diaspora include examinations of the diasporic island homelands of Puerto Ricans, Dominicans, and, in particular, Cubans. In their essay "Introduction. Latinos and Society. Culture, Politics, and Class" Latino/a critics Antonia Darder and Rodolfo D. Torres underscore the importance of reconceptualizations of diaspora to incorporate the experiences of Latino/a peoples with their assertion that "[w]hile paradigms founded on the notion of the diaspora have been quite abundant in the writings of African Americans, it is only recently that it has begun to emerge more consistently in the literature on Cubans and Puerto Ricans in the United States".[6] Their discussion of the importance of the concept of diaspora in regards to Latino/a peoples implicitly emphasizes the significance of geography and movement in the formation of inter-ethnoracial exchanges and identities: "the conditions faced by members of diaspora communities toss them into interactions with organizations which force them into constant negotiation of their identities and new ways of thinking about multiple identities".[7] These contentions relate back to Hall's arguments about the implicit fluidity inherent in identities formed within the diaspora. Darder and Torres acknowledge the influence of Hall's understanding of diasporic identity by stating that

[a] critical definition of 'ethnicity' is also of vital concern to diasporan scholars, particularly those who are rethinking notions of Puerto Rican, Cuban and Dominican identities here and in the homeland [...]. But the assumption that seems most promising to a radical politics of diaspora is the notion that ethnicity is "a mobile and unstable identity which contains many possibilities, including that of becoming a diaspora" (Toloyan, 1996: 27) [... W]e can draw from the work of Hall (1990) who argues that a critical notion of ethnicity is required in order to 'position' the discourse of racialized populations within particular histories related to the structure of class formations, regional origins, and cultural traditions [...]. As scholars attempt to move away from a language of 'race' and the common practice of negating the multiplicity of Latino identities, critically rethinking the category of ethnicity comes to the forefront as an important intellectual and political project.[8]

Darder and Torres connect the ways in which history, geography, and movement underscore the creation of ethnoracial identities within the diaspora. The instability inherent in identities formed in the diaspora allows for the formation of inter-ethnoracial alliances and the development of new types of cross-ethnoracial exchanges – hence, as they state, the category of ethnicity necessarily must be re-evaluated. Such understandings allow scholars to move beyond static notions of race to embrace more multiplicitous renderings of identity within and without traditional United States borders. The diaspora is also an important concept in understanding this new category of literature since it is within this space of cultural exchange and identity formation that interactions across customary ethnoracial and national borders often occur which, in turn, give rise to the development of new ethnoracial identities such as 'Afro-Latino/a'.

3. Nationhood, Imagined Communities, and Fictive Kinships.
  Forging Cross-Cultural Connections

In relation to issues of diaspora and the formation of Afro-Latino/a identifications, questions of community, kinship and nationality remain central in the work of both African American and Latino/a writers. Working within Benedict Anderson's theory of 'imagined communities',[9] I contend that, as African American and Latino/a communities in the United States merge, there arises a new 'Afro-Latino/a' community based on shared ideological concepts and experiences rather than on shared nationality. In his book *Beyond Ethnicity. Consent and Descent in American Culture*, Sollors purports to draw upon "more recent conceptualizations of kinship and ethnicity [...] and look[s] at the ways in which symbolic ethnicity and a sense of natural kinship that weld Americans into one people were *created*".[10] In my assertion of the formation of inter-ethnic alliances between African American and Latino/a persons, I am building upon Sollors's allusion to the creation of a 'symbolic kinship'. Although the writers I am working with all acknowledge the existence of cultural traits and traditions unique to each ethnoracial community, they also insist upon the creation of inter-ethnic alliances, such as I am terming 'Afro-Latino/a', on the basis of shared experiences of oppression, a working-class ideology, emphasis on speaking from and for 'the people', i.e., those average, regular folks on the streets, a desire to offer cultural alternatives to assimilation, and to express anger and outrage at the existence of oppressive ideologies.[11] My examination of the collective work of various authors of African American and Latino/a ethnoracial backgrounds that addresses such topics and is marked by this aesthetic supports my contention of the existence of an identifiable body of Afro-Latino/a literature.

Theories of fictive kinship are particularly useful in supporting my decision to link together African American and Latino/a communities via their respective literatures in which these writers espouse similar political ideologies and shared experiences of racial and gender oppression. In his essay "Racenicity. The Relationship between Racism and Ethnicity" critic Pepi Leistyna discusses the various applications of the term 'fictive kinship'. He states that

> Signithia Fordham uses the term 'fictive kinship' to describe the collective identity that develops among racially subordinated groups who are mistreated and segregated in society. She argues that this kinship is based on more than just skin color in that it also implies "the particular mindset, or world view, of those persons ..." (Fordham 56). George A. DeVos refers to this phenomenon as 'ethnic consolidation'.[12]

Working within these definitions of fictive kinship, I contend that many African American and Latino/a writers forge fictive communities of resistance based on their 'oppositional identities'[13] created in response to their marginalized status within the US and the subordination that has been forced upon them by dominant Anglo-American society. Notably, this fictive kinship is most often expressed by Latino/a writers who identify with African American writers and activists and cite specific influences in their work. Sollors also acknowledges the formation of fictive communities and summarizes the ways in which American ethnoracial groups have created symbolic kinships via their use of the language of consent and descent:

> The intricate ways persist in which a sense of kinship has been created by such elements as boundary-constructing antithesis, biblically derived constructions of chosen peoplehood, mixed rhetoric of melting pots, naturalization of love as a ligament, curses and blessings by adoptive ancestors, symbolic tensions of parent and spouse figures, regionalist ethics, and generational thinking. The language of consent and descent has been flexibly adapted to the most diverse kinds of ends and has amazingly helped to create a sense of Americanness among the heterogenous inhabitants of this country.[14]

As he suggests, ethnoracial groups in the United States have often recongifured their ethnic and racial status through the creation of inter-ethnic and inter-racial alliances based on various linguistic modes of consent in order to gain greater access to political and socio-economic resources. Sollors takes the purpose of these inter-ethnoracial alliances one step further with his assertion that such coalitions allow persons from various ethnic and racial backgrounds access to an American identity through their interaction with older, more established ethnic American communities. His argument is particularly relevant in regard to the ways in which some Latino/as, in particular Evelio Grillo and Piri Thomas, have integrated into African American communities as a means of acquiring acceptance and success in larger Anglo-American society.[15]

4. The Politics of Resistance in the Formation of Afro-Latino/a Literature. The Civil Rights Movements, Historical Context, and Time Frames

The 1960s and 1970s are particularly important time periods in which to begin my examination of Afro-Latina/o literature. It was during this era that both African American and Latino/a literatures began to gain prominence within the academy. There also existed a close connection between the Black Arts and Black Power Movements of the 1960s and the Chicano Rights Movement of the 1970s. In some sense, it could be argued that the Black Arts and Black Power Movements set the stage for the later Chicano Rights Movement. Additionally, similar to the rise in publication and popularity of African American female writers, there has been a gradual emergence of Chicana authors, although on a much smaller scale, since the 1970s and, in the last decade or so, they have become increasingly popular. Due, in part, to the influence of womanist

African American female writers, including Alice Walker, Audre Lorde, and Gayl Jones, Latina authors, such as Gloria Anzaldúa and Cherríe Moraga, likewise have incorporated strong feminist characters in their work who counter sexism within both Latino and Anglo societies. This leads to my final reason for locating this study within a relatively contemporary time frame, that is, the emergence of an identifiable Afro-Latino/a literature since the late 1970s.[16] Accordingly, my interest in exploring connections between African American and Latina writers under the rubric of 'Afro-Latino/a literature' necessitates that I limit my study to the last three decades.

Historical Connections

Although I am limiting this study to a contemporary time frame, there exist many historical alliances between numerous African American writers and Latino/a literature and culture and vice versa. Perhaps one of the earliest expressed connections between African American and Latino/a writers was that of African American author Martin Delaney's professed admiration for the Cuban poet Placído, who also appeared in his nineteenth-century novel *Blake, or the Huts of America. A Tale of the Mississippi Valley, the Southern United States and Cuba*. The figure of Arthur A. Schomburg (Arturo A. Schomburg), founder of the famed Schomburg Center for Research in Black Culture, also demonstrates significant links between African American and Latino/a communities. Although Schomburg has long been admired and revered for his pioneering research as a world-renowned owner and purveyor of one of the world's largest collections of African American books, prints and artifacts, as well as a prominent supporter and promoter of African American artists during the Harlem Renaissance, little has been written about his Latino/a heritage or his labor on behalf of working-class Puerto Rican communities within the United States.[17] Initially, Schomburg, born in Puerto Rico as the son of a mestizo German father and a freed black mother, was involved in political movements throughout the Caribbean, including Puerto Rico, Haiti and Cuba.[18] Once he had moved to the US, he quickly involved himself in advancing the plight of Puerto Rican and Cuban working-class communities in New York City. However, after visiting New Orleans and coming into contact with the African American community there, Schomburg shifted his allegiance to the black community and went on to make the aforementioned contributions to the research and preservation of African American culture.[19] As demonstrated, Schomburg readily made the transition from labor activism in the Latino/a community to cultural activism in the African American community, which suggests that he saw a logical connection between these two kinds of work. Schomburg's shift of allegiance demonstrates the overlapping concerns of both African American and Latino/a communities in response to socio-economic circumstances in the United States. Both of these communities have engaged in the use of minority culture as forms of political resistance. The case of Arturo/Arthur Schomburg and his move from Latino/a labor activism to African American cultural activism is especially relevant to this study because it exemplifies the symbolic and historical appeal of African American culture to those involved in minority activism in the United States. Schomburg's actions underscore the inherently political nature of the term 'Afro-Latino/a' through their demonstration of the power of an African American political identification. Additionally, an examination of the trajectory of Schomburg's political and cultural work reveals the Latino/a community's historic efforts to draw upon this force. The purpose of my 'uncovering' of Schomburg's Latino/a heritage and his work on behalf of that community, within the US and the Caribbean, is not to lessen his contributions to the African American community, as might be feared by some African Americanist scholars, but to demonstrate alliances between these two communities. Such an act of recovery broadens our understanding of Schomburg's work and depicts him in a more complex light. Although some critics may decry such work as undercutting the purity of Schomburg's status as a preeminent figure in African American literature and culture, I would argue that it is imperative to understand all aspects of Schomburg's heritage and affiliations in order to fully appreciate his work.

James Weldon Johnson, another early scholar and writer in the field of African American literature, also explicated significant links between Latin American and African American writers in his seminal work *The Book of Negro Poetry*. In the preface to this work, Johnson discusses the overlaps between various Negro and Latin American 'colored' poets. He focuses particular attention on Latin American writers of African descent such as the Brazilian poet Machado de Assís and the Cuban poet Plácido and places them on a par with the great African American poet Paul Laurence Dunbar. Significantly, Johnson proclaims that Latin American poets of African descent are superior to Negro writers in the United States because they do not have to contend with the racism and oppression rampant in US society and "can voice the national spirit without any reservations".[20] He also makes the prescient prediction that the first world-renowned Negro poet will be Latin American.[21] As these remarks suggest, Johnson affirmed connections between Latin American and African American writers and implicitly advocated forging links between these two groups in the future. Unfortunately, his remarks went unheeded as the consideration and validation of such connections is just now slowly beginning.

As previously mentioned, although it is hard to find definitive texts within the field of African American writers that proclaim themselves to be creating 'Afro-Latino/a' literature, numerous African American authors have professed affiliations with the Latino/a community and expressed such connections in their work. Some of these writers also were and/or are politically involved with the Latino/a community. Perhaps one of the best-known cases is the relationship between Langston Hughes and Cuban poet Nicolás Guillén in the 1940s. These authors were enamored of one another's work and visited each other on several occasions. There are also documented ties between Marcus Garvey and Claude McKay, Afro-Caribbean writers and activists, and larger Caribbean and Latino/a countries.[22] Amiri Baraka is another African American author who has not only been politically involved in the Latino/a community, primarily in his hometown of Newark, New Jersey and elsewhere, but has acknowledged that Latino/a writers and activists have impacted the development of his writing[23] and has been very involved in Miguel Algarín's Nuyorican Poets Café. Other African American writers demonstrate ties to the Latino/a community in their work, including Wanda Coleman, Rita Dove, Zora Neale Hurston, Sonia Sanchez, Ntozake Shange, and Jay Wright. Artists such as Hurston, Hughes, and Sanchez have spent time in Latin American countries and Mexico and have linked their struggles against oppression as African Americans to that of Latino/as. For example, Lorde not only spent time in Mexico (about which she writes in her 1982 biomythography *Zami. A New Spelling of My Name*), but also wrote a short unpublished prose piece, entitled "La Llorona", that centers on a legendary mythic figure (La Llorona) from the Chicano/a community that appears in the work of many Latina writers, including Sandra Cisneros, Ana Castilla, and Yvonne Yarbro-Bejerano. Sonia Sanchez, like Lorde, also has visited various Latin American countries, including Cuba and Central America, and has incorporated the concerns and culture of the Latino/a community in her work. Notably, she acknowledges the influence of Latin American poets Pablo Neruda and Nicolás Guillén on her work. Sanchez has also spoken openly about her interest in the relief of racial and political oppression on an international level, and this commitment is reflected in poems such as "M.I.A.", in which she makes references to the 'disappeared' villagers of El Salvador's repressive government. Poet Rita Dove has also demonstrated a similar commitment to representing the struggles of oppressed people of Latin American descent in her poem "Parsley", written about the murder of hundreds of Haitians who could not correctly pronounce the Spanish word for 'parsley' by Rafael Trujillo, the infamous dictator of the Dominican Republic. Still other African American writers, such as Ntozake Shange and Barbara Smith, have collaborated with Latina authors – most notably in works such as anthologies from the Women of Color Press and the Kitchen Table Press, including the well-known volume *This Bridge Called My Back. Writing by Radical Women of Color*.[24]

The Influence of the Civil Rights Movement

As many critics contend, the 1960s and 1970s were watershed time periods for the establishment of cross-cultural connections between African Americans and Latino/as. In particular, the Black Power Movement of the 1960s and 1970s was especially important in regard to its establishment of race as a means around which political movements could be articulated that later influenced the trajectory of Latino/a nationalism. Just as the Black Power Movement made 'black' a political term, the later Latino/a Civil Rights Movement of the 1970s used 'brown' as a term around which to rally in the struggle to attain political equality and socio-economic resources. Significantly, the decision of Latino/as to use race-based terms instead of ethnic ones denotes the impact of African American models of political resistance upon Latino/a scholarship and activism. Critics Darder and Torres contend that Latino/as shifted from using the term 'ethnicity' to using the term 'race' in the 1960s in an attempt to follow the use of the 'race paradigm' employed by scholars to "address the conditions of African Americans".[25] This switch distanced Latino/as from theories of ethnicity used to understand European ethnic groups and crystallized their identification as 'the brown race'. Such identification "provided a discursively powerful category of struggle and resistance upon which to build in-group identity and cross-group solidarity with African Americans".[26] In her essay "The Fiction of 'Diversity without Oppression'. Race, Ethnicity, Identity, and Power" Margaret L Andersen concurs by contending that

> [n]ew understandings of ethnicity first surfaced in the aftermath of the Black Power movement of the 1970s. The emergence of Black nationalism in the United States during this period also inspired other similar movements, such as La Raza and the mobilization of Asian American movements with a focus on pan-Asian identity.[27]

Accordingly, Andersen broadens the influence of the Black Power Movement to include its impact on the formation of other political groups around specifically ethnoracial identifications. Critic Acosta-Belén similarly locates the development of a specifically Puerto Rican ethnoracial identity in the United States within the context of the Civil Rights Struggles of the 1960s and 1970s during which time other ethnoracial groups emerged:

> [T]he affirmation of a Puerto Rican identity in the United States, a process similar to that undergone by other ethnoracial minorities such as the Chicano, African-American, and Native American communities, is part of the broader process of multicultural revitalization

among ethnic groups in many parts of the world, which had its most sparkling moments during the 1960s and 1970s.[28]

The end product of this multicultural revitalization has led to a critique of the myth of the American 'melting pot' theory. Instead, this has led to the "affirmation of a US society in which diversity, differentiation, and multiethnic interaction constitute its true cultural nucleus".[29] As these critics suggest, the Civil Rights Movement profoundly impacted the shape of Latino/a political struggles. Interestingly, the similarities between the black and Latino/a struggles for civil rights were not always positive as both groups, at times, exhibited negative practices in regard to women in their respective communities. In their essay "Merging Borders. The Remapping of America", critics Acosta-Belén and Carlos E. Santiago discuss the exclusion of Chicanas and Latinas within the Latino/a Civil Rights movement.[30] They compare the efforts of Latina women to enter the political arena to the struggles of African American women within the Black Power and Black Arts Movements who encountered similar sexism. The attempts of these women to combat overwhelming sexism within their respective communities of ethnoracial origin further underscore the significance of this time period in forging links between African Americans and Latino/as.

Afro-Hispanic Literature

The 1960s and 1970s are also particularly relevant time frames when examining the emergence of Afro-Latino/a literature since it was during this period that critical studies of Afro-Hispanic literature first began to be published. Critic Vera M. Kutzinksi carefully delineates the emergence of Afro-Hispanic literature from the early twentieth century up to the 1980s in her essay "Afro-Hispanic American Literature", in which she analyzes some major Afro-Hispanic writers including Nicolás Guillén, Nancy Morejón, and Carlos Guillermo Wilson (Cubena). According to Kutzinski, literary exchanges between African American and Latin American writers and scholars were frequent during the 1960s and 1970s, stemming from political interaction in the Black Power and Civil Rights Movements and the rise in popularity of the Latin American novel. Moreover, several well-known Afro-Hispanic journals, including "*Cuadernos Afro-Americanos* (Caracas, 1975), *Negritud* (Bogotá, 1977), *Studies in Afro-Hispanic Literature* (Purchase, New York, 1977), and the *Afro-Hispanic Review* (Washington, D.C., 1982, now located in Columbia, Missouri)", were established in the United States at this time as well.[31] During this time period, several Latin American presses reissued classic Afro-Hispanic novels including *Juyungo* by Adalberto Ortiz. Numerous texts examining the black presence in and black poetry by Hispanic writers were also published.[32] Kutzinski argues for the recognition of an Afro-Hispanic literary canon and contends that Afro-Hispanic writers such as Adalberto Ortiz, Manuel Zapata Olivella, and Placído must appear alongside celebrated ostensibly white authors such as Gabriel García Márquez. The ethnoracial essentialism of the 1960s Black Power Movement also shaped the development of the Afro-Hispanic canon in that the racial identity of authors and the "project[ion of] a unified cultural identity, a kinship based on a shared 'black experience'" were its main concerns.[33]

Several other well-known critics have explored Afro-Hispanic poetry and literature as well as the depiction of blacks in Latin American literature including Richard Jackson in his 1998 book *Black Writers and Latin America. Cross-Cultural Affinities*, Miriam DeCosta Willis in her 1977 collection of essays *Blacks in Hispanic Literature. Critical Essays*, Marvin A. Lewis with his anthology *Afro-Hispanic Poetry 1940-1980. From Slavery to "Negritud" in South American Verse*, and Rosemary Geisdorfer Feal in her essay "Afrohispanic Poets and the 'Policy of the Identity'", to name a few.[34] Thorough as these works may be, their aims differ significantly from my project in that they focus almost exclusively on Spanish-speaking authors and fail to include Anglophone US authors in their examination of Afro-Hispanic literature.[35] Their singular examination of texts written in Spanish necessitates their use of the term 'Afro-Hispanic', thereby emphasizing the Spanish language and Latin American nationality of such authors, in comparison to my use of the term 'Afro-Latino/a' in order to emphasize my project's focus on Anglophone texts written by US-based authors. Consequently, as of yet, little scholarship has been conducted in this emerging field of study. Scholars have considered the Africanist presence in Brazilian, Caribbean, and South American literature as evidenced by studies exploring Afro-Hispanic poetry or examinations of Blacks in Brazilian and Latin American literature. However, limited research has focused on either the Latin American presence in African American literature or the Africanist presence in Anglophone Latino/a authors. It is within this tangible gap in literary criticism that my project is situated.

5. Afro-Latino/a Alliances and the Creation of a Resistant Political Ideology

In regards to the terms under which I am bringing together African American and Latino/a literature, I am basing this alliance on shared experiences of oppression, discrimination, under-employment, overrepresentation in the American prison system, similar experiences of displacement from their cultural homelands, shared experiences of poverty, and lower standard of living as non-white peoples in the United States. In short, I link African American and Latino/a literatures on the basis of their similar creations of a literature that resists dominant Anglo-American ideologies that discriminate against persons of color. As far as explicating cross-cultural connections between these two groups beyond the mere fact that they are non-white peoples living in the US, I defer to critics Acosta-Belén and Santiago's description of links between non-white peoples in the US. They contend that "we find diverse populations bound by a shared legacy of colonialism, racism, displacement, and dispersion".[36] Acosta-Belén makes a similar statement in another essay, "Beyond Island Boundaries. Ethnicity, Gender, and Cultural Revitalization in Nuyorican Literature", in which she professes to "underscore[...] the 'anti-Establishment' character of this literature and its commitment to denouncing inequality and injustice in US society and as a consciousness-raising tool for promoting social change among the writers' respective communities".[37] Acosta-Belén and Santiago emphasize the politically radical component underlying Latino/a literature based on the desire of these authors to counter destructive ideologies in mainstream Anglo-American society. I contend that contemporary African American literature is also marked by a similarly radical political aesthetic in its depictions of the struggles of black Americans within an oppressive United States.

*Female Authors and the Creation of a Specifically
Afra-Latina Literary Aesthetic*

At times, women within both African American and Latino/a communities have expressed a greater willingness to address issues of racism, sexism, and classism in their writings in comparison to the male writers in those same communities. Female writers have also been more willing to espouse the formation of cross-cultural alliances between these two ethnoracial groups based on their collective efforts to identify and denounce oppressive Anglo-American ideologies. Several critics have acknowledged the politicism underlying Latina texts. For example, Darder and Torres assert that "Edna Acosta-Belén (1992) documents in her work the emergence of a literary cultural discourse among Latina writers that moved beyond national origins and more inclusively addressed issues of class position, sexual orientations, and racialized relations".[38] Furthermore, they refer to the groundbreaking anthology *This Bridge Called My Back. Writings by Radical Women of Color* that demonstrated that "Latina, African American, Asian, and Native American women were not only collectively challenging the language, style, and discourse of the patriarchy, they were actively involved in counterhegemonic activities that would open up political spaces where their particular issues and struggles would never again remain silent".[39] As Darder and Torres contend, the willingness of female authors from myriad ethnoracial backgrounds to openly acknowledge and criticize ideological ills within and without their respective cultures of origin effectively put an end to the silence that had previously surrounded such issues. They, in effect, paved the way for future politically radical texts to be written. An important distinction to note, though, is that my analysis here is specific to women writers from African American and Latina communities and not just about women of color writers in general. However, at times, my project does build upon previous critical examinations of women of color writers in general. It is about women of color uniting in general, and it is also about the unique unification of women from African American and Latina communities. In a sense, my examination of alliances between African American and Latina female authors is the same yet different than that which has been done before.

The foregrounding of a mixed American ethnoracial heritage is at the root of a radical political ideology espoused by many women writers of both African American and Latina descent. They argue for women of color to unite across racial and ethnic borders in order to eradicate racial and sexual oppression. Although these writers insist upon the unification of women of color, they also advocate the simultaneous maintenance of ethnoracial distinctions. The purpose is *not* to privilege one ethnoracial group over the other, but, instead, to embrace all groups in the struggle for equality as women and, more specifically, as women of color. Such an alliance between women of color is complex for, in the coming together, there must also be deep-seated respect for unique ethnoracial attributes of each woman. This is most specifically not a project of assimilation, as is often the case with multicultural endeavors. Although these writers call for cross-ethnoracial alliances to be forged, they do not advocate the privileging of one specific ethnoracial group over the other. Instead, they propose the recognition of shared similarities, including legacies of racial and gendered oppression, a female-based spirituality grounded in an African heritage, a privileging of an inclusive, communal perspective that opposes traditional Western systems of rationality, and an oppositional stance towards Anglo-American capitalism and imperialism. Activism is also an integral aspect of an Afra-Latina perspective. It is grounded in the belief that women of color must collectively unite in order to combat pervasive racism and sexism that threatens to destroy them. Within this perspective is a fervent call for women of color to unite across traditional ethnoracial divides in order to effect social change within and without the United States. African American and Latina women are urged to bond across shared stories of struggle in order to access a collectively greater power. Through the recognition of these similar experiences and beliefs, African American and Latina women of color can join together and form a stronger collective base of power from which they can work to oppose destructive racist and sexist ideologies. Consequently, these articulations are central to the creation of an Afra-Latina political ideology in that the texts, themselves, are calls to action – they demand that their readers acknowledge the racial and sexual oppression experienced by women of color. The articulation and subsequent recognition of such oppression is essential to its eradication.[40]

The alignment between African American and Latina women, which I am identifying as a specifically Afra-Latina political perspective, is grounded in a borderlands ideology as explicated by Anzaldúa's theory of a *'mestiza* consciousness'. According to Anzaldúa, this new mestiza consciousness, *una conciencia de mujer*, is "a consciousness of the Borderlands".[41] This consciousness is marked most specifically by its embrace of a cultural 'in-betweenness'. Anzaldúa contends that this includes an oppositional stance towards Western rationality in favor of "divergent thinking, characterized by movement away from set patterns and goals and toward a more whole perspective, one that *includes* rather than excludes".[42] As such, this consciousness privileges inclusivity, as can be seen in the writings of the authors examined in this chapter as they embrace both African and Latino/a heritages in their work. Bridges must be built, in the words of the editors of the seminal text *This Bridge Called My Back. Writings by Radical Women of Color*, in order to make this world a better place for women, in general, and for women of color, in particular. The future belongs to those who are willing to embrace a more complex, hybrid identity, according to Anzaldúa, who contends that "the future depends on the breaking down of paradigms, it depends on the straddling of two or more cultures".[43] Embracing an 'Afra-Latina' perspective, one that privileges both African American and Latina/o cultures, exemplifies Anzaldúa's charge that, in the future, one must be willing to embrace a multiplicity of cultures.[44] Significantly, Anzaldúa maintains that in order for Chicana/o peoples to move forward, they must "know our Indian lineage, our afro-*mestizaje*, our history of resistance".[45] This 'afro-*mestizaje*' of which Anzaldúa speaks is similar in theory to an Afra-Latina ideology due to its recognition of a hybrid ethnoracial category that encompasses African, Indian, and Latina/o cultures. For Anzaldúa, this borderlands ideology, although feminist at its core, is all-encompassing, and she proclaims that, in order to overcome prejudice that oppresses and divides, "we can no longer [...] disown the white parts, the male parts, the pathological parts, the queer parts, the vulnerable parts".[46] Instead, all components of a person, be they Mexican, Chicano/a, Anglo, African, queer, male, female, etc., must be embraced in order to achieve a healing wholeness in opposition to divisive racial and sexual oppression. According to Anzaldúa, this way is "the *mestiza* way, the Chicana way, the woman way".[47] Building upon Anzaldúa's mestiza/borderlands theory, I argue that women writers of African American and Latina descent call for alliances across ethnoracial divides in an embrace of an ideology that can be specifically identified as Afra-Latina.

6. Conclusion. Living 'in between'

Afro-Latino/a literature is emerging as an extremely relevant field of study when examining texts written by African American and Latino/a authors. To date, the term 'Afro-Latino/a' possesses marginal status and has not yet gained a wide audience. However, given the similarities in themes, political concerns and writing styles among writers of African American and Latino/a literature, this categorization proves to be very useful. Notably, when discussing both African American and Latino/a literature, critics and scholars often point to the cross-cultural components of both fields given their diasporic roots. Accordingly, the examination of similar concerns and characteristics shared by these literatures is not a new thing. The willingness of various Latino/a authors to use the term 'Afro-Latino/a' to describe their work testifies to this fact. Curiously enough, though, the category of Afro-Latino/a literature has yet to gain sufficient currency within the field of American literature. In my initial exploration of this term, I found that numerous Latino/a authors, including Rosario Morales, Victor Hernández Cruz, Sandra María Estevez, Tato Laviera, Piri Thomas, and Cecilia Rodriguez Milanés, repeatedly emphasized their African origins and/or readily acknowledged their incorporation of African mythology and culture in their writing. On the contrary, African American writers less readily acknowledge and/or deliberately incorporate Latino/a mythology or culture in their work. Perhaps due to the disjuncture in regard to the willingness of these two groups to acknowledge common cultural values and heritage as well as shared political concerns and themes, the category of Afro-Latino/a literature has yet to be fully established and stands as a field ripe for literary exploration and study.

In addition to work that centers on a non-fictional examination of the connections between African American and Latino/a communities, many Latino/a writers incorporate African mythology and culture in their work. This is best exemplified in the work of numerous Latino/a poets, including Morales, Laviera, Hernández Cruz, and Esteves. Significantly, several of these writers, including Laviera, Hernández Cruz, and Esteves, refer to their poetry as either 'Afro-Latin' or 'Afro-Caribbean'. The work of Cruz, for example, focuses on a wide range of multicultural and multiracial themes. Notably, one of his most anthologized poems, "African Things", is a tribute to the African spirits of his maternal ancestors. Although he is Puerto Rican, in this poem, he claims that being Puerto Rican "is all about the Indios & you better believe it the African things". The poem ends with him invoking his "black & shiny grandmother" to tell him about his African roots.[48] Poet and playwright Estevez foregrounds her Puerto Rican/African/Caribbean heritage in a similar vein. This is exemplified in her poem "From Fanon" in which she describes the enslavement of non-white peoples in the diaspora by "europeans thru power and fear". She laments that "as slaves we lost identity / assimilating our master's shadows".[49] As such, she unites the struggles of all enslaved peoples, most notably those of African descent. In her poem "It Is Raining Today", Esteves acknowledges the multiplicitous ethnoracial backgrounds of Puerto Ricans with her reference to their "Taino, Arawak, Caribe, Ife, Congo, Angola, Mesa/Mandinko, Dahome, Amer, African" ancestors.[50] Lastly, in her work *Getting Home Alive*, writer Morales includes a poem entitled "Africa" in which she asserts Africa as the source of her cultural roots. With the statement "Though my roots reach into the soil of two Americas, / Africa waters my tree" she insists that, although she is a Puerto Rican born in the United States (the 'two Americas'), Africa is the ultimate source of her cultural heritage.[51]

I use the term 'Afro-Latino/a' to underscore the in-betweenness of this category of ethnoracial identification in that it equally privileges 'African American' and 'Latino/a' cultures. This term is also intentionally broad in that I use it to refer to persons of myriad ethnoracial backgrounds including African American, Latino/a, Chicano/a, Afro-Caribbean, etc., to name a few. This term also refers to both male and female authors – hence, my decision to use 'Afro-Latino/a' instead of the masculinist term 'Afro-Latino'. The deliberate inclusiveness of the term Afro-Latino/a implicitly emphasizes the inherent fluidity of ethnoracial identities. In keeping with my disavowal of racial essentialism, this term also underscores the fact that borders are constantly in flux. Try as we might, we simply cannot keep rigid borders between cultural groups. Individual cultures eventually merge to form new ones, such as I am espousing in this study, in various contact zones – for example, in the multicultural neighborhoods of New York City and Los Angeles. The term, thus, represents this type of inter-ethnoracial amalgamation and engenders more complex examinations of ethnoracial identity that take into consideration the multiple ways in which people self-identify across seemingly fixed borders of race, ethnicity, class, and nationality.

In conclusion, I contend that the categories 'African American literature' and 'Latino/a literature' obscure the interchanges between these two literary traditions and fail to accurately describe authors whose work reflects an interest in both of these cultures. Moreover, as previously demonstrated, the category of 'Afro-Latino/a' is a most valuable tool when assessing connections and overlaps between African American and Latino/a literature. The literary examples I have analyzed in this study are but a few of the innumerable links between these two communities. Critics and scholars have just begun to recognize and explore this area. The field is wide open. However, given the disjuncture between some African American and Latino/a writers and scholars in regard to their willingness to acknowledge and embrace shared cultural roots and literary traditions, critical exploration in this field will surely be accompanied by some resistance. One of the ultimate outcomes of this project is to internationalize the African American literary canon and recognize authors who cross traditional literary and cultural borders.

Another significant goal of my study is the project of recovering and/or revealing heretofore untold or ignored stories, since inherent in these texts is the revelation of previously obscured histories of political alliances and connections between African American and Latino/a peoples. Consequently, these authors tell new tales about the Americas. Although the recognition of these connections is a relatively recent phenomenon, in reality, alliances between these two ethnoracial groups have existed for centuries both in the United States and on a much larger global scale (including the Caribbean, Mexico, Latin America, and Africa). Many of these writers reference these historical connections in an attempt to bring them to light in the present and to solidify such alliances for the future. In a sense, they are going back to the past in order to secure the future. In the end, examining texts from an Afro-Latino/a perspective propels scholarly debates about issues of nationality and ethnicity beyond conventional black-white dichotomies in order to render a more comprehensive understanding of the complex histories of African American and Latino/a persons in the United States.

Notes

1 See Rowell.
2 See Sollors (1986: 14).

3 Not surprisingly, their discussion kept returning to the work of Richard Jackson – a noted scholar of Afro-Hispanic literature. For example, see Jackson (1998).
4 In regard to my decision to use the term 'ethnoracial' in this article, I am borrowing this term from Latina critic Edna Acosta-Belén as articulated in her essay "Beyond Island Boundaries. Ethnicity, Gender, and Cultural Revitalization in Nuyorican Literature". I prefer to use 'ethnoracial' for its amalgamation of the terms 'ethnicity' and 'race' into one word, thereby symbolizing the inter-connectedness of these terms instead of conventional tendencies to separate the two. See Acosta-Belén (1992: 980). I am also drawing upon the distinctions between these two terms as articulated by Margaret L. Andersen in "The Fiction of 'Diversity Without Oppression'. Race, Ethnicity, Identity, and Power" (1999). Thus, although I personally prefer to use the term 'ethnicity', I have chosen to use the collapsed term 'ethnoracial' because I feel it best references the complicated experiences of both African American and Latino/a persons since both groups have been labeled as 'races', yet they are now often referred to as 'ethnic groups'. Additionally, each group has used each label at one time or another in their struggle for political and socioeconomic equality. However, when referring to cross-cultural connections between African American and Latino/a peoples, I prefer to use the term 'ethnicity' to describe such a group. The term 'ethnicity' makes most sense here because it allows for such connections not on the basis of shared physical characteristics, as the term 'race' does, but on the basis of common experiences of oppression and colonialism and a shared consciousness. Furthermore, ethnicity scholar Werner Sollors similarly addresses the discrepancies between the terms 'race' and 'ethnicity' and contends that 'race' and 'ethnicity' are not separable terms but, in the end, 'ethnicity' takes precedence as 'race' is, according to Sollors, but 'one aspect of ethnicity'. See also Sollors (1986: 39).
5 To date, the term 'Afro-Latino/a' possesses marginal status and has not yet gained a wide audience. However, given the similarities in themes, political concerns and writing styles among writers of African American and Latino/a literature, this categorization proves to be very useful.
6 Darder & Torres (1998: 17).
7 *Ibid.*
8 *Ibid.*, 9-10.
9 For a thorough explication of the creation of imagined communities see Anderson (1991).
10 Sollors (1986: 11, emphasis in the original).
11 Significantly, Edna Acosta-Belén describes Nuyorican literature in a similar vein, contending that it emerged out of the Civil Rights Struggles of the 1960s and 1970s and notes the "'anti-Establishment' character of this literature and its commitment to denouncing inequality and injustice in US society and as a consciousness-raising tool for promoting social change among the writers' respective communities" (1992: 980).
12 Leistyna (1998: 154).
13 Leistyna goes on to discuss the existence of 'oppositional identities' in accordance with scholar John Ogbu. He states that "John Ogbu makes reference to 'oppositional identities' and 'survival strategies', which he describes

as instrumental, expressive, and epistemological responses to cope with subordination and exploitation [...]. Both Ogbu (1987) and Fordham (1988) observe that generations pass down this fictive kinship – norms, values, and competencies, and that racially subordinated children thus learn different survival strategies and markers of solidarity from their parents or caregivers and peers." (*Ibid.*)

14 Sollors (1986: 245).
15 In making the transition to US life (after immigration), many Latino/as initially make contact with the African American community (in particular due to the geographic concentration of ethnic groups within similar locations, i.e. New York City, Los Angeles, Chicago, etc.). According to Werner Sollors, this group often serves as a means of acculturating new immigrants to the American way of life (1986: 17).
16 For a thorough description and delineation of the emergence of this literary category see Kutzinski (1996: 164-194) and DeCosta (1977).
17 In fact, although I have read some of Schomburg's work and have studied about him in several classes on African American literature, it was not until I began researching Afro-Latino/a literature that I learned of Schomburg's Latino/a heritage. Schomburg was born in Puerto Rico and later moved to the United States. His father was German and his mother was of African descent from St. Thomas.
18 For a brief autobiographical overview of Schomburg that underscores his Puerto Rican heritage see Knight (1995).
19 Augenbraum & Fernández Olmos (1997: 159-160).
20 Johnson (1922: 40). It is important to note that Johnson's contention that Latin American poets of African descent were not subjected to the same kinds of racism that African American poets were forced to endure is somewhat naïve and ill-founded. However, Johnson's assertions are in keeping with the common depiction of Latin American and Hispanic countries, such as Cuba and Brazil, as idyllic racial paradises.
21 *Ibid.*
22 Garvey tried unsuccessfully to involve persons of African heritage in Haiti and Cuba to join his 'Back to Africa' movement during the 1930s.
23 See his collection of essays: Baraka (1998).
24 Anzaldúa & Moraga, 1983.
25 Darder & Torres (1998: 9).
26 *Ibid.*
27 Andersen (1999: 9). Here Andersen is referring to Yen Le Espiritu (1992).
28 Acosta-Belén (1992: 986).
29 *Ibid.*
30 They include a brief historical overview of their involvement in various radical movements. See Acosta-Belén & Santiago (1998: 11-14).
31 Kutzinski (1996: 164).
32 *Ibid.*, 164-165.
33 *Ibid.*, 166-167.
34 For other examples of Afro-Hispanic literature see Adams (1998), Birmingham-Pokorny (1993), Birmingham-Pokorny (1994), LaCapra (1991), Miller (1991), Ortiz (1982).

35 Jackson (1998) is the exception to this rule as he includes a brief close reading of US authors Gayl Jones, Audre Lorde, Ntozke Shange, Paule Marshall and Toni Cade Bambara in his discussion.
36 Acosta-Belén & Santiago (1998:29).
37 Acosta-Belén (1992: 980).
38 Darder & Torres (1998: 13).
39 *Ibid.*, 13-14.
40 I am indebted to Dr Thomas Fahy for his input in helping me better articulate the theoretical framework for this section.
41 Anzaldúa (1999: 99).
42 *Ibid.*, 101 (my emphasis).
43 *Ibid.*, 102.
44 Significantly, Anzaldúa identifies the 'queer' as the person best equipped to cross borders (1999: 106-107).
45 *Ibid.*, 108.
46 *Ibid.*, 110.
47 *Ibid.*, 110.
48 Turner (1991: 30).
49 *Ibid.*, 182.
50 *Ibid.*, 188.
51 Levins Morales & Morales (1986: 55).

Bibliography

Acosta-Belén, Edna: "Beyond Island Boundaries. Ethnicity, Gender, and Cultural Revitalization in Nuyorican Literature", *Callaloo* 15, no. 4, 1992, 979-998.
Acosta-Belén, Edna & Carlos E. Santiago: "Merging Borders. The Remapping of America". – In Antonia Darder & Rodolfo D. Torres (Eds.): *The Latino Studies Reader. Culture, Economy and Society*, Malden, 1998, pp. 29-42.
Adams, Clementina R.: *Common Threads. Themes in Afro-Hispanic Women's Literature*, Miami, 1998.
Andersen, Margaret L.: "The Fiction of 'Diversity without Oppression'. Race, Ethnicity, Identity, and Power". – In Mary L. Kenyatta & Robert H. Tai (Eds.): *Critical Ethnicity. Countering the Waves of Identity Politics*, New York, 1999, pp. 6-12.
Anderson, Benedict: *Imagined Communities. Reflections on the Origins and Spread of Nationalism,* revised edition, New York, 1991.
Anzaldúa, Gloria, & Cherríe Moraga (Eds.): *This Bridge Called My Back. Writings by Radical Women of Color*, second edition, New York, 1983.
Anzaldúa, Gloria: *Borderlands/La Frontera. The New Mestiza,* San Francisco, 1999 [first edition 1987].
Augenbraum, Harold & Margarite Fernández Olmos (Eds.): *The Latino Reader. An American Literary Tradition from 1542 to the Present*, Boston, 1997.
Baraka, Amiri: *Hom. Social Essays*, New York, 1998.

Birmingham-Pokorny, Elba D.: *Denouncement and Reaffirmation of the Afro-Hispanic Identity in Carlos Guillermo Wilson's Works. A Collection of Criticism*, Miami, 1993.

–: *An English Anthology of Afro-Hispanic Writers of the Twentieth Century*, Miami, 1994.

Darder, Antonia, & Rodolfo D. Torres (Eds.): "Introduction. Latinos and Society. Culture, Politics, and Class". – In A.D. & D.R.T. (Eds.): *Latinos and Society. Culture, Politics, and Class*, Malden, 1998, pp. 3-26.

DeCosta, Miriam (Ed.): *Blacks in Hispanic Literature. Critical Essays*, Port Washington, 1977.

Dove, Rita: *Museum. Poems*, Pittsburgh, 1983.

Espiritu, Yen Le: *Asian American Panethnicity. Bridging Institutions and Identities*, Philadelphia, 1992.

Jackson, Richard L.: *Black Writers and Latin America. Cross-Cultural Affinities*, Washington, 1998.

Johnson, James Weldon: *The Book of American Negro Poetry*, New York, 1922.

Knight, Robert: "Arthur 'Afroboriqueño' Schomburg", *Civil Rights Journal* website, 1995, http://www.wbaifree.org/earthwatch/schombrg.html (accessed 17 February 2003).

Kutzinski, Vera M.: "Afro-Hispanic American Literature". – In Roberto Gonález Echevarría & Enrique Pupo-Walker (Eds.): *The Cambridge History of Latin American Literature*, vol. II, Cambridge, 1996, pp. 164-94.

LaCapra, Dominick: *The Bounds of Race. Perspectives on Hegemony and Resistance*, Ithaca, 1991.

Leistyna, Pepi: "Racenicity. The Relationship between Racism and Ethnicity". – In Mary L. Kenyatta & Robert H. Tai (Eds.): *Critical Ethnicity. Countering the Waves of Identity Politics*, New York, 1999, pp. 133-71.

Levins Morales, Aurora & Rosario Morales: *Getting Home Alive*, Ithaca, 1986.

Miller, Ingrid Watson: *Afro-Hispanic Literature. An Anthology of Hispanic Writers of African Ancestry*, Miami, 1991.

Ortiz, Adalberto: *Juyungo. A Classic Afro-Hispanic Novel*, Washington, 1982.

Rowell, Charles: "An Interview with Gayl Jones", *Callaloo* 5, 1982, 32-53.

Sanchez, Sonia: *Homegirls & Handgrenades*, New York, 1984.

Sollors, Werner: *Beyond Ethnicity. Consent and Descent in American Culture*, New York, 1986.

Turner, Faythe (Ed.): *Puerto Rican Writers at Home in the USA*, Seattle, 1991.

West, Cornel: *Prophetic Reflections. Notes on Race and Power in America. Beyond Eurocentrism and Multiculturalism*, vol. II, Monroe, 1993.

Merle Tönnies, Bochum

A New Self-Conscious Turn at the Turn of the Century? Postmodernist Metafiction in Recent Works by 'Established' British Writers

1. Well-known British Novelists at the Beginning of the Twenty-First Century

When thinking about the 'establishment' in contemporary British writing, one immediately comes up with a group of four authors who started writing in the 1970s or 1980s: Martin Amis, Julian Barnes, Ian McEwan and Graham Swift are interlinked by a complex network of personal friendships and animosities and respond to similar social and literary developments. Not surprisingly, this quartet was part of the selection when *Granta* first compiled its list of the 'best young British novelists' in 1983.[1] Focusing on the period immediately after the turn of the twenty-first century, however, the present paper has to go beyond this group, because until the beginning of 2003, only Barnes and McEwan had actually published a new novel.[2] Another quartet will therefore be created by including an equally 'established' but more 'popular' novelist, David Lodge on the one hand, and one of the most recognised representatives of women's fiction in the 1980s and 1990s, A.S. Byatt, on the other. In this way, the shared moment of writing is seen in conjunction with potential differences due to each particular writer's position and target audience.

These authors' twenty-first-century novels – Barnes's *Love etc* (2000), Byatt's *The Biographer's Tale* (2000), McEwan's *Atonement* (2001) and Lodge's *Thinks ...* (2001) – are without exception highly self-conscious works which use a number of devices to foreground the narrative process in their readers' perception. Fittingly, Lodge himself observed in a 2001 interview with Craig Raine that he not only deemed himself "a metafictional novelist", but considered this to be "generally true of the present literary period".[3] Such interests are very close to the 'postmodernist' approach that dominated especially American, but subsequently also British fiction from the end of the 1960s to the 1980s. In the 1990s, on the other hand, the synthesis of experimental approaches with realism was most characteristic in Britain.[4] This is perhaps why metaficationality has so far not been accorded too much importance in studies of twenty-first century fiction.[5] By contrast, the present analysis will examine in how far the turn of the century can be taken to coincide with a second 'postmodernist turn' among established British novelists.[6] Many definitions of 'postmodernism' after all understand the term as referring in the first place to a particular outlook or mode of writing, instead of constituting a temporally specific period designation.[7]

The four novels under consideration fall into two groups, according to the main focus of their narrative experiments. In each case, one author is prepared to go further than the other in the direction of truly postmodernist metafiction. Both Lodge and Barnes work with different voices which they intertwine with destabilising effects.[8] McEwan and Byatt, on the other hand, concentrate on stacking a number of narrative levels which are always likely to collapse into each other with a similar impact.

2. Self-Conscious Polyphony. Thinks ... *and* Love etc

As Lodge's tremendously successful university novels of the 1970s and 1980s already built up a reputation for combining metafictional and (meta)theoretical elements with accessibility and enjoyability, it does not come as a surprise that his postmodernism now remains more guarded than Barnes's. As Joyce Carol Oates concludes in her review of *Thinks* ..., Lodge is – just as in his earlier works – "a postmodernist writer in the affable guise of a reliable realist".[9] With *Thinks* ... he returns to the campus setting with which his *oeuvre* is most readily associated. In terms of narrative technique, however, the novel develops a tendency more characteristic of his 1995 *Therapy*: the first-person diary account. Whereas in *Therapy* the focus was on the protagonist's perspective and inserted passages apparently narrated by other characters afterwards turned out to have been written by him for therapeutic reasons,[10] *Thinks* ... has two first-person narrators of equal standing. In keeping with the university novel's general preference for portraying two diametrically opposed 'cultures',[11] these figures are a male cognitive scientist and a female novelist teaching creative writing. Their points of view alternate in the novel in self-contained chapters, often describing the same events and sometimes disrupting the chronological sequence. It is central to the effect of the novel that the two narrators seem to be as close to the reader as possible. Helen is writing a diary which the reader follows throughout the novel, and Ralph is producing similar records by means of a tape-recorder and, later on, voice-recognition software. In his case, the ambiguous status of the text constantly focuses our attention on the transmission process: The use of language and the references to the recording clearly mark the statements as oral (there is indeed one written entry by Ralph that serves as a contrastive foil),[12] while Ralph's thoughts about transcribing, especially about the representation of pauses by dots and paragraphs, make the reader realise that s/he is reading the result of this transfer. When Ralph uses the computer software, the documents seem to become a true mixture of oral and written text, with "the words appearing right in front of your eyes on the screen" while being pronounced (71). Even then, however, he explicitly points out that he is "able to correct and revise" as he goes along (72, 181), i.e. the "stream of consciousness" (116) that the reader absorbs may have been doctored by the speaker and thus be not so much more immediate (or 'authentic') than Helen's unequivocally written account after all. On the other hand, such subsequent interventions by the narrating I also support the impression that no other, higher entity has prepared the text for the reader. The two narrators indeed at times seem to merge with the recipient when they announce that they have been going through the previous section again – together with the reader who has just finished it.

There is thus clearly no overarching level which might unite the two standpoints, and this seems to have been very important for Lodge in writing the novel. When – feeling that his readership would like "some relief from the [two] solipsistic narratives"[13] – he included a number of third-person chapters, he took special care to avoid any sense of superimposed narrative authority. Apart from the deliberately conventional last chapter,[14] these parts consist almost exclusively of dialogue; the reader is not allowed access to the characters' consciousness here. As these sections are written in the present tense, they thus produce the impression of – as Lodge himself has called it – a "behaviourist account",[15] straightforward transcripts of the characters' speech and actions which efface the narrator level as far as possible. They can even take the form of e-mail exchanges between Ralph and Helen, seemingly 'reprinted' in the novel without any authorial intervention (like cutting the redundant address sections or correcting Ralph's typos). Lodge himself has indeed described the third-person passages as "documents",[16] 'found' pieces of writing mingled with the rest without any attempt to form a coherent whole. In this way, they only add yet another perspective and cannot be used to judge which of the overtly subjective interpretations is correct.[17] The presence of these chapters also means that the two first-person accounts do not alternate regularly but randomly, which strengthens the sense that there is no ordering authority above the isolated bits of text. In two cases, this polyphony is intensified further by pastiches in the manner of well-known contemporary novelists, which gives an intertextual dimension to the diverse voices and styles mixed in the novel and opens up the text to an endless series of cross-references. These sections "don't advance the story", as Raine put it to Lodge's complete satisfaction in their interview,[18] i.e. they constitute a typically postmodernist denial of linear development through digression, which fits in well with the time jumps between Helen's and Ralph's chapters. The reader thus seems to be confronted with a decentred fictional universe where all narration can only have subjective truth value and the absence of an omniscient narrator (apart from the last summing-up chapter) reflects the impossibility of obtaining a reliable version of events.

However, it is characteristic of Lodge's writing that this apparent narrative disorder – while having a much greater impact than potentially postmodernist elements in his previous novels – never seriously confuses the reader. Most reviewers do not even think the mixture of diverse perspectives worth mentioning in full, confining their remarks to the alternation of the first-person narrations.[19] Although there is no unifying narrator organising the sequence of chapters, one often cannot but feel the (implied) author's hand in their orchestration. Not only are the changes in style consistently provided with a plot motivation (Helen has just acquired e-mail access, the pastiches are written by her students), but the jumps in point of view and time are attenuated by quickly conventionalised markers of whose chapter one is reading. Ralph always begins his records with a 'testing' phrase, and Helen enters the date into her diary, which is incidentally included in most of Ralph's accounts as well to make sure that the reader feels sufficiently oriented. Moreover, a break in perspective regularly means a direct follow-up in terms of the narrated events. The combination of different chapters can even provide the reader with additional information and thereby facilitate rather than obstruct the reception process, e.g. when Ralph comments on the three pastiches that the reader has just seen and may not have been able to allocate on his/her own (170). When the same event is told from different perspectives, this can also allow the reader to see through the (self-)deception practised in the two first-person reports, so that the combination of more or less 'unreliable' narrators paradoxically makes him/her relatively sure about the 'real' course of events.[20] In the final result, the reader usually knows more than the narrator of the respective chapter and is able to "compare [the characters'] responses" (187), as Ralph imagines in his diary-swap scenario.[21] The priviliging effect of polyphony is also alluded to through the motif of the 'thinks bubbles' in comics – a recurring image (42, 220, 252) which is used to visualise the title on the cover of the 2001 paperback edition and stands for ideas inaccessible to the other characters but obvious to the reader. Such metafictional readings are encouraged by frequent passages that can be understood as joking references to the reader's activity. Both I-narrators state that they could not bear having their journal seen by anyone but themselves, which the reader reads together with the rest of their accounts (e.g. 61, 72, 182, 258), and Ralph explicitly wonders about himself "as perceived by others" when he fears his recording has been overheard (149).

More intensely than Lodge's previous works, the book can moreover be taken to betray an awareness of its own status as fiction. The reader is always tempted to apply Helen's remarks on novel writing and reading to the text itself (e.g. 15, 42, 62, 63, 82, 84, 123, 125, 316, 318), which for instance produces dramatic irony on more than one level when she discusses the uses of fictional adultery with Ralph's wife (211). In a novel plotted as intricately as *Thinks ...*, references to "coincidence" (187) or "fate" (306) acquire a metafictional sense as well, in which they draw attention to the (implied) author's decisions. Helen also fictionalises her own life, both in one of her novels, about which the reader learns from Ralph's summary (253-254, cf. 202-203), and in the diary entry about the beginning of her sexual relationship with Ralph. In the latter case, the guilt she feels towards Ralph's wife makes it impossible for her to write one of her usual first-person reports, so that she switches to a third-person limited perspective and produces the only example of her fiction that the reader gets to know directly in the book.[22] As with the fictional plot quoted by Ralph, the analogy between the embedded, hypodiegetic level and the 'reality' of the novel encourages the reader to play with ontological boundaries. The effect is reminiscent of the postmodernist potential of *mise-en-abyme*.[23] A related impact is obtained when Lodge's novel starts quoting itself. When Ralph reads sections from Helen's diary in the final chapter, they are made part of the third-person narration in bold type and quotation marks, which signals to the reader that a text with which s/he is already familiar is now removed to the level of fiction-within-fiction (335). On a broader scale, the book can be taken to allude to its own status when Helen publishes the literary result of her spell as a creative writing teacher. Like *Thinks ...*, her work comes out "[i]n the first year of the new millennium" and is "set in a not-so new greenfields university", and its stylistic features exactly reproduce those of the deliberately special concluding chapter that tells the reader about it: "It [is] written in the third person, past tense, with an omniscient and sometimes intrusive narrator" (340). In this way, the mirror effects even include the level of the reader's own reality.[24]

All in all, *Thinks ...* thus not only reflects on the status and effects of fiction through its destabilisation of absolute 'truth', but also presents itself more directly as self-conscious. Once again, however, Lodge stays relatively cautious. Despite the metafictional jokes, the characters themselves have no consciousness of their fictional status and do not try to interact directly with the reader. Similarly, games with hypodiegetic worlds within the fictional universe may playfully hint at possible mergers between the different ontological levels, but Lodge never genuinely confuses them (or his readership). By themselves, the metafictional techniques in *Thinks* ... might thus even be said to stop short of a postmodernist impact, though taken together with the postmodernist polyphony in the book they clearly intensify literary self-reflexiveness.

The relative guardedness of Lodge's postmodernist devices becomes especially obvious when we now use them as a contrastive foil for Barnes's *Love etc* of the previous year. This novel is also based on the intercutting of different voices, but compared with Lodge, the unsettling effect is maximised. Instead of two first-person narrators of equal standing Barnes has three, the members of an eternal triangle, and a number of secondary figures also contribute their versions at some points. There are no third-person passages which one might, at least initially, have credited with some degree of objectivity. In addition, the frequency of the switches is far higher; it is not whole chapters that are intercut but much shorter passages. They are always preceded by an indication of the speaker in bold type, which in a way makes the book look more like a drama (without stage directions) than a novel.[25] The status of the texts moreover remains much more ambiguous than in Lodge's work. At first sight, their style and presentation is reminiscent of Ralph's oral records; Barnes himself indeed reported in an interview that he had a sense of "taking the voices down by hand – as if I were taking dictation, or as if there was a physical link from their brains to my brain to my arm to the free-flowing ink".[26] At the same time, however, there are clear indications of the written nature of the contributions. Not only is there an abundance of brackets,[27] but the various narrators share a pronounced tendency to make lists (e.g. 96, 108-110, 115), always presenting them in a graphically attractive format with initial numbers etc. At one point, there is even a list of P.(P.P.)S.s (172), with the Latin designation itself signalling written instead of spoken text.

It adds to this fluidity of the textual snippets that, in contrast to Lodge, who is very specific about the gadgets used by Ralph, Barnes provides no information about what kind of (if any) transcription has occurred to bring the texts to the format in which they reach the reader. There is definitely no unifying narrator who might have been credited with this transmission process; in summing up an interview with Barnes, Thomas Sutcliffe describes the novel as a case of "authorial absenteeism".[28] The characters make clear from the very beginning that it is they who are in joint control of the narration. Gillian admonishes her husband Oliver and her ex-husband Stuart:

> Look, stop it, you two. [...] This isn't working.
> What sort of impression do you think you're giving? (7)

While the whole set-up and the topic of adulterous love is reminiscent of Beckett's *Play* – tellingly a drama rather than a novel –, it thus seems that the part of the ordering spotlight is absent; there may be "rules" (never described in any detail), but the characters break them whenever it suits their own intentions (7, 142, 239).[29] Compared with the (implied) author's palpable orchestration of the voices in Lodge's novel, Barnes's explicit empowerment of the narrators makes their input seem both more random, depending on their momentary desire to communicate, and (together with the ambiguous textual status) even less reliable. Indeed, the three protagonists can be called 'unreliable narrators' in a textbook sense,[30] lying to themselves as much as to others and admitting openly that even when they are genuinely trying to recall the past, their memory is often not up to the job (133, 143, 221). This repeatedly leads to a sense of vagueness in their narrations, especially when they jump back and forth between Stuart and Oliver's shared schooldays, the beginning of the triangular relationship and the immediate past. It almost goes without saying that the exact dates that mark the contributions in Lodge's novel are absent here, and the characters generally fail to refer to specific years with regard to past events as well. In addition to the other ambiguities, it is thus also much harder for the reader to keep the fictional time frame in perspective.

It has to be noted that all of these characteristics cannot simply be regarded as Barnes's response to a new postmodernist climate. They date back much longer in his writing, specifically to the novel *Talking It Over* of 1991, of which *Love etc* presents itself as a "sequel".[31] Not only is the title of the second book directly taken from Oliver's theory about different kinds of people in the earlier novel,[32] but the characters constantly allude to their first set of sessions and the events of that time. They assume that the reader is familiar with the plot of the previous book – although recalling it in such a way that *Love etc* is comprehensible for Barnes novices as well. With an evident metafictional subtext Stuart asks if the reader thought the final scene of *Talking It Over* "was the end of the story": "But life never lets you go, does it? You can't put life down the way you can put a book down." (93) In this way, one is encouraged to compare the techniques of the sequel with those of the 'original'. From our point of view, this leads to the observation that the (potentially) postmodernist elements have been intensified. The narrators of the first book seem much more certain of their memories (and also less inclined to lie about their lives, since they as yet lack the desperation with which they later try to convince themselves that their self-concepts are still valid). One may even sense an ordering level above the characters. When flower seller Michelle contributes her view in a one-off, a newspaper-style addition to her name informs the reader of her age, and Stuart and Oliver's friend Val is first presented as "... (female, between 25 and 35)".[33] Moreover, the status of the texts less obviously becomes a topic here. In keeping with the title, it is much easier to perceive the contributions (apart from one inserted written document) as oral reports, which leaves out an important source of the ambiguity that makes *Love etc* so deeply self-reflexive.

At the same time, the versions presented by the different narrators conflict with each other much more strongly in the second book. While *Talking It Over* does leave it open whether Stuart's or Olivers' memories of their schooldays are accurate,[34] most of the more immediately relevant events can be reconstructed by the reader quite confidently. At times, s/he can even enjoy a moment of superior knowledge similar to the ones produced by the plaiting of the different voices in Lodge's novel, e.g. when Oliver wonders about a poll-tax inspector whom the reader knows to have been investigative Stuart.[35] With regard to the climatic event at the end of the novel, the reader is only given Oliver's version, but it is confirmed both by what Gillian said beforehand about her plans and by the seemingly disinterested outsider Mme Rives. In *Love etc*, by contrast, the climax of the plot epitomises uncertainty. The reader is given three perspectives on Gillian's and Stuart's sexual encounter, first her version of passionate, youthful love-making, then his "rhapsodic account",[36] in which he is more active than in her preceding portrait, and finally Gillian's second report, describing straightforward, brutal rape. There are some clues that a character may be lying – Stuart, for instance, can be taken to insist a bit too much that his partner consented and enjoyed the experience (224, 226) –, but it is obvious that the reader will never be able to work out the exact truth from the characters' statements. It is not simply a question of "what is truth and what is falsehood", as Dominic Bradbury has put it,[37] but very probably the characters are mixing facts and fiction in all three versions.[38] Relativity is thereby pushed far beyond *Talking It Over*. It is certainly no coincidence that it is in the sequel instead of the original that Oliver presents his concept of "literary genre" by varying the story of the hare and the tortoise. The overview ends as follows: "Postmodernism: I, the author, made up this story. It's a mere construct. The Hare and the Tortoise don't actually 'exist', you realise that, I hope?" (157) The book thus metafictionally acknowledges its own self-conscious style and connects the vagueness with which the reader is confronted with the appropriate literary terms. Since the 'story' is not 'real' anyway but 'a mere construct', there is no point in insisting on one particular view, and different accounts can coexist peacefully with each other. As Gillian comments on picture restoring in the first novel: "There's no 'real' picture under there waiting to be revealed."[39] It is therefore possible to conclude that Barnes wrote the second book when he did not only because the 'confessional mode' of *Talking It Over* had now become the spirit of the age,[40] but also because the current developments in narrative technique encouraged him to bring out the postmodernist potential of the original to the full.

Compared with Lodge's *Thinks ...*, *Love etc* moreover goes much further with regard to transgressions against ontological boundaries. The characters are clearly conscious of their fictional status, constantly breaking the illusion of the plot. Throughout, questions and question tags addressed to the reader abound, and the characters regularly engage in full-blown dialogues with him/her which we can reconstruct from their replies.[41] Metafictional allusions like the incessant references to a "story" (e.g. 25, 35, 82, 136, 174, 182, 202, 233, 246) can thus clearly be attributed to them rather than to the (implied) author, as in *Thinks* .... As Barnes has put it, "[t]he membrane between the character and the reader is minimised",[42] which obviously links up very well with the complete abolition of an overarching narrator level through his uncompromising use of polyphony. At first sight, it seems as if *Love etc* transferred this unifying function to the reader position inscribed in the text, just as the spotlight in Beckett's *Play* can be seen as an on-stage representative of the theatre spectator. The characters indeed sometimes ascribe a privileged insight to the reader or ask him/her for help, since s/he is also familiar with their counterparts' points of view (e.g. 90, 176, 234). The reader is moreover explicitly shown to take control in the penultimate chapter entitled "Question Time". Weary of the conflicting versions, especially with regard to the sexual encounter, s/he here tries to investigate actively by asking the characters questions that can be reconstructed from their answers. However, just as the novel as a whole constantly frustrates the reader's attempts at finding out the 'truth', this intervention remains fruitless. The characters either cannot or will not provide more specific, unambiguous information, and sometimes they even refuse to answer at all (232, 238, 241). Thus, when the book draws to a close with their repeated question "What do you think?" (245-247, 248-249), this is clearly no appeal to the reader's superior knowledge, but an invitation to create yet another subjective version of the fictional events and their consequences. One can even feel the characters metafictionally alluding to the "wildly different" interpretations of subsequent events that readers gave Barnes after *Talking It Over*,[43] thereby perhaps hinting at yet another sequel.[44]

It should also be noted that the reader's presence in the text deepens the ontological vagueness of the different narrations. The characters and the reader seem to share the same 'reality', so that they can see his/her face (1-3, 9, 28, 30, 40, 63, 172), direct his/her perception (80) and establish a physical connection with him/her (142, 220-221). It also appears that this shared 'reality' extends beyond the scenes of direct contact, as Ellie for instance asks if the reader has also seen "this wildlife programme on the telly [....] about bowerbirds" (127). S/he is taken to have witnessed the plot of *Talking It Over* and then lived on for the same period as the characters, before now meeting them again. As Stuart puts it rather bluntly right on the first page of the book: "Oh, and by the way, *you*'ve changed too. You probably think you're pretty much the same as you were back then. Believe me, you aren't." (1, emphasis in the text) From this perspective, the characters' accounts look oral, delivered to the reader in face-to-face communication and often in response to his/her questions. It remains ambiguous, however, in how far all characters (or at least the three protagonists) are present in this 'reality' at the same time. In some cases, they explicitly signal that they have overheard each other's comments (3-4, 7, 172). At other moments, each character seems to be isolated from the others in a *tête-à-tête* with the reader, who takes certain statements with him/her to the next interview, for instance causing Stuart's ex-wife Terri to exclaim: "He actually *said* that?" (175, emphasis in the text) Still more confusingly, one can also find passages in which the characters are clearly part of a different world from the reader's, about which they can only guess. Gillian, for instance, wonders if the reader is "about to have [national average sex], when [s/he] finish[es] this bit" (61, see also 73) and imagines him/her reading the book in bed, next to a partner whose sex she deliberately leaves open (63). She thus breaks the fictional illusion, but at the same time demonstrates her awareness that she herself is fictional, part of a "bit" of text rather than a 'real' person like the reader and his/her potential partner. In addition, such instances mark the characters' contributions as written, just as unambiguously as the previous set of examples pointed to their oral nature.[45]

It is characteristic that *Talking It Over* goes less far in this respect as well. Just as this book contains fewer indications that the texts might be written rather than spoken, the characters stress their face-to-face contact with the reader. It moreover appears that they are all present together, 'on stage' as it were, since Oliver and Stuart can join forces to silence Val by physical violence, with her appealing to the reader to intervene (208-209). Oliver uses a graphic metaphor to sum up the shared situation of the protagonists and the reader in this book: "We're stuck in this car on this motorway, the three of us, and someone (the driver! – me!) has leant an elbow on the button of the central locking system. So the three of us are in here till it's resolved. *You're* in here too. Sorry, I've clunked the doors, you can't get out, we're all in this together." (75-76, emphasis in the text) Barnes's sequel thus deliberately pushes his familiar triangle further into the postmodernist domain, with polyphony combining with the most explicit metafiction to produce a playful denial of truth and ontological reliability which far surpasses Lodge's *Thinks* ....

3. Self-Conscious Play with Different Narrative Levels.
   Atonement *and* The Biographer's Tale

As analysed above, Lodge's *Thinks* ... also plays with different hierarchical levels. In the two books to be discussed in the following, however, this kind of destabilisation is the key narrative technique. The unsettling impact already becomes clear in McEwan's *Atonement*, which still remains more cautious than Byatt's novel and derives at least as much of its overall effect from the human interest of the story. The book consists of three parts of unequal length and an epilogue. In the first section, which is by far the longest, the topic of embedded narratives is introduced by the protagonist Briony, a thirteen-year-old aspiring writer who has decided to move on from her previous melodramatic stories to the adult world of "separate minds [...], struggling with the idea that other minds were equally alive": "That was the only moral a story need have."[46] This is why at that point in the summer of 1935 she is scrutinising the interaction of the other family members very closely, trying hard to understand what is going on, but remaining unable to apply any other model than the melodramatic one. Thus, she considers the confrontation between her sister Cecilia and Robbie, whom Cecilia loves without knowing it, to have an "illogical" "sequence": As Briony observes from afar, Cecilia jumps into the fountain (to rescue a broken vase) after the serious conversation between the two, whereas according to the rules Briony knows, "the drowning scene, followed by a rescue, should have preceded the marriage proposal" (39) Briony after all once staged a 'drowning scene' herself, when she had developed a crush on Robbie (230-232). She then challenges "existence" to produce some "real events" (77) and – seemingly in response – finds herself in possession of a sexually explicit love letter that Robbie has by mistake sent to Cecilia. As a consequence, she interprets the love scene between the two in the library as an assault (123-124) and determines to protect the family from this "maniac [a fittingly melodramatic term introduced by her cousin Lola (119)] treading through the night with a dark, unfilled heart" (157). She now considers herself "a figure in a richer story", of which she has "to prove herself worthy" (163), with the potential metafictional allusion drawing attention to the extent to which she is fictionalising her own life.

This is background of the third and most serious misreading that Briony performs. When Lola is sexually assaulted, she immediately concludes that she has recognised Robbie in the culprit, since this gives her the chance to prove herself both as an adult and as a writer: "She had no doubt. She could describe him. There was nothing she could not describe" (165, see also 167, 171) is how the omniscient narrator phrases her response.[47] Under the influence of the melodrama model, she sees the "symmetry" of her version as the key evidence for its "truth" (169), considering the whole turn of events "her story, the one that was writing itself around her" (166). Although this 'story' is not as such included in the novel but only emerges from the girl's answers to the adults' questions, it is clearly a case of the hypodiegetic level influencing the primary narrative. Briony's imagination produces 'facts' in the world of the novel.[48] Only Cecilia and Robbie can see through the real status of her 'story'.[49] It has to be noted that this merger between 'fiction' and 'reality' within the novel does not confuse the reader. Just as the ominiscient narrator provides unequivocally 'true' versions of the misinterpreted fountain and library scenes by showing them from the adults' perspective either before or afterwards, the reader is even less deceived by Briony's current 'story' than Robbie and Cecilia. In contrast to them, s/he "can deduce who attacked Lola":[50] Paul Marshall, the friend of Cecilia's brother, not only appeared with "a two-inch scratch" on his face after Lola had been assaulted for the first time, but was also slightly too eager to confirm her implausible report that she had been bruised by her two younger brothers (127, 141).

This superiority on the reader's part is then severely impaired by the next piece of embedded fiction – a narrative that Briony submits to the *Horizon* magazine in the third part, while training as a nurse to 'atone' for her "crime" (162, see also 285). Again the hypodiegetic level is not included explicitly,[51] but it can be reconstructed from Cyril Connolly's rejection letter, which is given in full. This source immediately encourages the reader to equate Briony's novella with the fountain scene in the first part of *Atonement*. The interaction between a "young man and woman by a fountain" and the uncomprehending "child at the window", who then decides to "abandon the fairy stories and home-made folk tales and plays she has been writing" (312-313), are as familiar from Part One as the stream-of-consciousness technique and the metaphor of "the long grass stalked by the leonine yellow of high summer" (38, 312). Other elements of *Atonement*'s first part seem to realise the changes that Connolly's letter advocates for Briony's work.[52] Most importantly, there is the "backbone of a story" that Briony's focus on her characters' thoughts in one particular situation makes impossible (314); as suggested by Connolly, McEwan's novel shows the girl being used "as a messenger" by the two adults and "com[ing] between them in some disastrous fashion" (313). Briony sees this section of the rejection letter as "a significant personal indictment" and realises that – like Lodge's Helen avoiding the first person when she feels in the wrong – she has been trying to "drown her guilt in a stream – three streams! – of consciousness": "Everything she did not wish to confront was also missing from her novella – and was necessary to it" (320). For the reader, this potential case of *mise-en-abyme*, with the embedded narrative together with Connolly's letter adding up to a central section of Part One, creates a less clear-cut situation. Is it not too much of a coincidence that the magazine editor should have guessed (and advocated) exactly those points that distinguish the apparently 'objective' omniscient narrator's text from Briony's? Therefore, could it not be that instead of Briony writing her novella on the basis of her own past, this past as the reader knows it was constructed in response to Connolly's suggestions? This would obviously turn her 'disastrous' intervention into nothing but 'fiction', the narrator's gratification of the audience's "childlike desire to be told a story" (314), which the reader of *Atonement* has been indulging in his/her turn during the first part of the novel. The book thus turns on itself in a constant circular movement, exploding narrative stratification in a truly postmodernist fashion.

This conundrum remains unsolvable throughout Part Three, indeed until the very end of that section. After the confrontation with the reunited lovers, Briony decides to write not simply the explanation that Robbie requires of her, "but a new draft, an atonement". It is then that the last lines give the initials "BT", followed by "London 1999" (349). Thus, not only the fountain scene of the first part but the whole of the preceding text, including Robbie's war experiences in Part Two, has been written by the character Briony. While on the one hand at least partly resolving the uncertainty created by the *Horizon* novella, this move at the same time constitutes a destabilising equation of ontological levels that far surpasses Lodge's tentative play with Helen's novel at the end of *Thinks* …. It gives a completely new interpretation to the title and retrospectively changes the reader's relationship with the omniscient narrator of the preceding parts. After all, Briony has revealed herself to be proverbially 'unreliable' as a narrator in Part One, "possessed by a desire to have the world just so" (4). With his/her new knowledge, the reader may moreover remember hints in Part Three that the plot is fiction (within fiction), deliberately selected and organised by a narrator instead of constituting a faithful reflection of 'reality'. When having decided to walk on to meet her sister rather than turn back, Briony feels "the distance widen between her and another self, no less real, who was walking back towards the hospital. Perhaps the Briony who was walking in the direction of Balham was the imagined or ghostly persona." (329) Similarly, Robbie's appearance immediately makes his potential death in the war "outlandish, against all odds": "It would have made no sense" – i.e. it was not available as a choice for the narrator anyway (338). It should also be noted that the year given at the end of the third part means that Briony has written the main body of the text from a distance of more than sixty years, which casts further doubt on the accuracy of her memories, even if she attempted to recreate past events faithfully.

The novel does not end on this surprising and deeply unsettling note, however, but adds an epilogue entitled "London, 1999", which is narrated by Briony in the first person and makes the issues implied in her signature after Part Three almost bluntly explicit. The relationship between the novella sent to *Horizon* and the first three parts of the book is spelt out; the manuscript was the first version of Briony's novel and they are the last, with "half a dozen different drafts" in between (369). At the same time, Briony clarifies her novel's relationship with 'truth'. While having regarded it as her "duty to disguise nothing" about the characters' 'real' names (369) and having tried very hard to capture the "truth" in all details with regard to war scenes (359), she admits having committed "offences against veracity", of which merging different places to concentrate her experiences was the least (356). The reader was thus absolutely right to mistrust the accuracy of the plot after having learnt about the narrator's identity. There is even a certain distinction here between plot elements that can be believed and purely 'fictional' ones. The narrator's cousin Lola appears in the epilogue, still married to Paul Marshall, now the famous Lord Marshall, i.e. these characters and their story are rooted in the 'reality' of 1999 London and given an existence independent from Briony's novel. Cecilia and Robbie, on the other hand, are said to "end well" only in "this last version" which the reader has read. "All the preceding drafts were pitiless", but now Briony "can no longer think what purpose would be served" by their permanent separation through death (370). The allusion to the above-discussed point in Part Three where Briony realises that Robbie's death 'would have made no sense' is obvious. But ultimately none of these representations has any reliable 'truth' value, which – quite in contrast to the reader's ability to see through lies and mistaken perceptions in Part One – mirrors the impossibility of deciding between different accounts in Barnes's *Love etc*. McEwan's epilogue even takes into account potential questions about "what *really* happened" put by "a certain kind of reader" (371, emphasis in the text). Apparently, this species is not too rare in 'real' life, as the author acknowledges that the postmodernist relativity of his ending has alienated "[s]ome readers".[53] They probably could not bear finding their emotional investment in the (truly engaging) character undermined in the end, i.e. the human level of the plot can be taken to intensify rather than marginalise the effect of the narrative techniques. Briony herself answers the reality question with a Shakespearean assertion of the power of fiction: "As long as there is a single copy, a solitary typescript of my final draft, then my spontaneous, fortuitous sister and her medical prince survive to love" (371), and – just as with the Shakespearean sonnet –, this is, of course, the effect of *Atonement*. The novelist is not only "God"-like in "her absolute power of deciding outcomes", as Briony puts it (371), but also in her power to give (fictional) life to characters and situations.

In spelling out the implications of Briony's signature at the end of the third part, the epilogue thus clearly makes one feel very strongly that one should read the book again in the light of its final revelations.[54] From this point of view, Briony's fictionalisation of her own life as a 'story' in Part One and her frequent thoughts about stream-of-consciousness techniques both here and in the third section (e.g. 40, 282) are given a second metafictional sense, commenting on the older Briony's novel as much as on McEwan's. Indeed, one can now observe Briony's concern with symmetry – restated in Part Three at the time of the *Horizon* draft (282) – making itself felt in the first three parts of McEwan's novel. He has after all himself expressed a profound interest in "'the geometry' of the scenes" and has been attested having achieved a "beautifully architectural" construction in *Atonement*.[55] Just as the epilogue still shows the narrator to some degree influenced by the character stereotypes of melodrama (she observes "a touch of the stage villain" in Lola's current appearance [358]), this section perfects the symmetry of the plot so completely that one is almost led to doubt again whether Briony is faithful to 'reality' here or to the laws of fictional construction: The play that she failed to put on at the age of thirteen is now staged for her 77th birthday. When she concludes the epilogue by taking her account up to the present moment, she thus gives the "tidy finish" that she professed to like at the beginning of this part a second metafictional sense as well (353).

Below this tying up of threads, however, the ending is pointedly 'untidy', as we have seen, stressing the destabilising implications of Briony's role as the omniscient narrator of the first three parts and deliberately refusing to provide closure with regard to the lovers' story. From this point of view, the novel as a whole can be said to mirror and transcend the development that the mature Briony ascribes to her own writing self: "she would describe how at the age of thirteen she had written her way through a whole history of literature, beginning with stories derived from the European tradition of folk tales, through drama with simple moral intent, to arrive at an impartial psychological realism" (41). As Evelyn Finger has pointed out, the first part starts out à la Jane Austen,[56] from whom the epigraph of the novel is taken, and the text then proceeds to literary models like Virginia Woolf and Elizabeth Bowen. Ironically, when these names appear in the book (see 282, 312, 314), 'psychological realism' has already been tinged with a fair amount of postmodernist vagueness through the *Horizon* manuscript. The epoch (if one can call it such) of postmodernism then clearly predominates from the end of Part Three onwards and retrospectively engulfs the first part as well: It becomes clear that the reader has been "deliberately [misled] into regarding an embedded, secondary world as the primary, diegetic world", as the absence of any initial equivalent to the epilogue made him/her unable to realise that s/he was reading a novel-within-a novel – a classic case of postmodernist *trompe-l'oeil*.[57]

Our fourth example, Byatt's *The Biographer's Tale*, also allows the reader to follow the development of an emergent writer. In contrast to McEwan's novel, this means a direct involvement in the writing process. In this respect, Byatt is thus closer to Lodge; as with his Helen, a first-person account is being written in front of the reader's eyes. Indeed, Byatt's narrator Phineas is as sure as Helen that his "manuscript, [...] for obvious reasons, cannot be public property",[58] and even repeatedly jokes about possible responses of "my non-existent reader" (175, see e.g. also 36, 141, 227) – with obvious metafictional implications. Lodgean allusions to "Providence, or Fate" and "coincidence" (149, 220, see also 105) are present as well. While Byatt clearly stops short of breaking the ontological boundary between the characters' and the reader's world, as Barnes does, Phineas's writing is, however, much more explicitly self-conscious than Helen's diary. He constantly refers to "this document" (e.g. 114, 188, 227), confirming its physical existence within the text by citing the current page of the manuscript version (214). Later on, in two final sections separated from the main text (and from each other) by a line of asterisks and reminiscent of the epilogue in *Atonement*, he spells out that the rest of his text is on his "machine (and backed up on disk) in London", while he is now writing "in a small notebook" (255), reading through the first entry (seemingly together with reader, like Lodge's two narrators), before starting the second (257). When he decides to "put away this notebook", this is therefore a fitting final sentence for Byatt's novel (260), just as the impending end of his 'document' announced that the main part of the novel was drawing to a close (249-250). In addition, Phineas is far more aware of his own writing than Lodge's Helen, questioning his use of language and metaphor with increasing frequency (e.g. 97, 122, 132, 168, 240, 250) and reflecting about his choice of the first person point-of-view (100, 214)[59] and about the structure of his narrative (152, 155). Byatt thus "purposefully prevents the reader becoming wholly involved in the writing", as Hal Jensen has put it.[60] This effect is still intensified by the handling of narrative time. Much more noticeably than McEwan's novel, *The Biographer's Tale* indicates that its events took place at some temporal distance from the time of writing, and Phineas disconcertingly jumps back and forth between the present moment of telling and the past tense of the narrative. This approach is continued right up to the two 'epilogues', which confine themselves to the present and the immediate past – another parallel with McEwan's ending.

Phineas's manuscript is also given a physical presence within the novel through the inclusion of countless documents (written and pictorial) which he sometimes explicitly describes as "attach[ed]" to his narrative (112). The most extensive example even uses a slightly different font to signal that another voice is incorporated into Phineas's text (37-95), and in other instances indentation serves the same purpose (with one apparently genuine oversight [230]). Due to the great number of embedded texts, the book clearly comes across as a "patchwork", as the author herself put it in her acknowledgements (264). It is important to note, however, that in contrast to the genuine polyphony of different voices in Lodge's and Barnes's novels, the first person narrator constitutes an overarching level which unifies the narrative. Instability is nevertheless introduced here in a classic postmodernist fashion. Byatt constructs a complicated hierarchy of recursive strata, only to create analogies that link different levels and allow the reader to make ontologically impossible equations.[61] Phineas describes how he is trying to put together a biography of the (imaginary) biographer Scholes Destry-Scholes, who wrote the seminal biography of the (equally imaginary) Victorian explorer and writer Sir Elmer Bole, which makes Phineas "the third in line" (24). Since Destry-Scholes had a special ability to "write[…] as though he were looking with [his subject's] eyes" (13-14, see also 20), it is always hard to determine who is speaking in excerpts from his works, especially of course since the information reaches the reader summarised "from the point of view of [Phineas's] initial interest" (15). Problems multiply with the inclusion of Destry-Scholes's unfinished biographical sketches about Carl Linnaeus, Francis Galton and Henrik Ibsen, followed by selective 'reprints' of the index cards that seem to have prepared these drafts. Quotations from texts written by the biographical subjects or other biographers and parenthetical remarks by both Desty-Scholes and Phineas make the reference of personal pronouns highly doubtful here, particularly when parts of letters are included (see e.g. 176). Phineas indeed at one point feels called upon to clarify who is speaking: "Phineas G. Nanson, that is, the ur-I of this document" (162). Thus, the definite article in the novel's title can only be understood as a joke – highlighting the impossibility of applying the phrase with any definiteness to either Phineas's or Destry-Scholes's 'tale'.

Indeed, going far beyond *Atonement*, confusion not only encompasses the stratification of narrative levels in Byatt's novel, but makes identity itself increasingly fluid. Linnaeus, Galton and Ibsen were apparently selected by Destry-Scholes for "what they had in common [rather] than [for] what made them unique" (239); far from being individualised, they are not even given names in the drafts but are referred to by initials. As Phineas notes, their stories have "intriguing, pointless symmetries" (98, see also 236), of which the most striking one concerns accounts of spirit journeys (49-50, 75, 235). It thus certainly has a 'metafictional' significance for Destry-Scholes's writing that he was interested in Galton's 'composite' photographs of criminals and family members – with one example in Destry-Scholes's collection mysteriously showing female members of Linnaeus's family. Phineas explicitly wonders "that the three personages [in the biographical drafts might be] like stripes or bars behind which lurked the figure of Destry-Scholes" (98, see also 238). After all, in a conversation between Ibsen and his son that Destry-Scholes presents like a playscript, the dramatist's statement that he "was always particularly good at last acts" ends not only the encounter and the dramatic snippet, but also – in a *trompe-l'oeil*-like effect – the whole biographical sketch (95). More unsettlingly, Phineas senses that the voices from the embedded narrative levels infiltrate his own text; he is for instance "becoming infected by the Victorian sonorous reasoning of Pearson", Galton's biographer (165). Even without noticing, he takes up the term "strange customer" used by both Ibsen and Desty-Scholes (128, cf. 89, 150) and the latter's abbreviation "wch" (74, 230). In addition, he collects sentences that Destry-Scholes "lifted" without acknowledgement from his subjects' work, "intending, when my time came, to redeploy them with a difference" and thereby provide a fitting illustration of "[p]ostmodernist ideas about intertextuality and quotation of quotation" (29). Indeed, it must prove impossible for Phineas to develop "a style *of* [*his*] *own*" (165, emphasis in the text), as his very personality is invaded by the 'characters' of his narrative. Not only does he see a vision that Galton had (201), but he notes how Destry-Scholes's information on Galton and Ibsen interlinks with the appearance of Fulla in his own life (230).[62] In a similar gesture of *mise-en-abyme*, he constantly equates himself with Destry-Scholes, from the size of their handwriting (142) to their (potentially shared) attitude to photographs (141), to the fact that they are both writing "for no reader" (237). It seems that by "rewrit[ing] his writings in my writing" (142), "cop[ying] his copies" (149), Phineas to some extent becomes (like) Destry-Scholes. Therefore, it appears only logical that – towards the end of the novel – he thinks that "the composite portrait" of the three biographical sketches might also show his face rather than Destry-Scholes's (236-237), trying to reassure himself by stressing his own identity as "me, myself" (200).

In contrast to the parallels between past and present in Byatt's 1990 novel *Possession*,[63] the overlaps between the different ontological levels in *The Biographer's Tale* thus pointedly do not provide the "delight[...]" of "facts slot[ting] together", as the text itself describes the response it refuses to its readers (10). On the contrary, human subjectivity "keep[s] sliding in and out of focus" (238), and – just as McEwan's epilogue brings the postmodernist play with narrative levels out into the open – Byatt makes Phineas comment explicitly on this destabilisation process. In the final result, there is no unifying level that can hold the novel's diverse voices together, as the first-person narrator's self dissolves in the act of narrating. It therefore hardly comes as a surprise that he is an extremely unreliable narrator. In contrast to Briony, this is not due to a desire to distort the 'truth'; on the contrary, Phineas deliberately sets out to work on a biography (rather than write a piece of fiction, as she does), because he wants "facts" (4, 167). The novel quickly makes clear, however, that he is not very well equipped for this job. His very desire to be precise constantly makes him reveal how unsure he is about certain details (128, 142, 152, 175, 201), with the time difference adding to his uncertainty (143, 152, 187, 214). In addition, Phineas repeatedly confesses himself to be "slow to read signs" (215, see also 143, 188), i.e. readers are warned that they may do well not to trust his interpretation too much, and he often finds the development of his narrative trapped in – of course typically postmodernist – digressions (e.g. 130, 168). Nevertheless, his ultimate failure to establish and relate the 'necessary' facts is by no means only his fault. It proves impossible to ascertain the most basic information about Destry-Scholes and his life; no photograph can be found (249), and the source of his eccentric name remains in the dark as well (133). Phineas even states at one point that he has "to respect [Destry-Scholes] for his scrupulous *absence*" from his (Phineas's) writing and work (214, emphasis in the text). As in the passage from *Peer Gynt* copied out by Phineas, the peeling of the onion does not reveal the "heart" but leaves the researcher with nothing (235) – or with the "fictive" image of the biographer with which he started out (35).

'Factual' reliability is moved still further out of reach by the tendency of both Destry-Scholes and his triad of subjects to mix fact and fiction. As Destry-Scholes himself notes, Linnaeus's "published account of his travels" may have been "to some extent mendacious" (52), a view that is later corroborated by Fulla (111). Phineas moreover finds out that Destry-Scholes added further fictive elements to this account and to the other two sketches (112, 126, 164-165, 236), creating "a tissue of truths and half-truths and untruths" (118) that makes it as completely impossible to establish a 'true' version of events as it is for Barnes's and McEwan's readers. In his quest for 'facts', Phineas indeed quickly acquires the slightly paranoiac sense that Destry-Scholes is "trying to deceive or illude [him] personally" (119). Since there is no usable information in the outside world, it is inevitable that Phineas's attempt at piecing together a biography turns into what he "detest[s]", an "autobiography" (250, see also 214). Ironically, however, the subjectivity on which this form rests is itself subject to the above-discussed dissolution process. Thus, his text ultimately becomes a "story" (247, 250), a fictional work. Byatt thereby far surpasses contemporary biography's wariness of constructing too linear and too unequivocal narratives, finally affirming the all-pervasive predominance of fiction over any kind of truth value.

Indeed, in Phineas's account one repeatedly feels the writing itself asserting its power, driving the writer to set down events that did not take place and that he therefore puts 'under erasure' immediately afterwards (e.g. 122, 186-187).[64] Fiction even seems to be exercising an increasing influence on his 'real' life. He feels that he has "in a way *invented* Vera and Fulla", as their likeness to "a goddess of the night, and a goddess of the daylight" makes them seem more 'fictional' than 'real' (237-238, emphasis in the text) – which, of course, they are in a metafictional sense. Similarly, by thinking about "the '1920s' version of Phineas G. Nason", he recognises a Joycean "epiphany" in his life (251). Ironically, this literarily inspired moment constitutes a renunciation of literature for nature, which provides a fitting ending for the main part of the manuscript. 'Fiction' is not so easily put down, however, and Phineas spends the two 'epilogues' trying to "stop writing" (256, 260), in each case attempting to blot out the allure of fiction with the 'real' presence of one of his lovers. But the reader has seen enough of the "liberation" that he has felt in developing a "lyrical" mode (215, 240) to suspect that this resolution will not last long. Despite his "nausea" at the thought of becoming a "Writer" (251), one anticipates a continuation similar to Briony's life. It is indeed possible to draw a parallel between the desire of McEwan's character for a turning-point in her life and Phineas's account – with the crucial difference that Briony deliberately shapes her life according to fictional models and later perfects this correspondence retrospectively, whereas Byatt's hero feels such patterns imposing themselves on his life and writing in spite of himself. Equating the development of his life 'story' with the manuscript's, he concludes that "this story has funnelled itself into a not unusual shape, run into a channel cut in the earth for it by previous stories" to become "a *writer's story*" (*ibid.*, emphasis in the text). He has "somehow been *made* to write [his] own story", "driven" by the predominance of 'fiction' over 'reality' to take a path that runs counter to his conscious plans for his life (237, emphasis in the text). Phineas regards this fundamental powerlessness as another parallel with Destry-Scholes, who was 'driven' towards fiction writing in exactly the same way (237). His "fabrication of Linnaeus's fabrication of his visit to the Maelstrøm was [after all] a pastiche of Edgar Allan Poe" (256). Byatt's reinterpretation of intertextuality thus bodes ill for human free will and by its very force emphasises the relative harmlessness of Lodge's use of pastiche.

4. Postmodernist Concerns in the New Millennium

All in all, the present analysis has shown a spectrum of established British writing in the first years of the twenty-first century, stretching from Lodge's comparatively mainstream postmodernism to Byatt's disturbing destabilisation of narrative levels and identities. Despite all differences in the exact techniques employed and in the intensity of their impact, the four novels – taken together – demonstrate that postmodernist concerns are high on the agenda of well-known fiction writers in Britain immediately after the turn of the century. Readers seem to share this interest, as is proved by the immense success of McEwan's *Atonement*. It should be noted, however, that their willingness to engage with the complexities of postmodernist texts does not necessarily stretch as far as the writers' exploratory tendencies. It is probably no coincidence that the most successful novel of the quartet, McEwan's, does not push postmodernism to its absolute limits, though challenging readers more profoundly than Lodge's extremely cautious *Thinks* .... Reviewers of Byatt's novel have after all rather consistently reported a lurking sense of alienation "as the barrage of disparate information becomes numbing".[65] In the slightly less fundamentally disconcerting forms found by Barnes and McEwan, on the other hand, postmodernist destabilisation has provoked no such rejection on the critics' part. The questioning of concepts like reality, certainty and linearity thus seems to have a relatively broad appeal in today's society. Perhaps secret anxieties connected with the beginning of a new millennium have ushered in another postmodernist decade, although it obviously remains to be seen how these tendencies will develop.

Notes

1. See *Granta* 7 (1983). With regard to this collection Swift has talked about an "extraordinary coincidence of talent at the time": "I never thought it was a conspiracy, a movement, a collective endeavour. It was a group of individuals coming together." (as quoted in Tonkin 2003: 18)
2. Since then, Amis has produced *Yellow Dog* and Swift *The Light of Day* (both 2003).
3. As reprinted in Lodge (2002: 296).
4. Bruno Zerweck indeed sees what he calls 'experimental realism' as a literary response to postmodernism (2001: 284).
5. See Nünning (2003) and Lane, Mengham & Tew (2003). Characteristically, the latter's stocktaking does not include any of the novels analysed here.
6. The phrase is taken from the title of Hassan's famous analysis of postmodernist fiction, which locates the first turn at the end of the 1930s (1987: 30, 88).
7. A representative case is Brenda K. Marshall's concept of the "postmodern moment [...] which demands an awareness of being-within a way of thinking" (1992: 2) and – judging by the examples she analyses – is relatively extensive in temporal terms. Peter Brooker solves the problem of the mixture of qualitative and temporal elements in the term by introducing a second notion. 'Postmodernism' is reserved "for a set of particularised artistic, philosophical and cultural modes, self-consciously but not exclusively adopted in the historical period of postmodernity" (1996: 26).
8. As pointed out by Raine in the above-mentioned interview, see Lodge (2002: 294-295).
9. Oates (2001: 21).
10. Lodge (1995: 212-214).
11. See the title of Thomas Kühn's study of the university novel – even though he reduces all such oppositions to the one treated in *Thinks* ... (2002: 39-40).
12. Lodge (2001: 250-257). Further references to this edition will be included in the text.
13. As quoted by Walsh (2001: 9).
14. As pointed out in Lodge (2002: 295).
15. *Ibid.*
16. *Ibid.*
17. See Raine's point that "polyphony means [that] the reader has to decide" for himself/herself (in Lodge 2002: 287).
18. *Ibid.*, 285.
19. See e.g. Oates (2001: 21), Tague (2001: 48), Emery (2001: 52).
20. The third-person perspective on Helen showing Ralph round her house

(chapter 17) is for instance followed by her view and then by his. Thus, the reader's suspicions that the tidiness of the place and the elaborate meal provided were the result of extensive preparation are confirmed by her subsequent diary entry. Chapter 19 then rounds off the picture by informing the reader that Ralph, too, noticed the trouble taken in his honour.

21 This is so much of a rule in *Thinks ...* that Walsh even considers it exceptional that the reader does not get a special insight into Helen's decision to sleep with Ralph (2001: 9).
22 As Raine points out in the interview reprinted in Lodge (2002: 287-288). Lodge himself adds a note to this section of the reprint specifying that Helen does not tell this experience "'as fiction', because she refers to herself by her own name, but in the style of fiction" (*ibid.*, 288).
23 On the use of *mise-en-abyme* in 'classic' postmodernist fiction see McHale (1987: 124-125).
24 Similar effects occur when readers recognise that Robyn Penrose, the academic invited to give a lecture at Ralph and Helen's university, comes from an earlier Lodge novel, *Nice Work*, and that – as Lodge himself has pointed out – the example from Henry James's *The Ambassadors* that Helen rejects for her lecture because "it's been done" (314) was previously used by the author who invented her (see Lodge 2002: 297).
25 A *Guardian* review of *Love etc* indeed lauds "Barnes's mastery of the dramatic form" (anon. 2000: 16).
26 See anon. (n.d.).
27 There is even a case of square brackets within round ones (Barnes 2001: 244-245). Further references to this edition will be included in the text.
28 Sutcliffe (2000: 7).
29 Even the chapter headings are taken directly from the contributions making up the respective part, and the selection seems to be in the characters' hands: While agreeing that Stuart starts off the next chapter, Oliver makes one request: "Please don't call this next bit 'The Story So Far'" (9). When exactly this title appears after the reader has turned the page, it seems only logical to read this as a manifestation of spite on his rival's part.
30 The term is indeed employed in one review (anon. 2000: 16).
31 This term is used by Barnes himself (see Sutcliffe 2000: 7).
32 Barnes (1992: 132-133). This title was already adopted for the 1996 French film version of *Talking It Over*.
33 Barnes (1992: 84, 173). It has to be noted, though, that *Love etc* at one point phrases a contribution from Oliver as "[*declined to answer any further questions*]" (241), which can be read as a narrator reporting a past response to the reader.
34 See e.g. *ibid.*, 16-18, 25-26.
35 *Ibid.*, 123-124, 140.
36 Imlah (2000).
37 Bradbury (2000: 12).
38 It is for instance extremely confusing that Stuart says Gillian bit his hand (226), while she, in her second account, claims she did not see "any point in biting it" (228), even though such an act of resistance would obviously have increased the credibility of her rape story.
39 Barnes (1992: 114-115).

40 As pointed out by Adams (2000).
41 The reader constructed by the book is clearly a British one (34, 152, 164). It might thus seem doubtful whether non-British audiences will actually identify with this role offered by the text. However, while the explicit comments on national identity might alienate them (see Roberts 2000), these passages are too isolated to prevent them from being drawn in by the direct addresses in the text.
42 As quoted in Wroe (2000).
43 Barnes, quoted in Sutcliffe (2000: 7). See also anon. (n.d.).
44 The opinion that the ending leaves open the possibility of another sequel is indeed held by some reviewers, see e.g. Imlah (2000) and anon. (2000: 16).
45 With similar clarity, Stuart at one point advises the reader "to skip the next bit unless you've got a strong stomach" (195).
46 McEwan (2002: 40). Further references to this edition will be included in the text.
47 This formulation echoes Briony's earlier view of such a 'description' of 'real' events as the proof of her new identity (156-157).
48 The narrator indeed describes her as "build[ing] and shap[ing] her narrative in her own words and establish[ing] the key *facts*" (180, my emphasis).
49 When writing to her beloved, who has become a soldier in France in the second part, Cecilia sees the rejection of one of Briony's fictional narratives by the *Horizon* magazine as a sign that "at least someone can see through her wretched fantasies" (212). Robbie in turn equates the romantic "stories" that he thinks the girl constantly made up about him with the "story that saw him all the way to Wandsworth prison" (233-234) – thereby incidentally misreading events himself, since Briony immediately forgot again about being in love with him (342).
50 Tonkin (2001).
51 The text does have a physical presence in the book, however, as "the completed pile of pages – one hundred and three!" that Briony hands in at the magazine's office (281).
52 This holds true for a number of details: The location of Bernini's *Triton* is given correctly (in contrast to Briony's novella), a Meissen vase is included instead of the too costly Ming, and the reader is given the "flavour" of the young writer's previous works (18, 23, 313-314). Moreover, "the watching girl" does "not actually realise that the vase ha[s] broken" (313, cf. 38-39). Her account follows rather than precedes Celia's (and there is no section from Robbie's perspective), which can be taken to reduce the redundancy criticised by Connolly.
53 As quoted by Cohu (2001).
54 See Lovenberg (2002: 42). Retrospectively, one can thus sense the presence of Briony the older narrator in the brief moment in the first part when the time frame is momentarily widened to include her life and career "[s]ix decades later" (41). McEwan himself has also pointed out in an interview with John Sutherland that in writing the first part, he took great care to reproduce the reticence of "a 77-year-old woman" in creating the love scene and to adopt the perspective of someone who takes "everything in [her time] [...] entirely for granted" and "describes virtually nothing that is specific to the time" (2002).

55 See Cohu (2001) and Sutherland (2002) respectively.
56 Finger (2002: 45).
57 The quotation constitutes McHale's definition of this technique (1987: 115).
58 Byatt (2001: 245). Further references to this edition will be included in the text.
59 The interest in perspective forms an obvious parallel with Helen's text, though Phineas's reflections involve the status of his whole narrative, rather than the isolated diary entry discussed by Helen.
60 Jensen (2000: 23).
61 The postmodernist nature of "the interconnectedness of things made possible by the power of analogy" in the novel is pointed out *ibid*.
62 Hermione Lee also mentions that after he has started his work on the biography, Phineas's life, "with his two loves, his travels and his new interest in nature", starts to resemble Elmer Bole's (2000: 11).
63 The contrast has been noted by Owen (2000: 66).
64 Placing narrative events *sous rature* is, of course, a classic technique of postmodernist fiction (see McHale 1987: 99-106).
65 Owen (2000: 66). See also Lee (2000: 11); Williams (2000: 56); Mattingly (2001).

Bibliography

Adams, Tim: "The Eternal Triangle", *The Observer*, 23 July 2000.
Anon.: "Careless Talk Costs Wives", *The Guardian*, 5 May 2000, 16.
–: "A Conversation with Julian Barnes", Random House website, n.d., http://www.randomhouse.com/catalog/display.pperl?isbn=0375411615&view=qa (accessed 13 March 2003).
Barnes, Julian: *Talking It Over*, London, 1992 [first edition 1991].
–: *Love, etc*, London, 2001 [first edition 2000].
Bradbury, Dominic: "Talking It Over about Writing, etc", *The Times*, 2 August 2000, 12.
Brooker, Peter: "Introduction. Reconstructions". – In P.B. (Ed.): *Modernism/ Postmodernism*, London & New York, 1992, pp. 1-33.
Byatt, A.S.: *The Biographer's Tale*, London, 2001 [first edition 2000].
Cohu, Will: "'I Thought I Was Going to Screw It Up'", 22 September 2001, http://www.arts.telegraph.co.uk (accessed 5 July 2002).
Emery, Michael: "Finding Soul in Science", *Birmingham Post*, 10 March 2001, 52.
Finger, Evelyn: "Eines langen Tages Reise in die Nacht", *Die Zeit*, 19 September 2002, 45-46.
Granta 7 (1983).
Hassan, Ihab: *The Postmodern Turn. Essays in Postmodern Theory and Culture*, Columbus, 1987.
Imlah, Mick: "Revenge of a Tortoise", *Times Literary Supplement*, 28 July 2000.
Jensen, Hal: "Unexaggerated Lions", *Times Literary Supplement*, 2 June 2000, 23.
Kühn, Thomas: *Two Cultures, Universities and Intellectuals. Der englische Uni-*

versitätsroman der 70er und 80er Jahre im Kontext des Hochschuldiskurses, Tübingen, 2002.
Lane, Richard J., Rod Mengham & Philip Tew (Eds.): *Contemporary British Fiction*, Cambridge, 2003.
Lee, Hermione: "Just Get a Life. Have You Read as Widely as A.S. Byatt?", *The Observer*, 28 May 2000, 11.
Lodge, David: *Therapy. A Novel*, London, 1995.
–: *Thinks .... A Novel*, London, 2001.
–: *Consciousness and the Novel. Connected Essays*, Cambridge, Mass., 2002.
Lovenberg, Felicitas von: "Vergiftete Zeilen. Lesen gefährdet den Charakter", *Frankfurter Allgemeine Zeitung*, 31 August 2002, 42.
Marshall, Brenda K.: *Teaching the Postmodern. Fiction and Theory*, London & New York, 1992.
Mattingly, Daniel: "The Postmodern Biographer. A.S. Byatt's Newest Novel Ponders the Perils of Theory", *The Yale Review of Books* 4, no. 2, 2001, http://www.yale.edu/yrb/summer01/review08.htm (accessed 18 June 2002).
McEwan, Ian: *Atonement*, London, 2002 [first edition 2001].
McHale, Brian: *Postmodernist Fiction*, New York & London, 1987.
Nünning, Vera: "Beyond Indifference. New Departures in British Fiction at the Turn of the 21st Century". – In Klaus Stierstorfer (Ed.): *Beyond Postmodernism. Reassessment in Literature, Theory and Culture*, Berlin, 2003, pp. 235-254.
Oates, Joyce Carol: "Hot-Blooded Brits", *Times Literary Supplement*, 23 February 2001, 21-22.
Owen, Katie: "This Student Is too Clever", *Mail on Sunday*, 28 March 2000, 66.
Roberts, Ryan: "*Love, etc*, etc.", Julian Barnes website, August 2000, http://www.jbarnes.com/fb/005.html (accessed 4 August 2000).
Sutcliffe, Thomas: "I Met a Man Who Wasn't There", *The Independent*, 1 August 2000, 7.
Sutherland, John: "Life Was Clearly too Interesting in the War", *The Guardian*, 3 January 2002.
Tague, John: "Prison House of Language", *The Independent*, 4 March 2001, 48.
Tonkin, Boyd: "*Atonement* by Ian McEwan", *The Independent*, 15 September 2001.
–: "Distant Voices, Still Lives", *The Independent*, 1 March 2003, 18.
Walsh, John: "David Lodge. Nice Work for Body and Soul", *The Independent*, 3 March 2001, 9.
Williams, Zoe: "The Biographer Biographised", *Evening Standard*, 5 June 2000, 56.
Wroe, Nicholas: "Literature's Mister Cool", *The Guardian*, 29 July 2000.
Zerweck, Bruno: *Die Synthese aus Realismus und Experiment. Der englische Roman der 1980er und 1990er Jahre aus erzähltheoretischer und kulturwissenschaftlicher Sicht*, Trier, 2001.

Christoph Ribbat, Bonn

The Washcloth at the Bottom of the Pile.
A Conversation with Jonathan Franzen

"All of my stuff is a joke", Jonathan Franzen tells his interviewer. And he adds: "A serious joke." It is this ambivalence, apparently, that has made Franzen one of the most interesting novelists of the twenty-first century. *The Corrections*, published in September 2001, was praised by both audiences and literary critics and seemed to accomplish an extremely rare feat: it pleased its readers with slapstick comedy and absurd, sit-com style family relations and at the same time managed not to alienate readers interested in the complexities of the literary imagination by unfolding an extremely ambitious, panoramic vision of the forces threatening to obliterate the authentic individual as such in contemporary American culture. With a first sentence destined to join the American novel's pantheon of great openings ("The madness of an autumn prairie cold front coming through"), *The Corrections* could even be understood by readers so inclined as a prophetic text for the troubled first years of a new decade.

The following interview documents a conversation with the author in late January 2002, when Jonathan Franzen's international career was just taking off. The author was visiting the American Academy in Berlin, and this conversation took place on a rainy morning following a public reading of *The Corrections* by the author. The interview does not appear in its entirety. The passages selected here focus on some of the issues most relevant to Franzen's work and his public persona: his first two novels (*The Twenty-Seventh City*, 1988, and *Strong Motion*, 1992) and his essays from the 1990s (among them, the most well-known piece: "Perchance to Dream. In an Age of Images, A Reason to Write Novels", 1996). In conclusion, the conversation touches on his role in what was known as 'Oprahgate' and his position in debates on literature's role in the aftermath of September 11.

When your friend and fellow novelist Jeffrey Eugenides introduced you last night, he said about the two of you that as a generation you were deconstructing stories before you told them. That didn't really convince me.

A little too much irritating self-consciousness? No, I was telling stories first – in college. I came over after college, to Berlin, with a Fulbright grant and with a suitcase full of books. I believe I had one novel, *Gravity's Rainbow*, and this huge stack of these theory books that I intended to read. And I did read Auerbach then, I did read Fredric Jameson. I had these dense Derridean and Lacanian texts because I'd been in love with that stuff the previous year. By the end of that fall I was begging my then-fiancée, soon-to-be wife, to bring over novels. She brought about ten novels, she brought *Anna Karenina* and *Middlemarch*, for instance, and I never read the Lacan, never read the Derrida. They were so boring.

It's true, though, that the one novel I did bring initially was Pynchon's *Gravity's Rainbow*. My thinking even in *The Twenty-Seventh City* was: Well, Pynchon is about the ambiguity of whether there is a conspiracy or not. And I, theoretically self-conscious, said: Let's just make conspiracy absolutely real and upfront from page one. Much more than this. It seemed to me that the problem of coincidence in the nineteenth century novel was solved by this sort of light-hearted assertion by Pynchon and others. They said: Well, nothing is a coincidence, it all hangs together, we're all being manipulated in this conspiratorial way. And because coincidence was such a part of the nineteenth century books that I loved I decided: Well, let's just take it as a given. Let's take it a step further. The thing becomes perfectly circular. Everything in my experience is a constructed narrative, but it's still my experience. Fine, all right, signifier and signified are not in a meaningful relationship, it's all a play among the signifiers. And so forth. That's just sort of an entertaining and useful excursus. But it gets you back to the same point. We still have these lives.

> *In your essays from the 1990s – in "Perchance to Dream" as well as in other pieces – it seems as if you attack academia not so much for its obsession with postmodernism, but rather because of the way in which you perceived it as being dominated by feminist and multicultural theory.*

I now see that nonfiction of mine from the mid-1990s as being totally about personal fear and resentment. It was my own desperate struggle to reclaim something that I felt had been taken away from me. I really was trying to say – to the extent that I continue to stand by that publicly and intellectually – that I think people read for a connection and that the problem with tribal identity and the problem with the philosophy of multiculturalism is that it seems to say you really are speaking to your tribe, for your tribe, as a member of your tribe. And that's just not how I feel when I'm reading Jane Austen. Yes, Austen, OK, maybe we are of the same tribe, but maybe even Zora Neale Hurston ... We've got the tribes set up all wrong. It's not about black or white, male or female.

It's about: Does the world seem ridiculous and tragic to you? Does it seem a lot more complicated than the popular entertainment and popular discourse will have you believe? And if it does, if the answer is yes, then that fact, I think, matters more than anything else, really. Which is not to discount, it's merely to be suspicious of, writing that is promoted merely because of the identity of the writer.

The Lamberts in The Corrections: *would it be accurate to say that you see them not so much as white Americans, but as Midwesterners? That place is more important than ethnicity or class?*

No, obviously they're white. Even though maybe not economically, but certainly by education, they are upper middle class. And I think those things are of significance. Somebody who came from an utterly different background can certainly be forgiven for not finding much of interest to him in these worries. So I always recognize that. I recognize that one of the reasons that Paula Fox's novel *Desperate Characters* meant so much to me as it did was that it was about a marriage at a point that my marriage was at. Accidents do matter in how you read a book.

One thing I have noticed about the way The Corrections *has been read is that some people read it as a treatise on the 'typical' American family, or the 'typical suburbanite'.*

Certainly I realize it's out there because I get asked the question a lot. Is this a typical American family? Chip Lambert [a college professor in *The Corrections*] in his classroom discussion deliberately tries to avoid a conversation about art's responsibility vis-à-vis the typical ... It's not an interesting concept. Suffice it to say that I and other writers I know are not thinking in terms of the typical. That sounds like some sort of Soviet project.

One of the terms I *am* thinking about is suburban versus urban. It seems to me that the suburb is set up to obviate or avoid precisely the stark difference, that sense of cultural entropy that characterizes the city. I want to be able to continue to tell interesting stories and to build novels that give me a certain kind of feeling, and that which seems to smooth things over and eliminate conflicts, whether it's the uniformity of suburban life or the medication toward the norm or American penetration of every global market – that is about the erosion of difference, that's what I'm about resisting as a novelist. Hence the idea of the typical, the label of functional or dysfunctional, those are all, broadly speaking, what I'm in resistance to.

The Corrections is such a fast-paced novel that the first brief chapter – "St. Jude" – seems, strangely enough, a little slow, almost a little hard to read. As if you were consciously making it hard for your readers to get over the beginning of the book ...

I've thought about the fact that this idea could be directed against *The Corrections*. I worked on the book hard, so pretty much everything you could think of along those lines I've thought of.

The book was begun anew with shards of a different project. Those shards had to be there. The St. Jude opening had to be there. I had to start with this academic romance [Chip Lambert, the college professor and key protagonist, has an affair with one of his students]. I was really unhappy about both those things because I thought these were the most familiar parts of the book. Like: Oh my God – another story of an affair between a college professor and a female student! Oh my God – another wry account of the desolation of suburban retirement! And I was unhappy to be having them right upfront. But [laughs] ... I got over it. I stand by it. It's of a piece with the rest of the book. Nonetheless, it took me the longest writing the Chip chapter. It was difficult trying some reasonably fresh take on that very familiar story.

Whereas some parts of The Corrections *are just plain funny, I was struck by the bitterness of your second novel,* Strong Motion.

It's an angry book. A very, very angry book.

The sex parts ...

I agree.

What I found extremely interesting was the chapter in Strong Motion *that uses the point of view of a racoon.*

I was after something. I didn't have a real program there. It's just something I wanted to do. Part of what made *Strong Motion* fun to write was fooling around with nature – suddenly shifting to other points of view, for instance. Or Louis's thinking that if only we could really be waiting for an earthquake all the time, we'd never have an earthquake because they only happen when we're not looking. That's his theory: something's always waiting. That is tied in my mind to Renee's huge self-consciousness, the sense of how self-consciousness freezes you. It replaces action. And then there's this thing which in spite of her best effort to be self-conscious happens anyway. Who knows what that's about. It's there.

It's funny that you would rather use the point of view of an animal than first person.

In the case of *The Corrections*, the first, the unwritable version, one of the things that was making it unwritable was the first-person narrator. I came to think that first person is incredibly overused. First person almost always should be in third person. Only if you have a voice or an unreliable narrator ... *The Catcher in the Rye* should be in first person. *Lolita* should be in first person, *The Great Gatsby*. I studied and studied *The Great Gatsby* thinking, how does he do this? Such a perfect voice! And yet I could never find a reason to have it in *The Corrections* and eventually I thought: Well, I don't have anything to prove because I've used the first person voice in my nonfiction and that's actually my first person voice and I don't feel like I'm a lesser novelist because I can't do first person.

Third person seems the better option to represent a family, as in The Corrections?

It's multivalent. Because it's difficult for me to take sides. And actually to try to create an entirely authentic voice for each perspective would be this monstrously challenging thing that would seem 1920s-ish any way. Would seem very *The Sound and the Fury*. One of the things I find off-putting is a literary novel ... A novel that sets itself up as literary. My heart sort of sinks when I open a book and it's: Oh, this book has three sections, each has a voice, one is the sailor, one is the sailor's wife, one is the daughter ... It's like, awwwh, alright, fine ... If it's a good story, you don't really need that.

One of the things I was trying to learn how to do in *Strong Motion* was to write from outside of perspective. I was very taken with Flannery O'Connor the year I started the book and she really rigorously stays outside the character's perspective much of the time. One thing that forces her to do is to be extremely precise in describing people's gestures. And I kept slipping into Louis's point of view for instance and I also tried to get outside of him and to describe him. Seemed to make a livelier page. Another thing: if you allow yourself to fall into perspective too much its very hard work to really imagine a scene, to get it right gesturally. In gestures that are described as metaphors that are thematically interesting and useful. But if you do the work ... All of Flannery O'Connor shows the payoff if you're rigorous about making yourself invisible. But these are all crafty things that are probably not critically significant.

To return to cultural context then: would it be accurate to explain the success of The Corrections *with the growing importance of family and the private sphere after 9/11?*

In a time of peace the novelist is probably going to be thinking about war. In a time of war, the novelist is going to be thinking about these domestic things. Just as a sort of corrective. But I don't think that's how it's being read. The reports I'm getting from readers are things like: I made the mistake of reading the book right before Christmas. In the end, the book probably does come down on the side: Well, like it or not, these are connections that are real. It's very hard to locate sorts of meaning elsewhere. But to read it as a family values book ... that would be an extremely rich irony.

Is there anything you can say about the effects 9/11 might have on American literature?

I don't think the country has changed that much since 9/11. And: there was no good fiction being written about Vietnam when Vietnam was happening. 1944 was not a great time for World War II novels. So why is there this idea we ought to be looking for good writing about September 11 now? We don't even know what happened yet. As [American novelist] Donald Antrim said: it's the 12-year-olds on whom it's going to have a big impact. It's not going to change me. It confirmed things for me. It didn't seem like an interesting event per se. A terrible event, yes.

What's somewhat more interesting, is, say, with respect for the United States trying to be a country that stands for the rule of law and also deals with lawless people, the POW in Guantanamo Bay. Or following the oil trail through the last decade, through Saudi Arabia, Pakistan, Afghanistan, Iraq. Those things are interesting. But as an event? What was striking to me about 9/11 was that within two days the nation was told that it needed psychotherapy and began to receive psychotherapy. For this terrible trauma. You didn't see that after Pearl Harbor. It was like: We're adults, what are we going to do about this problem? Now: You poor children, now this terrible thing has happened, and now we sort of have to worry about our feelings. And the instant transformation of terrible event into media package: 'America Fights Back', 'America Under Attack', these graphic frames on CNN and all of the network coverage of it. It seems to me that the constant drumming of questions to writers – well, what do you have to say about 9/11? – is part of that packaging, part of that instant analysis. And, you know, the writers who interest me, they don't have a clue or else they are simply not interested because its already been tampered with. DeLillo has written about terrorism 20 years ago, I've written about terrorism in the American heartland in the *Twenty-Seventh City* 15 years ago. I mean what do you want me to say except: Yeah, it was a long time coming. Boy, am I not surprised. And it was a terrible, terrible thing.

One of the first responses by intellectuals to 9/11 and how it might change our culture was the argument that the time of obsessing about simulacra was over. Baudrillard, at least to some, seemed terribly passé. This was real, this was not a construction. The events urged us to come back to real objects, real things. I'm not really making a connection to your work, but one of the things I noticed about your novels are the long, very detailed lists of objects. Of real things. There is one long list in The Twenty-Seventh City *when a house burns down and you enumerate almost all of the things inside of the house. And in* The Corrections, *also, lists of objects seem central – all of the things that Enid keeps in the St. Jude house, for instance. I was wondering why these everyday objects are important to you.*

A great deal of thought went into the book and the thought always had the same goal, which was: how am I going to get this thing written? The novel as grail, as thing that I have unreasoned faith, just plain-old loving faith in, care about tremendously, want to take on the enemies and perceived enemies of – even if they are in my own heart, where I feel like: I don't have sufficient confidence or I'm not sufficiently mature to write this. So I thought a lot about those things, but something like the list of objects? I could talk about what stuff like that comes from emotionally. When I was 10, 12 years old I used to feel sorry for the washcloths at the bottom of the pile of washcloths that didn't get used very often and I would deliberately sometimes take them from the bottom because I felt like they'd been forgotten. I had this tremendous childish sympathy with objects and I think that was because it was a way of dealing with the fact that everything was so emotionally latent in my own childhood, my own family, that I couldn't possibly deal with the emotion in direct form with another person. I could have a feeling for them that was just completely impossible and unsafe to have about my mom.

I was also thinking of the lists of brand names and celebrities in Bret Easton Ellis's novels.

I like Bret a great deal. I liked *American Psycho*, though I liked the movie more than I liked the book itself. Because I felt that, since it's about surface, it seemed to lend itself so much better to a superficial medium like film. It's about the visual impact of these things. Listing the words, listing the designer names … I find that tedious as a reader. Bret's very smart, he's really on to something. But it's no accident that he's very much associated with the magazine *Artforum*. Those kinds of works are in the same discourse as a lot of visual art in the last couple of years – rather than in the much more conservative, conventional tradition of fiction writing that I feel like I inhabit. So: intellectually very interesting, but not affecting.

> *Ellis has great influence on a group of younger German authors: Christian Kracht, Benjamin von Stuckrad-Barre, the creators of a genre briefly known as 'Popliteratur', detested by some, yet praised as new and comparatively original by others. Do you follow the German literary scene at all?*

I've been hearing about it. With the German stuff I'm always in this terrible bind because I feel this responsibility to read it in German and yet it's still a chore for me. Especially the younger writers. And a lot of it is not available in the States – we get Bernhard Schlink and that's about it. But we don't get ... Can you write down some names for me?

> *Sure. Funny that you mention Bernhard Schlink, whose novel* The Reader *was an Oprah Book Club selection long before* The Corrections *was selected. Winfrey pulled back the selection of your novel after you made some comments that she misinterpreted as criticism of her book club. You've said in later interviews that you didn't handle the media too well in that case.*

I think it can safely be said that I didn't do a great job with the media when it came to the Oprah stuff. [laughs] Although some people claim that it was a brilliant marketing ploy on my part, that it was all deliberate, but that's patently ridiculous.

> *Did your angry voice of the 1990s come through in that conflict?*

Right. There was a sense of lingering ... resentment. All of that anger, that sense of isolation. For better and for worse, that sense of isolation. And that powerful sense of: It's me against the world. That sustained me through the writing of the book. It was like I was a month late in realizing that was no longer really appropriate in a conversation. Something else had happened with the book. But again it took about a month to realize that. Which is also why I've gone back and rewrote "Perchance to Dream" [for a 2002 volume of essays – *How to Be Alone* – the essay was retitled: "Why Bother?"].

> *Gender played an important role in that controversy.*

Taken out of context. Because I was used to having a conversation with a small community. For instance: I upset a lot of women by saying on National Public Radio that I had heard that the Oprah label on a book scared off male readers and that I hoped to actually reach male readers with this book. Well, behind that for me was what everybody knows.

Which is: men over 30 don't really read books in America. If they do, they might read Tom Clancy. Or *How to Grow in the Business World.* In other words: I'm fully aware that most novels are bought and read by women and so when I say I had hoped to reach a male audience I was hoping this book might actually appeal to a lot of different people. Including finding some way to make this book relevant and interesting to men, not simply to women who I take for granted as part of the audience. Of course I didn't say any of that, I merely said I hoped to reach a male audience. Of course that then gets heard – when you're talking not to *Harper's* readers but to several million listeners on National Public Radio – that gets heard as: Franzen doesn't care about women readers. The readers he cares about are male. It's so much the opposite of that, I don't even bother saying it.

Astrid Böger, Düsseldorf

Making the Best of It.
New American Short Stories after 9/11

Every year a handful of collections of short fiction are produced in the United States which claim to contain the best of what the field has to offer. Having undergone rigorous selection processes, these stories can be read as literary litmus tests of the historical moment during which they were written, of its specific cultural weight and density and of its degree of acidity. Short by definition and nowadays generally favoring psychological realism over the more fantastic and romantic origins of the genre,[1] short stories have the capacity to engage more directly with the world than most other literary formats. Perhaps more significantly, even though the stories themselves do not usually make explicit references to particular historical events, they are often read and interpreted as being somehow in resonance with such events. This has certainly been the case with the three recent publications I want to discuss here: *The Best American Short Stories 2002*, *The O. Henry Prize Stories 2002*, and *Best New American Voices 2003*.[2] In their introductory comments, the editors of all three collections establish some connection between the stories they selected and what is now ritually referenced as 'the tragic events of September 11', even as they acknowledge that most of the stories had actually been written *before* the attacks on the World Trade Center and the Pentagon that the date now seems doomed forever to connote. And even if we were not explicitly reminded of the larger cultural context in which these stories appeared, there is no denying that a striking number of them deal with such sobering themes as violence, death, and other, more sweeping traumas including war, while evoking an atmosphere bound to remind readers of some of the most troubling concerns of today, both in America and elsewhere.

In the aftermath of the September 11th attacks, a group of fifteen writers "who have attained a certain stature for their work"[3] was commissioned by the US Department of State's newly recreated Office of International Information Programs to submit short pieces that would elaborate on the question of "what it means to be an American Writer".[4] These pieces were to be included in a publication entitled *Writers on America* which would then be distributed internationally. Stressing such core American values as diversity, economic opportunity, freedom and democracy, the propagandist purposes of this publication are hard to overlook. Most of the authors, however, while affirming said values, also gesture toward more universal aims, as seen, for instance, in Robert Olen Butler's concluding sentences reminiscent of Walt Whitman, "I am an artist. I look at my country and I seek the human soul."[5] Both of these seemingly contradictory impulses appear throughout these essays: the exploration of an identifiable American *way of life*, with its own core beliefs and values, and at the same time the transcendence of any particular properties of American-ness toward a more universal vision. These "reflections", as is explained in the introductory statement, thus continue "a long tradition of literary self-analysis in the United States", from J. Hector Saint John de Crèvecœur to Ralph Waldo Emerson and Ernest Hemingway.[6] Here, I am bringing *Writers on America* into dialogue with the texts collected in the recent collections of short fiction mentioned above, in an attempt to show how these contemporary texts reflect on the art of writing and, simultaneously, strike notes which resonate richly with the present world-historical moment. Autobiographical rather than fictional – though autobiography is best understood as a form of fiction in itself – the narratives in *Writers on America* can help us appreciate the realities presented in those other stories, and vice versa.

1. *Hitting Home.* The Best American Short Stories 2002

It is important to consider where these stories come from, as each venue of origin and each selection process puts its own mark on the final product, i.e. the publication we hold in our hands. Entries for *The Best American Short Stories* undergo three such processes of selection: First, only stories written "in English by writers who are American or Canadian, or who have made the United States or Canada their home"[7] are considered. Furthermore, these must have already been published over the course of the year in one of the eligible magazines, with *The New Yorker* clearly heading the list in 2002, since eight out of the twenty stories that made it into the final selection first appeared there.[8] Series editor Katrina Kenison limits the qualified entries to about 120, from which the guest editor finally picks the stories that are then reprinted in the actual book – a task writer Sue Miller took on for 2002. Kenison admits that she let her choices be guided by the political events of the fall of 2001 when she offers, "I came to see in some of these works nothing less than an antidote to terror."[9] The criteria Miller gives for her selection are more general, claiming that in fact she sees "excellence" as the stories' only commonality: "In the aggregate they had no voice, they didn't speak; separately, they certainly did – but each was a perfect representative only of its own instance."[10]

However, when reading these stories, a common theme does emerge: the home, including the people who make up a home, or who are absent from it. In other words, the majority of these stories deal with family relationships. Typically, a commonplace American setting is used as a backdrop for some unfolding drama. Michael Chabon's opening story "Along the Frontage Road", for instance, depicts a father and his young son going to "a vacant lot between the interstate and the Berkeley mudflats" (1) in order to pick a pumpkin for Halloween – a rather unspectacular undertaking in nondescript surroundings. But then it is gradually revealed, through the boy's choice of a tiny pumpkin that he wants to give a name – despite his father's initial refusal – that the family is having to deal with the trauma of a recent abortion. As in most of the stories in the collection, the underlying themes here are loss, mourning, and, ultimately, forgiveness. At times, the need for forgiveness assumes a cosmic quality, as in Jill McCorkle's "Billy Goats". This story is told from the perspective of a group of pre-adolescent children aptly described as "too old for kick-the-can and too young to make out". (202) Not knowing what to do with themselves turns out to be the least of their problems, however, as it soon becomes apparent that the actual, day-to-day violence surrounding them surpasses even the darkest childhood nightmare. There has been a recent murder-suicide in their town which extinguished a whole family; they have seen one young man slowly lose his mind; an unnamed 'freckled boy' is sexually abused by some of the older boys and kills himself out of shame; another man who is said to have been queer also ends his own life. In addition to these gruesome deaths, the children realize their own parents' mortality: "We had learned that alcohol and cigarettes would begin to kill off people we loved. Some of the grownups who sheltered us were disappearing from their windows like fade-outs." (202) The second half of the story is told from the perspective of one of the children, now a young woman in college, who has a fantasy of calling up all the now-dead people she grew up with in their graves, culminating in a poetic vision that expresses the sense of control over her own life she has finally achieved as well as a universal notion of forgiveness: "[L]ike a director, I would call for lights to come on in every house in town and for every person who had ever lived there to step outside and take a long deep breath on this average summer night." (208)

Besides death and fear, other, less morbid themes occur throughout *The Best American Short Stories*. In particular, ethnic and cultural differences are frequently negotiated. This can occur in simple cross-cultural encounters, such as in "Along the Frontage Road", in which appears a cashier "of indeterminate ethnicity – Arab, Mexican, Israeli, Armenian, Uzbek", (4) or in Leonard Michaels's "Nachman from Los Angeles", which centers on a deal gone awry: an American graduate student has promised to write a term paper for a wealthy Iranian fellow student and then fails to deliver it. Other stories frame cultural differences as more complex narratives of immigration, assimilation, and their bearing on family and community relations, as in Meg Mullins's story "The Rug", in which an Iranian carpet-dealer is trying to make a living in America even as his marriage at home is falling apart, or Melissa Hardy's "The Heifer", in which a Finnish couple emigrates to Canada where they struggle with farm life as well as with each other. It is striking that both these stories end in catastrophic failures, both of the marriages *and* the negotiations of cultural difference. Several other stories treat cultural difference as something that is passed on through family lineage, almost like genes. In Beth Lordan's "Digging" this is an unconscious process involving three generations of two Irish families. The families are united when two of their youngest descendents living in the United States fall in love and marry, in the process inheriting an endless array of family secrets and hidden treasures to be dug up or not. The couple's mutual attraction is largely based on their Irish-ness ("he tells her about Irish politics, and she tells him droll bits about Irish people", 185) but ultimately their happiness together is founded on life and prospects in America, not Ireland. This sense of having 'the best of both worlds' creates a sharp contrast with the last story in the collection, Mary Jukari Waters's "Aftermath", set in post-WWII Japan. A Japanese woman whose husband was killed in the war by American soldiers has to come to terms with her son's growing up in an environment increasingly influenced by American mass culture. In the context of traditional Japanese society, still based on strongly patriarchal values, the son's eroding memory of his father stands for the much-feared loss of cultural identity.

While almost all the selections included in *The Best American Short Stories* deal with terrible losses, there is in them also a potential for the transformation of pain – which is perhaps what Kenison means when she suggests that they served as an "antidote to terror". Such redeeming moments occur either within the narrative itself – the pumpkin is named, and so is the loss it stands for, so that mourning can begin; the memory of the father is given a proper place; the dead are called up for a final blessing of the place where they were once alive – or on a meta-level, in the form of a pure, creative impulse. Arthur Miller's "Bulldog" is such a story, as is Alice Munro's "Family Furnishings". The latter can be read as a story about the impulse to transform experience into a work of art, to be creative. Chronology is carefully eschewed and the truths that are at the heart of the story are never fully revealed. Instead, all the *stuff* that comes from decades of accumulating family furnishings, standing for too many traumas and untold secrets along with a few pleasant memories – and above all else the inability to let go – fills up the narrative space. Literally overstuffed, the narrator finally leaves it all behind or, rather, she experiences a moment of self-creation that seems programmatic for the mood that prevails in most of these stories:

> Such happiness, to be alone. [...] I did not think of the story that I would write [...] but of the work I wanted to do, which seemed more like grabbing something out of the air than like constructing stories. [...] This was what I wanted, this was what I thought I had to pay attention to, this was how I wanted my life to be. (302-303)

2. *Please Do Disturb.* The O. Henry Prize Stories 2002

"Interesting and unconventional", according to the blurb on the 2002 edition's back cover, *The O. Henry Prize Stories* are also one of the most important publication and award-giving institutions for "the very best in American and Canadian fiction". A great effort is made to include in the annual anthology established writers along with new talents, whose work has appeared over the course of the year in literary magazines of greater or lesser renown.[11] Twenty out of thousands of such stories were selected for the 2002 collection by series editor Larry Dark, which were then submitted to the prize jury members (Dave Eggers, Joyce Carol Oates, and Colson Whitehead) whose choices determined the three ranked winners.[12] Additionally, *The New Yorker* received the Magazine Award 2002 for "publishing the best fiction during the course of the previous year" (vii).

At first sight, there are striking similarities with *The Best American Short Stories*, all the more so as two stories appear in both collections (Alice Munro's "Family Furnishings" and Edwidge Danticat's "Seven") and two other authors (Mary Yukari Waters and Richard Ford) have entries, though different ones, in each. But there are some important differences. Generally speaking, *The O. Henry Prize Stories* are more experimental. Thus, a story titled "Scordatura", which won the second prize, is written in the second person singular, the 'you' throughout making for a conversational, even intimate tone as it seems to imply a direct conversation with the reader. "Memento Mori" is narrated from the point of view (or split consciousness, it's left unclear which) of someone who has lost his short-term memory due to trauma and subsequently goes through obsessively repetitive behavior loops, and is at the mercy of the few certainties he believes there are (namely, that his wife was killed some time ago and that he has to find her murderer). In "Speonk" an anecdote is told in three variations leaving it to the reader to figure it all out; and finally, "Good Old Neon" is told from the perspective of someone dead. Whereas the majority of *The Best American Short Stories* reveal a deep need for redemption of some kind (which is usually satisfied), any such hope is rarely granted in *The O. Henry Prize Stories*. This has much to do with the O. Henry tradition of storytelling itself, which favors dark ironies, surprising plot twists and uncertain outcomes over soothing comforts of closure (v).

In fact, some of *The O. Henry Prize Stories* have a double-edged quality that almost turns them into the literary equivalents of optical illusions, where one shape turns into another depending on the way one looks at it. A good example of this is Munro's "Family Furnishings". While the reading offered above, focusing on the narrator's slow growth toward creativity and self-awareness, is the one that immediately suggests itself, there is another, much darker side to the story. If certain past events, never made explicit but always lurking below the surface, are filled in by the reader, the effect is devastating, leaving nothing standing that previously passed for truth. In *The O. Henry Prize Stories*, too, marriage and family life are important themes, but harmony is rarely achieved and relationships tend to be doomed in spite of good intentions. The unsettling quality of these stories is the one thing they have in common, even though there are some thematic brackets as well. Larry Dark singles out travel, marriage, and writing as such common themes – broadly conceived so as to encompass their inherent potential for conflict as well, due to displacement, troubled intimacy, and the harms of self-expression at the expense of others, respectively. While Dark insists that none of these themes "necessarily sweep up all of the stories in the collection" (xix), sometimes a particular story may sweep up all the themes. In A.M. Homes's "Do Not Disturb" all three come together when a writer and his estranged wife (who finds out she has terminal cancer) try to save what is left of their marriage by taking a trip to Paris. In the end, though, their efforts fail. All that remains is a deep mutual resentment which leaves the husband fearful for his own life as well as his wife's, physical and emotional paralysis and, perhaps most disturbing of all, a deadly closure worthy of Edgar Allan Poe.

A sense of impending disaster within or without the domestic sphere reappears throughout *The O. Henry Prize Stories*. Judged by certain standards proposed by Raymond Carver, this would mark them as good stories indeed:

> I like it when there is some feeling of threat or sense of menace in short stories. I think a little menace is fine to have in a story. For one

thing, it's good for the circulation. There has to be tension, a sense that something is imminent, that certain things are in relentless motion, or else, most often, there simply won't be a story. What creates tension in a piece of fiction is partly the way the concrete words are linked together to make up the visible action of the story. But it's also the things that are left out, that are implied, the landscape just under the smooth (but sometimes broken and unsettled) surface of things.[13]

The jurors may have had Carver's recommendations in mind when they gave the first prize to Kevin Brockmeier for "The Ceiling", for there is more than a little menace in this story; it is also very visual and, in its own unique way, progresses dramatically. Set in an average small town and opening with a birthday party for the narrator's seven-year-old son, what appears at first to be a rather idyllic community soon becomes literally overcast when an "object in the sky [...] large enough to eclipse the full moon" (8) begins to slowly descend upon, and ultimately threaten to annihilate, the town and its inhabitants. Throughout, any comforts to be had from home life are undermined by this imminent threat as well as a sense of alienation among the individuals exposed to it. For instance, at the first sighting of the then still slight celestial abnormality, the wife suddenly remarks, "My life is a mess". For the next several weeks, her husband "watch[es] her fall into a deep abstraction", (7) their relationship slowly eroding in the process. Finally, when 'the ceiling' has dropped so low that people can no longer move around but have to lie on the ground immobilized, the wife says to those around her as much as to herself, "Do you ever get the feeling you're supposed to be someplace else? [...] It's a kind of sudden dread" (16). Made under such extreme circumstances the effect of this statement is surreal, even funny. Considering the course of the story, however, the sobering question imposes itself at what point and to where she should have escaped.

Brockmeier's dark tale "powerfully conjoins the parable and the realistic short story, the horrific and the domestic", (3) as Joyce Carol Oates points out in her admiring introduction. Going well beyond the more purely realistic conventions, the story defies straightforward interpretations. Obviously, the familiar theme of estranged spouses reappears in it, as does a general sense of doom and claustrophobia. Not surprisingly, though, considering its dramatic *mise-en-scène* and especially the apocalyptic ending, in which structures are collapsing all around, the story has also been placed in the context of 9/11 and may even owe some of its obvious appeal to the jurors to this fact. As Oates suggests:

Though "The Ceiling" was written before September 11, 2001, it can now be read as a poetic meditation upon that tragic and unfathomable event in our history: an acknowledgement of our common humanity in the face of terror, and an eloquent if heartrendering testimony to the resilience of the human spirit in extremis. (3)

But perhaps Oates's comments in turn need to be understood as a testimony to the human need for reassurance *in extremis*, as nothing in the story itself would suggest such a hopeful message. In fact, the people in it seem doomed precisely because they are all too willing to accept their lot, as absurd as it may seem, whereas the active search for a solution – or collective escape – might have been a more appropriate response: "[I]f the ceiling were simply to hover where it was forever, we might come to forget that it was even there, charting for ourselves a new map of the night sky." (11)

3. *The Art of Madness.* Best New American Voices 2003

Joyce Carol Oates was also the guest editor of the last anthology of short fiction considered here, *Best New American Voices 2003*. Only in its third year, the series fittingly includes stories by younger and little known authors, which appear in print for the first time. According to the series editors, nominations are sought "from graduate writing programs, art organizations, workshops, and summer conferences",[14] most of which are located in the US, and a few in Canada (vii). Moreover, as this particular collection was prepared about a year after the others, it contains (with one exception) stories that were written in 2002, i.e., during the months following the September 11th events. This fact may or may not have guided Oates in "looking for works of fiction that involve the reader in dramatically realized, emotionally charged situations of significance" (ix). Given this motivation, though, it should have come as no surprise to her what she found. Still, she writes that she "was struck by the high percentage of stories in which extreme or grotesque imagery figured" (xi). And indeed, many of the fifteen stories included display a large measure of such imagery. At the same time, several focus on realities that feel quite imminent, as two of the openings Oates singles out for being "wonderfully diverse and imaginative" illustrate (ix):

> Four days before the UN Security Council resolution will turn Desert Shield into Desert Storm, the team waits for the scouts on the south side of a dust-covered washout deep in the Iraqi desert. Their operation is illegal, but necessary ("The Storekeeper" by Otis Haschemeyer, 149).

They are excavating the bodies at night, a few hundred yards away from our house. The bright halogen from the spotlights seeps through cracks in our closed windows and doors ("Everything Must Go" by Barry Matthews, 261).

Despite similarities with the other stories discussed here in terms of general subject matter, and in particular a prevalence of themes related to death, there is in the *Best New Voices* an insistence on pressing realities such as war, life under military occupation, mental illness and death from HIV/AIDS not often found in the other collections. At the same time the *Best New American Voices* are not only those of gloom and doom, but in fact some of the stories have a humorous quality rarely encountered elsewhere. For instance, Caimeen Garrett's "Circuits" opens with the line "Our sex life suffered terribly the summer my boyfriend competed on the amateur tug-of-war circuit." (183) If one looks for real diversity in a short story collection, the *Best New American Voices* seem to be the way to go.

Perhaps the most striking difference between this volume and *The Best American* and *O. Henry Prize Stories* is the fact that most of the stories leave the domestic realm behind. Even where familial relationships play a role, as in Cheryl Strayed's "Good" and Jenn McKee's "Under the Influence", family ties are violently compromised, such as by a mother's death of cancer, or when a couple's son is sent to prison for killing a man while driving intoxicated, respectively. Both stories center not so much on relationships but on the characters' growing awareness of the ultimate *unknowability* even of those closest to them (as expressed in the father's helpless realization: "I didn't even know Max drank", 109). Both stories share with most others in the collection a deep concern with 'doing the right thing', i.e. questions of morality. Intricately connected with this is another theme reappearing throughout, namely the question of normalcy and its opposite, madness. Or, more appropriately put, the troubled line between what is considered right and normal and what is not, and under what circumstances such qualifications might shift.

The protagonist in "April" is a young woman named Angie, who was hospitalized and misdiagnosed with schizophrenia after a complete mental breakdown, and then transferred to a 'farm' for the mentally ill, where she now struggles to regain control of her life. There are precious few meaningful ties with friends and family in her life, but it is unclear if this is the outcome of her breakdown or its cause. Reminiscent of Holden Caulfield's dilemma in *The Catcher in the Rye*, the suggestion throughout is that it is not so much the patients, but "the world that's crazy" (58). Unlike Salinger's discontented hero, however, the protagonist in "April" is all too eager to fit in, and to appear as normal as possible. This becomes painfully apparent when she nervously anticipates the first visit by her best high school friend, whom she has not seen since the breakdown:

> Angie was bent over, arms around herself, face against her thighs. Nothing, she was thinking. Nothing, nothing could make her fall apart in front of Jess again. She would be okay as long as she was careful, as long as she kept her hands out of sight, as long as she kept her thoughts on track. As long as she focused on the small details, as long as she made that be enough, as long as she made that be everything. (53)

In the end, Angie's efforts prove vain and her relationships remain strained at best. But the story is not without hope, as friendship and normalcy and perhaps even intimacy may eventually be found within the secure confines of "this odd new life" (55) of hers.

The borderline crossed in "The Storekeeper" – the earliest story in the collection, written in 1998 – is of another order entirely. In spite of Hays's rational outlook on life, things spiral out of his control when his wife leaves him for no apparent reason: "[S]he snapped right then and there. She blew a fuse." (154) Subsequently, he decides to leave his children with his parents and join the Navy as a 'storekeeper' of a supply center. Military life appeals to him because it appears to eliminate irrationality. When his knowledge of firearms (precision tools) and shooting (rational calculation) are noted, he enlists for a Sea-Air-Land (SEAL) team lacking a sniper for 'special operations' in Iraq on the eve of the 1991 gulf war. Even though there is no legal basis for these liquidations without UN backing, Hays does what he believes is his duty which is, in this case, to kill a man:

> [A]s I lined up the shot, the thought that it was illegal didn't cross my mind. The thought that I shouldn't be there didn't cross my mind. The thought that this guy was going to die didn't cross my mind. The only thought that went through my mind was, I can't let this SEAL team down. I would be devastated to let them down. (164)

To make sure the first strike hits its target – an unsuspecting observation guard in the desert "a little over a kilometer away" (150) – Hays goes through a lengthy process of various scientific calculations, including:

> The ballistic tipped bullet needs contact with a sturdy bone structure to explode. In humans, bone ossification is completed about the age of twenty-five. [...] The target looks about twenty. Hays would like

to take a sternum-to-spine shot, but the man faces due east. The bullet will be coming from the southwest at approximately a thirty-degree angle. He decides his trajectory should meet the target just below the man's right pectoral muscle. (159-160)

Hays functions as automatically as his high-tech weapon and kills the man with scientific precision. A crucial line is crossed – something snaps – the moment where all human concerns and emotions are taken out of the equation, the single-mindedness of the sniper translating into a form of insanity. Years later, Hays lives with his grown children again and, by all appearances, "[a]ll is well" (168). He never questions his actions from a moral or any other standpoint. But – still fixated on his 'target' – his unconsciousness forces him to re-enact the perfect shot:

> At night he dreams repeatedly of the man smoking his cigarette, [...] perhaps because Hays is smoking again himself. Then he looks for the lack of surprise in the man's eyes. [...] But as he watches, the image starts to skate away. That is generally when Hays realizes that he is viewing the man through a scope, that its reticle superimposes the image – crosshairs that for years were made from a black widow's silk webbing. (168)[15]

4. No Place like Home. Writers on America

When asked to elaborate on the question "In what sense do you see yourself as an American writer?", most of the authors included in the collection responded by writing about slightly different things probably more interesting to them, such as how they came to be Americans in the first place, and what America means to them, or when and why they took up writing (no surprises there – they were all avid readers first, which somehow gave them the idea). This being a publication sponsored by the US Department of State's Office of International Information Programs, it was hoped that "the results could illuminate in an interesting way certain American values – freedom, diversity, democracy – that may not be well understood in all parts of the world".[16] And indeed, some pieces respond to this call rather closely. Furthermore, there are some common themes strikingly similar to those appearing in the short story collections discussed above, namely the home and home life, and the experience of growing up in America. Even though this experience is without doubt more complicated for children coming from cultural backgrounds other than the United States, it is the first generation immigrant writers' narratives that strike the most patriotic notes. Interestingly, they are also the most poetic. Thus, Elmaz Abinader's

"Crossing the Threshold" uses the metaphor of the 'magic door' that separated her Arab-American family's house from the outside, expressing her sense of isolation from mainstream culture – a feeling only writing could help her overcome. Julia Alvarez is a native of the Dominican Republic, which she describes as "a repressive and dangerous dictatorship". She discusses her experiences of "prejudice and playground cruelty" after her arrival in the United States, and feeling "homesick and heartbroken" (2). But these negative feelings were gradually transformed when she began studying American poets – Walt Whitman and Langston Hughes figuring most prominently – which allowed her to develop her own sense of freedom to express herself as a pan-American writer, culminating in a bilingual poem alluding to both of her poet-heroes, "I, too, Sing América." (6-7) Naomi Shibab Nye grew up in Jerusalem as the daughter of a Palestinian father and an American mother. After their emigration to the United States, she was struck most by the religious freedom and the sense that "[e]verything was possible on the page" (2). She sees her writing as a "daily declaration of independence, saying, I am part of this magnificent diversity and intricate texture" (4).

These celebratory texts appear ritualistic in their invocation of American values and how centrally these affected the writers' lives. It is implied in all these texts that without coming to America, personal fulfilment could not have been found. America, in other words, figures as a symbol of everything that is desirable. It is striking that all these strongly affirmative narratives were written by women; most of the men – especially those born in the United States – submitted somewhat different, rather complex, and decidedly more sceptical responses.

Richard Ford describes his patriotic feelings at a young age, and how these were more related to being a Southerner than an American (1-2). The turmoil that gave rise to and surrounded the civil rights movement in the 1950s and 1960s, however, complicated his sense of both. As a writer, he has found a way to negotiate the ambivalences inherent in cultural identification:

> [C]onsonant with my American experience [...] (contested, complex, ambiguous, diverse, often disharmonious to the point of profound unsettlement), I have always *tried* to write stories and novels that testify to the nature of human kind as it is displayed by the purifying heat of adversity and disharmony and interrogation – lovers seeking but failing to find intimacy, mutual understanding, sympathy, consolation; fathers and sons, sons and mothers viewing one another longingly but imperfectly across gaps of misunderstanding [...]. (4, his emphasis)

Among other things, this pattern, which is closely followed in the stories by Ford included in both *The Best American* and *O. Henry Prize Stories*, shows the intimate connection between cultural identification and the *family plot* that is at the core of most of the short stories published in the recent collections. Robert Creeley, too, emphasizes the connection of family, writing, and being American, albeit more tentatively: "[W]riting was to prove the one constant in a life marked with endless shiftings of place and relationship [...]. Is that an American habit, I wonder?" In general, texts as these resist any singular notion of America or American-ness: "America, whatever it is, cannot be taken to be a single place", writes Creeley (3). As for the role of American literature, he has only modest hopes at best, which is made clear in one of the very few places where the September 11th events – the hidden agenda of *Writers on America* – are explicitly brought into the narrative:

> Poets are so very low in the ranking of public performers or those providing the body politic with material of their interest and desire. If the sad events of September 11, 2001, provoked a remarkable use of poems as a means wherewith to find a common and heartfelt ground for sorrow, it passed quickly as the country regained its equilibrium, turned to the conduct of an aggressive war, and, one has to recognize, went back to making money. (4)

Despite Creeley's verging on cynicism here, the very appearance of this passage in what is, after all, essentially a government-sponsored propaganda project makes one hopeful for the survival of some core American values. And, while his observation that America has gone back to 'business as usual' is certainly correct, one should not overlook the places where pain and trauma are dealt with. The 'unsettling' short stories published in recent American collections are a place to start.

Notes

1 See, for instance, Marler (1994: 165-181).
2 Miller & Kenison (2002); Dark (2002); Oates, Kulka, & Danford (2002).
3 See Clack (2002).
4 *Ibid.*
5 *Ibid.*, 4.
6 *Ibid.*, 1-2.
7 See foreword by Katrina Kenison (2002: xi).
8 Eight of the twenty *Best American Short Stories 2002* were previously published in *The New Yorker*, two in *Zoetrope*, and one each in *Agni Review*, *McSweeney's*, *The Southern Review*, *Descant*, *The Atlantic Monthly*, *Ploughshares*, *Bomb*, *The Iowa Review*, *Harper's Magazine*, and *Manoa*.

9   Kenison (2002: x).
10 See introduction by Sue Miller (2002: xiv-xv). Further references to the stories in each collection and the introductions preceding them will be made parenthetically in the text.
11 Four of the twenty *O.Henry Prize Stories 2002* had previously appeared in *The New Yorker*, two in *The Atlantic Monthly* and *McSweeney's*, and one each in *Ontario Review*, *Esquire*, *Zoetrope*, *Bamboo Ridge*, *Tin House,The Threepenny Review*, *Agni Review*, *GQ*, *Epoch*, *DoubleTake*, *The Oxford American*, and *Conjunctions*.
12 These were Kevin Brockmeier (first prize for "The Ceiling"), Mark Ray Lewis (second prize for "Scordatura"), and Louise Erdrich (third prize for "The Butcher's Wife").
13 Carver (1994: 276-277). Carver here implicitly acknowledges and comments on Ernest Hemingway's 'iceberg theory', according to which "[t]he dignity of movement of an ice-berg is due to only one-eighth of it being above water", in other words, the surface of a story always conceals much greater, and typically abysmal, depths. Cf. Zapf (1997: 264-265).
14 The institutions under whose tutelage the stories were produced and selected are printed underneath each title (paralleling the other publications' format, which lists the magazine titles in a similar way). In 2003, these were Syracuse University, Johns Hopkins University, Michener Center for Writers, Stanford University, Sewanee Writers' Conference, Fine Arts Work Center in Provincetown, Pennsylvania State University, 92nd Street Y, University of Montana, Florida State University, University of California at Irvine, University of Iowa, Cornell University, Naropa University. Also included is a list of participating institutions complete with contact information.
15 From a purely literary standpoint it does not matter, but a biologist might object here that black widows, being predatory spiders, do not weave webs.
16 See Clack (2002: 1). References to the individual narratives are included in the text. However, as the online publication is not consecutively paginated, each text starts at page 1.

Bibliography

Carver, Raymond: "On Writing". – In Charles E. May (Ed.): *The New Short Story Theories*, Athens, Ohio, 1994, pp. 276-277.
Clack, George (Ed.): *Writers on America*, 2002, http://usinfo.state.gov/products/pubs/writers/ (accessed 20 July 2004).
Dark, Larry (Ed.): *The O. Henry Prize Stories*, New York, 2002.
Marler, Robert F.: "From Tale to Short Story. The Emergence of a New Genre in the 1850s". – In Charles E. May (Ed.): *The New Short Story Theories*, Athens, Ohio, 1994, pp. 165-181.
Miller, Sue & Katrina Kenison (Eds.): *The Best American Short Stories 2002*, Boston & New York, 2002.
Oates, Joyce Carol, John Kulka & Natalie Danford (Eds.): *Best New American Voices* 2003, San Diego & New York, 2002.

Salinger, J.D.: *The Catcher in the Rye*, Harmondsworth, 1986 [first edition 1951].
Zapf, Hubert (Ed.): *Amerikanische Literaturgeschichte*, Stuttgart & Weimar, 1997.

Nicole Schröder, Düsseldorf

'Love Across a Distance'.
Friendships and Family Relations in Twenty-First Century American Short Stories

distance:
1. the amount of space between two places or things
2. being far away in space or in time
3. a point that is a particular amount of space away from sth else
4. a situation in which there is a lack of friendly feelings or of a close relationship between two people or groups of people[1]

As the *Oxford Advanced Learner's Dictionary* tells us, distances come in various forms, ranging from geographic or temporal distances to those of an interpersonal and emotional nature. These distances have to be crossed all the time. As the news illustrates every day, it seems that in the twenty-first century these distances are not only growing but also multiplying, despite the often celebrated 'space-time compression', 'technological advancements', and social 'progress.' This essay looks at a selection of recent American short stories that mirror the diversity of people's experiences in the twenty-first century and that span vast distances around the globe. The authors selected are quite diverse, in particular with regard to their ethnic backgrounds; nevertheless, it makes sense to look at them as a group since their literary intentions and concerns are quite similar and, I would add, point to a larger trend in American literature.[2] Their stories grant insights into lives as different as that of a family who tries to establish a new life after the nuclear disaster in Chernobyl, the unusual situation of two old women in a picturesque, albeit eccentric Basque community, and the life of a middle-class couple in Seattle. What connects the protagonists in their different locations and situations is that they continuously try to reach across the distances that open up between them and their friends, children, lovers, and neighbors, sometimes unsuccessfully, but nevertheless persistently. The reason these people are so persistent in crossing geographic, temporal, or emotional distances is love, an emotion that also comes in different shapes and guises, ranging from parental love and the platonic love of deep friendship to passionate feelings between lovers. In the following, I analyze and compare the variety of distances and emotions, which both separate and unite the stories' various protagonists.

I would like to begin this comparison with Sherman Alexie's short story "Assimilation".[3] Here, an interracial (Native American/white) couple has drifted apart not so much because of a lack of love and affection but due to norms and values that society imposes upon them. Specifically notions of race and ethnicity restrict their personalities and thus limit their relationship:

> During the course of their relationship, Mary Lynn and Jeremiah had often discussed race as a concept, as a foreign country they occasionally visited, or as an enemy that existed outside their house, as a destructive force they could fight against as a couple, as a family. But race was also a constant presence, a houseguest and permanent tenant who crept round in all the rooms in their shared lives, opening drawers, stealing utensils and small articles of clothing, changing the temperature. (14)

The story manages to show that race, although an invention or, rather, a construction, still very much plays a decisive role as a visible, even tangible force that the two characters, Mary Lynn and Jeremiah, have to deal with every day: "race, whatever its construction, was real" (*ibid.*).

"Assimilation" evolves around the central event of Mary Lynn's unfaithfulness to her husband caused by her dissatisfaction with their relationship. Mary Lynn concludes that it is the issue of race that has come between them: "Yes, she was a Coeur d'Alene woman, passionately and dispassionately, who wanted to cheat on her white husband because he was white." (3) She herself "only wanted to be understood as eccentric and complicated" rather than being characterized by her ethnicity and cultural background since "that wasn't the only way to define her" (2). Yet she cannot help referring to race and ethnicity as important, almost essential parts of her relationship to Jeremiah. Looking at their family, two boys who resemble herself, dark hair and skin, and two girls who resemble their father, blond hair and light skin, she suggests that they should have another kid, "so we'll know if this is a white family or an Indian family" (13). When Jeremiah answers that "[i]t's a family family" (*ibid.*) they both know from experience that this conceals the problems they have to face as a so-called interracial family. 'Race' is their constant companion, an expression of society's construction of an essentialist difference which can not be grasped and which is always elusive, a difference which is never really there but which can nevertheless be constantly felt.

A seemingly rational and objective concept, race is intertwined with their whole life and comes to dominate their relationship, widening the gap between them and building up an emotional and cultural distance that seems absurd. While Mary Lynn "wanted to go to bed with an Indian man only because he was Indian" (1), Jeremiah is "in love with the idea of a white woman from a mythical high school, with a prom queen named *If Only* or a homecoming princess named *My Life Could Have Been Different*" (9, emphasis in the original). Their different cultural backgrounds did not even play a role in their meeting and falling in love, but nevertheless their love has become entangled so much with issues of race and ethnicity that they cannot think about their relationship without essentializing themselves. Race, "the Frankenstein monster that has grown beyond our control" (14), comes to play such a decisive role that they become unfaithful to each other and also to themselves.

Right after she has cheated on Jeremiah with an unknown "flabby Lummi Indian" (3), Mary Lynn meets him for dinner. Since they unsuccessfully wait for a table at a restaurant, presumably because the place "discriminates against white people" (11), they decide to drive home. When they get stuck in a traffic jam on a bridge, Jeremiah walks to the other side of the bridge in order to find out the reason for the congestion. The bridge not only represents a real spatial distance between him and his wife but turns into a metaphor for the emotional gap that has opened up between them. While Mary Lynn watches her husband disappear on the other side of the bridge, she is suddenly "slapped by the brief, irrational fear that he would never return" (17). Unable to articulate her thoughts, her fears, and her feelings to Jeremiah, she starts to honk their car's horn, using it as a substitute language and hoping that he will "recognize the specific sound of their horn and return to the car" (*ibid.*). When he does not come back, she starts to weep and realizes "she loved him, sometimes because he was white and often despite his whiteness" (19). Jeremiah, however, continues walking and disappears to the other end of the bridge, where he witnesses a suicide. The jumper, a woman, keeps screaming a name, presumably her lover's, before she jumps from the bridge. And while Mary Lynn becomes "suddenly and impossibly sure that her husband was the reason for the commotion" (*ibid.*), Jeremiah, shaken by the stranger's suicide, realizes all of a sudden how much he loves his wife and confesses abruptly to another onlooker. "'My wife', said Jeremiah, strangely joyous. 'I'm never leaving her'." (*ibid.*) He finally finds his voice and "shouted out his wife's name, shouted it so loud that he could not speak in the morning" (*ibid.*). Although the paramedics arrive too late to rescue the woman, Mary Lynn and Jeremiah find each other just in time to rescue themselves and their love and to articulate their feelings. Finally, they can reach across the gap that has opened up between them: "Jeremiah ran across the bridge until he could see Mary Lynn. She and he loved each other across the distance" (20).

Although the story remains open as to whether the couple will manage to overcome their estrangement, it becomes very clear that at least they try to reach across the distances that make their love difficult. It is here that the story's title "Assimilation" attains a deeper meaning, apart from its most common definition "action of making or becoming alike".[4] The word can also designate a "process whereby a person acquires new ideas through comparing experience with the existing content of the mind" and Mary Lynn and Jeremiah have assimilated in this sense.[5] They have discovered that "the Frankenstein monster" (14) might be controlled in spite of everything, in that traditional, essentialist concepts of race and ethnicity can be 'assimilated', changed by new ideas and viewpoints.

Another love relationship affected by distances is explored in Edwidge Danticat's "Seven".[6] The story deals with a couple from Haiti that has been separated since the day after their wedding, when the husband left for the US expecting to be joined by his wife as soon as he would attain his green card. Unfortunately it takes almost seven years until he receives the document and, thus, it is almost "seven years since he'd last seen his wife" (35). The story explores the nature of the unnamed couple's relationship, which has been affected very much by this long geographic and temporal distance. Furthermore, both husband and wife have had extramarital affairs to fill the loneliness that the absence of their spouse has left them with, which adds guilt to the complicated nature of their relation. We witness their reunion, which is almost like a meeting of strangers. Although the husband had hoped that the marriage would hold their relationship together, so that "even if their union had become a victim of distance and time, it could not have been easily dissolved" (41), the formal bond of marriage is not enough to bridge the emotional distance.

Nevertheless, both husband and wife try to reach across the emotional gap, which extends from the beginning of their marriage to its ending: "Someone had said that people lie only at the beginning of relationships. The middle is where the truth resides. But there had been no middle for her husband and herself, just a beginning and many dream-rehearsed endings." (43-44) The actual ending resembles a beginning as it entails a number of radical changes for both of them. Whereas "he wasn't going to tell her about those women who had occasionally come home with him in the early morning-hours" (37), his wife cannot tell him about "that neighbor who had slept next to her for those days after he'd left and in whose bed she had spent many nights after that" (43). Their reunion changes their lives significantly. The husband cannot have "those nights out" with his friends any more – "[g]one were the late-night domino games. Gone was the phone number he'd had for the past five years" (37). The changes she has to undergo seem more radical, as her new life is made difficult by the racism that she experiences as soon as she arrives at the airport. Her meager belongings are searched and most of her things, harmless gifts of food intended to remind her and her husband of their Haitian home, are thrown away. In contrast to that "a man pushing a cart, which tipped and swerved under the weight of three large boxes" (39) can pass customs unharmed.

It is significant that the spouses long for each other's company despite their estrangement. Whenever his wife leaves their room, he "couldn't stand to watch her turn away and disappear" (40-41). Similarly, "[s]he was happy when the weekend finally came" (44) to explore the city together with her husband. The walk through the foreign city conjures up memories of the Haitian carnival during which they met and during which they performed a traditional wedding ritual. The couple has to walk around in their wedding garments and ask strangers to marry them. The joke of this carnival theater is that the couple usually switches roles, "that the bride was a man and the groom a woman. The couple's makeup was so skillfully applied that only the most observant could detect this" (46). They, however, added their own twist to this ritual as she played the part of the bride and her husband that of the groom, "forgoing the traditional puzzle" (*ibid.*).

The Haitian carnival and the wedding game come to symbolize their relationship and its new beginning in New York in a special way. As husband and wife walk through New York as if in search of a new beginning, a new basis for their relationship that takes "the many dream-rehearsed endings" (44) as a starting point, the wife wishes they had not burned their wedding clothes so that they could perform their ritual in this city, "among the stony-faced people around them", and complete "their wedding march in silence, a silence like the one that had come over them now" (46). The carnival, symbol of cheerful exuberance and the possibility of foregoing and challenging traditions, rules, and norms, here turns into an image of the impossibility of change, into a silence in which the nameless wife and husband try to come to terms with their new situation – they cannot but walk around silently in New York. The anonymous city and its inhabitants, whose stony faces resemble carnival masks, therefore turn into a carnivalesque scene, yet one in which traditional structures are not challenged by laughter but reinforced by silence. The story, too, leaves open whether the couple will manage to overcome the distances that have grown between them. Nameless, wife and husband come to signify 'types' – they, too, wear carnival masks to symbolize the fate of numerous immigrants who try to start anew in a strange country, a foreign city, a new culture. The reality of migration and displacement not only creates physical and temporal distances between people. In "Seven" this distance has turned into a solid wall of silence, a silence not only between husband and wife but also between the couple and the stony-faced inhabitants of the city. Yet the couple is shown walking hand in hand – despite the silence, their physical closeness suggests that there might be a way to overcome the gap. Maybe they will manage to add yet another twist to the Haitian wedding game, with a second beginning after seven years, and turn the streets of this foreign city into their own carnival and their silent walk into a new beginning.

Jhumpa Lahiri's "Mrs. Sen's" also deals with the physical separation from home.[7] Here, too, a wife has followed her husband, leaving her beloved India to live in an American university town, where her husband hopes to get tenure. Again economic opportunities are entangled with cultural and emotional issues of finding a new home away from home. The main focus of the story lies on Mrs. Sen, who works as a babysitter in her own home, and Eliot, the boy she looks after while his mother works during the day. Both Mrs. Sen and Eliot are lonely in their own peculiar ways, Eliot since his mother has to work long hours and consequently leaves him to the care of babysitters and Mrs. Sen since her family lives in India. Although she has lived in America for quite some time, she is lonely and homesick, and for her, home is still India, not the new apartment in the US. Isolated as she is, Mrs. Sen's immobility is signified by her inability to drive.[8] She knows how to operate a car – she practices together with her husband – but the pace and rhythm of American traffic confuse her and she does not dare to drive beyond their apartment block, so that she is confined to her apartment.

Her apartment appears to be an ambiguous place, a mixed blessing. On one hand, it is a safe haven, a fortress against the dangers of the American outside world. Here, Eliot's mother, a symbol of independence and mobility, comes to look strangely out of place: "it was his mother, Eliot had thought, in her cuffed, beige shorts and her rope-soled shoes, who looked odd [...] and in that room where all things were so carefully covered, her shaved knees and thighs [were] too exposed" (112-113). Just as Mrs. Sen feels uncomfortable and isolated in her American surroundings, Eliot's mother feels (and looks) uncomfortable and displaced in Mrs. Sen's little world.[9] Moreover, in her apartment, Mrs. Sen can momentarily forget her homesickness and loneliness when she prepares elaborate Indian meals. Eliot looks forward to the daily ritual of food preparation, which is so different from the ordered pizza that he and his mother have every evening:

> He especially enjoyed watching Mrs. Sen as she chopped things, seated on newspapers on the living room floor. Instead of a knife she used a blade that curved like the prow of a Viking ship, sailing to bat-

tle in distant seas. [...] Each afternoon Mrs. Sen lifted the blade and locked it into place, so that it met the base at an angle. Facing the sharp edge without ever touching it, she took whole vegetables between her hands and hacked them apart: cauliflower, cabbage, butternut squash. She split things in half, then quarters, speedily producing florets, cubes, slices and shreds. (114)

The blade, almost like a weapon, is her defense against loneliness. Its form is compared to a ship's prow and hence it can be read as a symbol of traveling across the ocean, an emotional means to go home for brief periods of time. The food and its elaborate preparation signify the degree of homesickness Mrs. Sen feels. The apartment is temporarily turned into an Indian cooking place, where Mrs. Sen prepares the vegetables, her homemade sauces, broths and pastes. Yet it remains essentially sterile with plastic covers on the sofas, chairs, and lamps. Here Mrs. Sen is alone cutting her food while in India the neighborhood women might come together and "sit in an enormous circle on the roof of our building, laughing and gossiping and slicing fifty kilos of vegetables through the night" (115). Although she uses the space of her apartment in her own way to suit her food preparation ritual, she does not really manage to feel at home there. The fact that she asks Eliot whether anyone would come if she screamed – he answers that, if they reacted at all, people would probably complain about the noise – shows how much she misses India, where you "just raise your voice a bit, or express grief or joy of any kind, and one whole neighborhood and half of another has come to share the news, to help with arrangements" (116). Moreover, the blade, which is truly Indian in its form and dimensions, comes to signify something forbidden. Although Mrs. Sen takes great care that "[b]y the time Eliot's mother arrived at twenty past six [...] all evidence of her chopping was disposed of" (117), Eliot feels that "he and Mrs. Sen were disobeying some unspoken rule" (118). The blade does not conform to American norms and values (symbolized in that it is used in a completely different way) and its almost archaic form poses a threat to the orderly American apartment world.

Mrs. Sen rarely leaves the security and isolation of the apartment. One errand that requires her to go out is the buying of fresh fish. Since the fish shop is quite far away, she has to depend on Mr. Sen to drive her there. These trips seem almost like holidays, especially since they sometimes include short walks at the seaside. One day, however, when the shop calls to offer her the last fresh fish of the season and her husband is not able to drive her, she decides to drive on her own. Although she has practiced a lot, Mrs. Sen really hates driving – her fast and skilled handling of the cutting blade contrasts sharply with her fearful and insecure driving.[10] Her anxiety and lack of self-confidence that becomes obvious in the car mirrors her situation in America, and it is not surprising that the "accident occurred quickly" (134) after she and Eliot had left the apartment. Nobody gets seriously hurt but nevertheless, the accident is the end of Mrs. Sen's driving as well as Eliot's visits. In the face of this accident, his mother decides that he is a "big boy now" (135) and that he can stay home alone. Mrs. Sen's prediction with regard to Eliot's situation finally comes true: "When I think of you, only a boy, separated from your mother for so much of the day, I am ashamed. [...] When I was your age I was without knowing that one day I would be so far. You are wiser than that, Eliot. You already taste the way things must be." (123)

"Mrs. Sen's" explores relationships between people with different ethnic, cultural, and social backgrounds and the situations they find themselves in. Mrs. Sen cannot break through her own isolation as she has no possibility of finding a replacement for the extended family that she is used to in India. Her only friend is Eliot, who is also isolated and lonely. The elaborate food preparations and the fresh fish are only poor substitutes for a home. Moreover, her specific situation in America, which is epitomized in her inability to drive, isolates her not only from her Indian home but also prevents her from establishing any contacts or friendships in America. Since Mr. Sen is not yet tenured, the couple lives in a kind of in-between state, a never-ending transition between 'here' and 'there'. While family and friends in India think that Mrs. Sen lives like a princess, she herself feels trapped since she lacks something that the American Dream does not provide: friends and family. Eliot is the only one who understands her. Moreover, he mirrors Mrs. Sen's isolation and loneliness, and in the story's last scene, we see him waiting for his mother in their tiny beach house, looking at the ocean. Although the thought of missing his mother "had never occurred to him" earlier (122), his visits to Mrs. Sen have changed him. He has been confronted with alternative ideas of home and family and now he seems to be as trapped in the isolated beach house as Mrs. Sen is in her apartment, and suddenly the world of a little American boy at home is not so different from that of a married Indian woman in a foreign country.

In Katherine Shonk's "My Mother's Garden" we encounter yet another kind of distance.[11] Here, too, family members are separated from each other, and although the spatial distance is not as big as the one that separates Mrs. Sen from India, notions of home and mobility play a quite important role. The story is set in the Ukraine twelve years after a meltdown in the local nuclear power-station and its characters have to deal with their loss of home, the subsequent resettlement, and the omnipresent threat of death and disease.[12] "My Mother's Garden" opens with the narrator's visit to the contamination zone, where she is going to see her mother, who has left the "new home" (275) in order to spend the rest of her life together with her friend in her old one. The relationship between Yulia and her mother is tense, due to their disagreement concerning the danger of living in the contaminated old place. When Yulia meets the two old women, she knows that "[t]hey were waiting for me to touch them, a kiss or a pat, but I hesitated, and the moment passed" (276). The fear of contamination and the resulting danger are closely connected to the longing and refusal to touch each other, and a gap opens up between mother and daughter emotionally and physically, a gap that cannot easily be crossed. It seems that Yulia, who is torn between the desire to visit her mother and her concern for her family's health, cannot reach across this distance to her mother, who denies and ignores the danger of living in her old beloved homeplace. Thus, while the narrator tries to convince her mother that their old home is contaminated by radiation, her mother insists that everything is normal, even healthy, since the produce of her garden grows more abundantly and bigger than ever before. For Yulia's mother the garden signifies home, a paradise where she lives peacefully, growing vegetables that taste better than ever. For Yulia herself, the garden symbolizes not only the exact opposite, the loss of paradise and home, it furthermore stands for the insidious, invisible, and inexorable death the atomic monster of progress has brought to its inhabitants. Whereas for the older generation the garden is a symbol of paradise, for the younger generation it acts as a constant reminder of the accident, a fall from grace, which has banished them from the Garden Eden. The dispute over the contaminated vegetables signifies helplessness vis-à-vis a generation of parents who cannot be convinced of the dangers they live in: "Mama showed me a bucketful of green onions she'd grown in her garden. 'Delicious,' she said, chomping on one. 'Here, you try.' 'Mama, you know I won't eat that,' I said." (276) Yulia keeps refusing these gifts, just as her mother keeps giving them, and both are convinced that they are doing the right thing. Just as Yulia cannot understand the importance the home has for her mother, the mother cannot grasp the deadly threat of the invisible contamination. In their attempts to reach out to each other – the mother's gifts, the daughter's well-meant provisions of uncontaminated food and her insistent pleas to leave that place – they actually seem to widen the distance that separates them.

A physical and emotional distance has developed – not only between Yulia and her mother. Yulia's daughter, Halynka, who has been raised by her grandmother, feels betrayed by both her mother, who forbids her to visit her, and the grandmother herself, who has simply left the family to live in the old place. Moreover, Halynka has lost her best friend, who died of cancer, and in a more indirect way her father, who tends to live in his own world due to his extended exposure to radiation right after the accident. Halynka is worried about herself as much as about her father, mother, and grandmother, and feels alone. Her life revolves around the central event of the accident, which she experienced as a baby, but whose significance she does not really understand. The whole family has been affected by the accident, which they nevertheless cannot fully comprehend – almost all of them live in a state of denial, dazed by this nightmare that looms above their heads as an ever-present threat and a traumatic memory. Yulia, for instance, is not able to talk to her daughter about her own fears of losing her and her husband to the radiation. Similarly, she cannot convey these sorrows to her mother, who not only refuses to leave the place but consistently invites her granddaughter to visit her. Therefore, Yulia emerges for her daughter as well as her mother as an insurmountable wall that stands between them as she refuses to let Halynka visit her grandmother.

Not until the end can the three women literally cross the geographic distance and approach each other. The scientist George Hayes, who researches the effects of the nuclear disaster on the environment, can provide adequate information for Halynka to understand the scale of the disaster and its aftereffects. Furthermore, he can visualize the radiation with the help of a special camera as tiny but all-pervasive snowflakes, so that the grandmother sees the contamination of her home with her own eyes. Suddenly the grandmother understands Yulia's precautions, she even asks her to stop coming. In this moment, when the distance between them becomes almost graspable due to its necessity and its urgency in terms of health, Yulia and her mother can reach out to each other. This understanding becomes visible in physical closeness: "I held her tight, wanting to both shake her and kiss her. After twelve long years, she finally understood. She had only needed to see it with her own eyes." (289)

Hayes can provide yet another bridge with which to cross the distance between the contaminated zone and the new home, a distance that is so much larger than the 50 kilometers that separate the two places. He gives Yulia his tape recorder so that Halynka and her grandmother can actually talk to each other, with Yulia functioning as a messenger between them. Hence, the grandmother can explain to her granddaughter why her longing for home is stronger than her fear of radiation and why she does not want Halynka to visit any more. Even more importantly, the tape recorder can also function as a communication channel between Halynka and Yulia, who has not been able to verbalize her fears. Now Yulia can walk through the old hometown on her own and face her past and her lost home while talking to Halynka about what she feels and remembers about the catastrophe. Going back to her own "old home" for the first time in twelve years, Yulia is finally able to describe her memories of this place and what it looks like now. Furthermore, she understands her own silence with which she has surrounded this event: "I was afraid to come here, to see our old home looking so empty and desolate." (292)

Whereas the accident symbolizes the dangers of progress and the careless use of science, the tape recorder plays a more positive role. The women use it to communicate across the distance that separates them, upholding a certain distance between speaker and listener; the device enables communication without direct confrontation. Yulia uses the tape recorder to relive her memory and tell her own story: "And, I confess, I was eager for my daughter to hear my own story for the first time." (296) For her, this is a relief, and afterwards she can run back to the bus that will take her home feeling "as if in my rush to leave the town I had forgotten myself, just for a moment, and thought that I was still a young girl" (*ibid.*). It seems that Yulia has not only crossed the distance to her mother and her daughter but also the one to herself, dealing with the traumatic experience of losing her home and living with the threat of radiation.

Family relations are also central to Louise Erdrich's short story "The Butcher's Wife".[13] The story's main character is Delphine Watzka, daughter of the town's drunkard, who becomes friends with Eva Waldvogel, wife of the town butcher, shortly before Eva is diagnosed with cancer. It is this fatal illness that affects not only the friendship between the two characters but also their relation to their families. The characters cope in very different ways with Eva's illness and her rapidly declining health. In an attempt to ease her friend's pain, Delphine takes care of her and her family, "just as Eva had done" (51). Eva, who has been hiding her pain for months, faces her diagnosis with black humor and tries not to give in to a feeling of hopelessness. To Delphine, "who cleaned up shameful things in her father's house" (43), Eva is a perfect being – "Eva appeared so fantastically skilled a being, so assured" (*ibid.*) – and the friendship with Eva instills new self-confidence in her. Eva regards her as a friend, not as the pitiable but nevertheless shunned daughter of an alcoholic as other villagers do. Therefore, although Delphine also suffers during Eva's treatments – "shooting pains stabbed her own stomach when the needles went in; she even had a sympathetic morphine sweat" (50) – she does not leave her friend and continues to nurse her. She administers the pain-reducing morphine although "she secretly hated needles, abhorred them, grew sickly hollow when she filled the syringe, and felt the prick in her own flesh when she gave the dose to Eva" (55); she tries to "divert her friend by massaging her sore hands" (*ibid.*) and she cleans away the signs of Eva's illness, "the sheets, the sweat, the shit, and the blood, always blood" (51). Delphine turns her traumatic experiences with her father, the burden of taking care of him, into a positive skill, a gift that she can give to her friend, who can accept it due to Delphine's own history.

As the women spend more and more time together, they grow closer, although it is not necessarily through words that their thoughts and feelings merge: "Delphine's sense of time passing had to do only with the duration of a dose of opium wine [...] or of the morphine that Dr. Heech had taught her to administer." (55) It is almost as if Eva's pain had become part of Delphine's own body as much as it has become a part of her daily routine. Nevertheless, the women cannot talk about Eva's death in a straightforward and unveiled manner. If they talk about it, it is in an attempt to submerge Eva's imminent death and their subsequent separation in a bout of morbid laughter. When Eva wonders what will happen to her mind after death, Delphine tries to reassure her:

> "Your mind stays itself," Delphine said, as lightly as she could.
> "There you'll be, strumming on your harp, looking down on all the foolish crap people do."
> "I could never play the harp," Eva said. "I think they'll give me a kazoo."
> "Save me a cloud and I'll play a tune with you," Delphine said.
> It wasn't very funny, so they laughed all the harder, louder until tears started in their eyes, then they gasped and fell utterly silent. (53-54)

Similarly, other people are helpless vis-à-vis the illness, notably Eva's husband Fidelis, a man who "shed power, as though there were a bigger man crammed into him" (44). He cannot find words to express his feelings either but finds other ways to do so. A public display of his physical strength is not only an attempt to distract Eva and show her his love (cf. 54-56). It also signifies his utter helplessness, "[s]howing clearly that all his strength was nothing. Against her sickness, he was weak as a child" (56). Delphine's father Roy is similarly helpless in the face of Eva's illness. Due to the sudden and early loss of his wife, Delphine's mother, Roy has become an alcoholic. For Delphine, Roy has become a synonym for shame and a burden, a helpless person whom she has to take care of, clean up after, and keep out of trouble. Yet now Roy comes to Eva's house every day to repay her friendliness towards him, "sometimes stinking of schnapps. But, once there, he'd do anything. He'd move the outhouse, shovel guts" (51). He, too, tries to distract Eva from her pain by telling her stories about his life, something he has never done for his own daughter.

The story's crucial event happens one day when Delphine discovers that the last vial has disappeared shortly before Eva's next dose of morphine is due. She assumes correctly that Fidelis's sister Tante Marie-Christine has taken it in her hypocritical religious fervor, damning her sister-in-law's 'addiction' to the medicine. With no chance of getting a new prescription on a holiday, Delphine drives straight to Tante's house and confronts her. Since Tante Marie-Christine has thrown away the morphine, Delphine has to try to find someone who can give her a new prescription. When she has to return empty-handed after hours of searching, she sees her father staggering along the road. Delphine, who has had to deal with her father's drunkenness and his unreliability all her life, is suddenly seized by "an all-seeing rage", and "she suddenly wanted to run him over" (59). Seeing her own helplessness vis-à-vis her friend's illness mirrored in her father, she ponders killing him with the car and imagines that it would mean a new beginning and erase the memories of her chaotic life. Yet when she "drew alongside him, she was surprised to meet his eyes and see that they were clear" (*ibid.*). Even then she thinks the bottle in his hand is booze, but this one time, Roy is more reliable than anyone would have thought possible. He hands her "a brown square-shouldered medicine bottle labelled 'Sulphate of Morphia'" (*ibid.*) that he has stolen from the drugstore. Despite his own need to drown his pain, Roy has surmounted his self-denial and pain-relieving stupor to help Eva.

When Delphine returns, Tante Marie-Christine is "slumped useless in the corner of the kitchen" and Eva's sons are "weeping and holding on to their mother" (60), who is about to kill herself, crazy with pain. Delphine manages to remain calm and administer the painkilling morphine: "She'd come upon so many scenes of mayhem in her own house that now a cold flood of competence descended on her." (*ibid.*) Finally Delphine can take confidence from her own life experience; she turns her shame, her traumatic memories, and her helplessness into strength and competence to help her friend and in a way also herself. Taking the knife away from Eva, she can promise her "not now. Soon enough" (*ibid.*), ambiguously referring to both the medical relief and Eva's coming death. In her friendship to Eva, Delphine has managed to grow beyond herself and see a future for herself, not just a shameful past. Although the two women have not known each other for a long time, their relationship proves to be very deep. While Delphine is given self-confidence and the feeling of being part of a family for the first time, Eva can accept her friend's care and nurturing without embarrassment and the feeling of being a burden. Eva's illness, her growing dependency, and her imminent death complicate their friendship, but both women do not perceive this as a gap or a distance between them. They substitute the words they lack to talk about this with a feeling of care that brings them closer together and that helps even Delphine and Roy to reach momentarily, silently, across the void that the loss of Delphine's mother has created between them. Emotional communication, acts of caring and nurturing prove to be just as important as words to bridge the distances between them.

This friendship can be contrasted with another quite unusual relation described in Trevanian's "The Apple Tree".[14] This story explores a love-hate relationship between two old women who live in a small community in a Basque village, a community which follows their rivalry in an attentive and yet bemused manner. Both women continually insist on being different from each other, but their lives are nevertheless astonishingly similar, a fact on which the narrator comments indirectly and ironically. The story's opening line introduces the object around which their rivalry culminates and which at the same time comes to signify the futility of their competition:

> The Widow Etcheverrigaray took great pride in the splendid apple tree that grew on the boundary of her property, just beyond the plot of leeks that every year were the best in all the village; and her neighbor and lifelong rival, Madame Utuburu, drew no less gratification from the magnificent apple tree near the patch of *piments* that made her the envy of all growers of that sharp little pepper. (311)

Although they would never admit this, both women take pride in the same things, symbolized in the apple tree, which they in fact share. As we follow the "bitter rivalry the two women cultivated and nourished for most of their lives" (*ibid*.), more and more correspondences and parallels between their characters and their lives emerge. The more any one of them points to their differences, the more alike they become, and in the end it is clear that they indeed need each other for luck and happiness.

While the narrator illuminates this need for the other, the need for competition and the feeling of difference, he also makes clear how constructed this rivalry is. In a delightfully naïve and comic way he explains that "[w]hen young, one of them had been accounted the most beautiful girl in our village, while the other was considered the most graceful and charming – although in later years no one could remember which had been which, and, sadly, no evidence of these qualities remained to prompt the memory" (*ibid*.). The narrator undermines the women's efforts to be different by showing instead how similar they are. Thus, the reader gets to know that both Widow Etcheverrigaray and Madame Utuburu were in love with "the cheeky rascal" Zabala, but that the two women married two "simple shepherds far beneath their expectations" instead (312). Again we learn a lot about village life as well as about human nature in general as the narrator points out that

> both women had given birth to babies after only seven months of gestation. Short first pregnancies do not occasion criticism in our valley, for it is widely known that the good Lord often makes first pregnancies mercifully brief as His reward to the girl for having preserved her chastity until marriage. […] Is it not marvelous how one finds justice and balance in everything? (*ibid.*).

The human search for other people's faults, the urge to judge shortcomings as well as the attempt find excuses for them is beautifully exposed; even more importantly, the arbitrariness of certain human norms and values is uncovered.

Even after their marriage, both women's lives are parallel. Their husbands die quite soon and both have sons who leave the village as soon as possible to become famous and successful elsewhere. Widow Etcheverrigaray's son is a "clever and hardworking scholar" (313) and Madame Utuburu's son is in contrast "the most powerful and crafty player of jai alai our village ever produced" (314). Both sons send their mothers tokens of their achievements, Etcheverrigaray receives a boring and complicated book written by her son, whereas Utuburu gets a silk cushion with "a beautiful (if rather immodest) woman painted on it" (315). As a sign of their pride and, more importantly, as a sign of their superiority vis-à-vis the other, Etcheverrigaray and Utuburu miss no opportunity to show off these tokens of "prodigal generosity" (*ibid.*) and brilliance. Of course, both women criticize the other's behavior: while Utuburu cannot understand why someone would show off "a stupid old book" (*ibid.*), Etcheverrigaray is annoyed by "the way some people forever lugged about a dusty old cushion" (316).

This rivalry belies a dependency on each other, which culminates when the women end up as next-door neighbors. While the garden produce, which is "the finest (or second-finest) […] in our village" (316), is a sign of their competition, the apple tree, which grows exactly on the border between their gardens, signifies their similarities and the fact that their lives are closely intertwined. It is around this tree that their rivalry reaches its peak. When they pick apples on the same day, they get into a dispute that quickly turns physical before the neighbors can intervene. This direct and physical confrontation has disrupted an invisible rule – had the two rivals until then only referred indirectly to each other, complaining about nameless people whose description and behavior innocently and quite accidentally matched the other, Utuburu and Etcheverrigaray now openly disparage each other. This open rivalry adds a lot to the village's amusement, but it takes a tragic turn when

Zabala suddenly dies. Their competition takes on an absurd quality when both women remain standing at the grave in full rain after the funeral to "win" the honor of being the "chief mourner" (351). They remain there until the priest leads them away to put an end to this game. When the Widow Etcheverrigaray does not go to mass the next morning, the reader already suspects that there is something wrong with her. Madame Utuburu, however, reads this behavior as yet another trick to win the honor of being the chief mourner and is quite shocked when the Widow is found dead in her kitchen, due to a fever she caught at the funeral.

As a result, it is after her rival's death that Madame Utuburu "sat in her neighbor's kitchen for the first time in her life" (323), observing the traditional mourning ceremony. She is urged by the other mourners to "follow the ancient tradition and take some little trifle from the house as a memento of the Departed One" (*ibid.*). After some hesitation, Madame Utuburu indeed takes a memento that gives the whole village much food for thought – her rival's beloved book. However, not until after the funeral does Utuburu realize the extent of her own loneliness. Suddenly, even "the task of planting a garden at all seemed terribly heavy and unrewarding" (324) without a neighbor to show it off to.

"The Apple Tree" makes quite clear that Widow Etcheverrigaray and Madame Utuburu cannot live without each other. Like close friends, even a loving couple, they depend upon each other; literally, they are each other's death, but in a sense, they have also provided for themselves "not something to live for, but maybe something to live *against*" (*ibid.*, emphasis in the original). Their relationship is of a peculiar sort – in their lifelong attempt to create a distinguishing gap between them, they have really become more similar. Only in the end does Madame Utuburu realize that she needs her 'other,' Widow Etcheverrigaray, to define herself, as a 'vexing incentive' to push herself to greater achievements than otherwise possible. Therefore, the next time Madame Utuburu visits the village, she carries not only her beloved cushion but also, to the astonishment of the whole village, "The Book" (325), her memento of the Widow. As always, she talks about her own son's achievement, only this time she adds to it by praising Etcheverrigaray's son and his success as well. As a result, "Madame Utuburu kept the Widow Etcheverrigaray alive for several years longer. And herself too" (*ibid.*). The story is a clever and charming comment on the human character and its insistence on essentialist differences, on a strict opposition between self and other. At the same time, it is a portrait of an unusual friendship, which is all the more touching and true as it points out the inconsistencies and illogical behavior that are so often a part of human relationships. The women's relationship is characterized by closeness as well as by a well-kept distance that 'hides' this closeness only to a certain extent. Only when Etcheverrigaray's death enlarges the gap between them infinitely can Utuburu reach across the distance, admit their similarity, and weave a connective thread out of an emotion that lies somewhere between love and hate.

These stories concentrate on human relationships and processes of (mis)communication. Their focus lies in the private realm of home and family; nevertheless this allows the authors to comment on larger issues of society. The stories' characters struggle with their everyday lives as well as with their more or less successful attempts to relate to and communicate with other people. Distances, voids, and estrangements of all kinds figure prominently. They can be of a geographic or temporal sort (e.g. in "Seven") or an emotional one (as in "The Apple Tree"). They can be constructed culturally or socially ("Assimilation") or caused by concrete forces like migration and displacement ("Mrs. Sen's"). Moreover, quite often the distances these characters attempt to bridge are intricately intertwined with their search for a place, geographic, emotional or otherwise, where they feel at home ("My Mother's Garden"). It seems that in our age of globalization and technological progress, when geographic distances decrease with the possibility of instant (virtual) travel, when capitalism, war, and economic need increase migrations around the globe, distances more than ever play a vital role in human relationships. As has been frequently observed, globalization not only leads to extended possibilities of cultural exchange, hybridization, and border transgressions; it also kindles opposing phenomena like nationalism, (cultural) conservatism or the (re-)drawing and enforcing of rigid borders. As the world moves closer together, the safe distance and clear separations between 'here' and 'there' and between what is perceived as self and as other decrease, something which requires new, additional skills of communication and of living together. The authors analyzed here turn to the private realm to discuss these issues and use the private realm to exemplify the problems of larger society.[15] It is 'at home' that we learn how to communicate, how to bridge distances to others, and how to negotiate boundaries and differences between ourselves and others. Society, networks of human relations are made not in the abstract realm of the 'out there,' but more immediately at home. Vis-à-vis growing conflicts on a global, international level, a great number of short stories seem to turn to a more 'local' level to scrutinize human relationships. In the stories, the protagonists attempt to bridge the gaps that open up between them and others, their spouses, lovers, friends, children, parents and neighbors. Although they are not always successful, "their need […] to form meaningful connections with others" is stronger than their fear of failing.[16] What these disparate stories can teach us is that there is always the possibility and the necessity to reach out, to love "each other across the distance" (Alexie, 20) even though this might involve leaving behind the safe position of what we consider 'our self', or a stable sense of identity.

Notes

1. *Oxford Advanced Learner's Dictionary of Current English.* 6th Edition. Oxford: OUP, 2000. I would like to thank Stefanie Eversberg for her critical comments on this essay.
2. Cf. e.g. recent novels like Jonathan Franzen's much celebrated *The Corrections* (2001), which is also deeply concerned with family relationships. See also Astrid Böger's essay in this issue, in which she observes that a lot of recent American short stories are concerned with the relationships between family members.
3. Alexie (2001: 1-20). Further references to this edition will be included in the text.
4. *The New Shorter Oxford Dictionary* (1997).
5. *Ibid.*
6. Danticat (2002: 35-46). Further references to this edition included in the text.
7. Lahiri (2000: 111-135). Further references to this edition included in the text.
8. It is quite ironic that a woman who has traveled thousands of miles is immobilized in the very country that symbolizes freedom and unlimited space.
9. Another decisive difference between the two women is their mobility: "It seemed so simple when he sat beside his mother [...]. Then the road was just a road, the other cars merely a part of the scenery. But when he sat with Mrs. Sen [...] he saw how that same stream of cars made her knuckles pale, her wrists tremble, and her English falter" (120-121).
10. Being able to drive does not really solve her problem. Eliot suggests that she "could go places" but to her question "Could I drive all the way to Calcutta?" (119) he knows no answer. Her network of friends and family cannot be replaced by a car.
11. Shonk (2001: 275-295). Further references to this edition included in the text.
12. The story refers, of course, to the nuclear catastrophe that happened in Chernobyl.
13. Erdrich (2002: 41-60). Further references to this edition included in the text. This story, which won third place in the O. Henry Awards, is part of Erdrich's most recent novel *Master Butcher's Singing Choir.*
14. Trevanian (2001: 311-325). Further references to this edition included in the text. Trevanian also writes under the pen names Rodney Whitaker and Nicholas Seare.
15. Cf. David Morley, who points out the various links between "micro structures of the home, the family and the domestic realm" and the "macro debates about the nation, community and cultural identities" (1999: 271).
16. Shonk (n.d.).

Bibliography

Alexie, Sherman: "Assimilation". – In S.A.: *The Toughest Indian in the World*, London, 2001, pp. 1-20.

Danticat, Edwidge: "Seven". – In Sue Miller, Katrina Kenison (Eds.): *The Best American Short Stories 2002*, Boston, 2002, pp. 35-46.

Erdrich, Louise: "The Butcher's Wife". – In Larry Dark (Ed.): *The O. Henry Prize Stories 2002*, New York, 2002, pp. 41-60.

Lahiri, Jhumpa: "Mrs. Sen's". – In J.L.: *Interpreter of Maladies. Stories*, London, 2000, pp. 111-135.

Morley, David: "Bounded Realms. Household, Family, Community and Nation". – In Bundesministerium für Wissenschaft und Verkehr und das Internationale Forschungszentrum für Kulturwissenschaften (Eds.): *The Contemporary Study of Culture*, Wien, 1999, pp. 271-287.

Shonk, Katherine: "Artist's Statement. Prose Fellowship Recipient of the Illinois Arts Council Artist Fellowship Program", http://www.state.il.us/agency/iac/IAC%20Fellowship%20Web%20Pages/Prose%20Recipients/Shonk/Home.htm (accessed 11 March 2004).

–: "My Mother's Garden". – In Barbara Kingsolver & Katrina Kenison (Eds.): *The Best American Short Stories 2001*, Boston, 2001, pp. 275-295.

Trevanian: "The Apple Tree". – In Barbara Kingsolver & Katrina Kenison (Eds.): *The Best American Short Stories 2001*, Boston, 2001, pp. 311-325.

Christoph Ribbat, Bonn

Reading Novels for the *Boston Globe*.
A Conversation with Gail Caldwell

The following conversation took place a stone's throw from Harvard University, in a restaurant on Brattle Street in Cambridge, Massachusetts. Gail Caldwell, who lives five minutes from here, is not an academic, though: her employer is the *Boston Globe*, one of the major daily newspapers in the US. More than 20 years ago, Caldwell dropped out of the Ph.D. program in American Studies at the University of Texas in Austin, and moved to the Boston area to become a writer. (According to Caldwell, a guest lecture by Gayatri Spivak on Carson McCullers served as a key event in making her decide she was unhappy with the way academics approached literary fiction). After freelancing for a while, Caldwell joined the *Globe* staff. Today, she ranks as one of the most important North American book reviewers, an author whose pieces are run by several newspapers across the country. As the *Globe*'s chief critic, Caldwell has reviewed many of the most important American novels of the last decades. And, after serving for many years on several juries and committees for prestigious American literary awards, Caldwell herself received the Pulitzer Prize for criticism in 2001 – for her 'insightful observations on contemporary life and literature'. At the time this interview took place, in the summer of 2004, she was on leave from the *Boston Globe*, working on a memoir to be published by Random House.

In spite of her uncompromising love for novels both contemporary and classic (the book in the handbag sitting on the seat next to her was *Mrs. Dalloway*), Caldwell has to cope with the problematic aspects of reviewing literature in contemporary America. On the one hand, publishing houses flood the market with novels, since state-of-the-art technology makes the production of books ever cheaper. On the other hand, the space newspapers allow for reviews of serious fiction gets smaller and smaller. The *Globe* is no exception. In the following conversation, though, the larger issues of fiction, publishing, and the media do not play a central role. The interview revolves around more personal issues of reading and writing – issues that will most probably be the key subjects in Caldwell's forthcoming book.

In a way, this must be a really good time to be a book critic. Franzen's The Corrections, *Chabon's* The Adventures of Kavalier & Clay,

Eugenides's Middlesex ... *It seems as if the 'big novel' was back. Do you agree?*

I did admire *Middlesex* a lot. I think what you're saying is true about the return to the big novel but I'm always so loath to make such a commentary on zeitgeist possibility, because for every one of those that we talk about there may be seven people out there with a totally different idea.

I hope that there is a critical demand or a kind of mass culture appetite for the big, dramatic, ambitious novel. I think that may be true. I also don't think that it means a damn thing in terms of how good something might then be. That's the odd thing. I was glad that Franzen got the attention he did. I was hugely glad that *Kavalier & Clay* got the attention it did – I love Michael Chabon. I also think that on the other hand something like Michael Cunningham's *The Hours*, which is a much smaller perfect little glass sculpture of a novel, provides such enormous pleasure. I mean: I love that book. But it is so difficult to know what to leave out. I guess I'm a little bit shocked by the egocentrism of a lot of novelists who believe that the more you put in the better. You know, the vast: 'Let's get all of America badly' instead of one town beautifully. So there's always the vision things that can be a problem.

Let's talk about individual cases then – and about your role as a critic. You have been judging 'how good something might be' for a fairly long time now. Have you made mistakes in that time that you are aware of? Errors of judgment that you later regretted?

Probably. Oddly, I would say now that if I've made errors of judgment they have been probably too kind rather than the opposite. I look back at things that I was reviewing when I was younger and there are things like dear little domestic novels that I perhaps took to a higher plane than they warranted. I don't think the opposite has happened often. But I'd rather love the field and fall a little shy of the mark than I would slaughter somebody who doesn't deserve it. It's too hard to write well.

There have been books that I loathed that I tried to be at least respectful of. Because, God knows, I have an understanding of the effort involved. And if it were really a dog ... There was a book by Robert Coover in the first five years I was at the *Globe* that I was just cross-eyed over. I'm trying to understand why anyone could enjoy reading it: *The Public Burning*. I wrote a very negative review of it. And my editor called me in. He had loved this book and loved Coover. He asked me what I thought. It was after the review had run and I was new enough to be always on my toes about such things. He asked me about the review and about the novel and I defended what I'd written. And then I was leaving his office and he said to me: "What about *Rites of Spring*?", referring to Stravinsky who was totally panned in the beginning. And I paused and said: "What do you mean?" And he said: "Don't you ever worry about being wrong?" And I was new enough that I was like: "Oh God, do they fire you for being wrong?" And I took a deep breath and I said: "Honestly, I worry all the time about being wrong, all the time!"

I told a male critic that story later because I thought it was so revealing and he said: "Huh, I never worry about being wrong. I don't think I've worried about being wrong in ten years." And I thought: "There is the difference between you and me!"

It must be difficult to go against the current, though. This was the case with Charles Frazier's best-seller Cold Mountain *in 1997, which was a sensational success with both readers and many critics, and which you apparently did not like at all.*

Well, at least Charles Frazier didn't need me. He was already on the bestseller lists by the time. In fact, I wrote that piece as a response to the mad publicity he was getting. It was more of a kind of send up of pop culture's alligator appetite for this novel, which seemed to me very similar to *The Bridges of Madison County*. A Dixie-Odyssean *Bridges of Madison County*. And I read it as somebody who grew up with Faulkner – Faulkner was my bible for a long time ... I certainly think *Cold Mountain* was a dramatic and engaging narrative, but it was not great literature and that was really all I was responding to.

The *Globe* got a reader response to the piece that I wrote about *Cold Mountain*: a phone call from a person saying: "You New Englanders think you know so much! It's this provincialist Yankee snobbery!" And I thought: "Honey, if you only knew ... If you had gotten me on the phone you would have known from my accent." That was not where I was coming from.

Does your immersion in Faulkner also inform your reviews of Toni Morrison's work?

I certainly see her as an heiress to Garcia Marquez and Faulkner, which is a tradition I love. I think that Morrison is quite uneven, unfortunately. I mean, I adored her early work and *Beloved*. And there's been other stuff I've not been so impressed by in the last several years. I think she can have her off times, as we all can. But when she reveals that kind of beautiful mythic tradition of what I suspect is a combination of those people whom she adores and admires – Virginia Woolf is another one, I think, in her legacy. And then her own oral tradition of storytelling ... I think she has done some exquisite stuff.

> Toni Morrison represents that rare case of a contemporary American author whose works are both dependable bestsellers and the subject of an enormous amount of critical work by the academic community. There certainly seems to be, and Jonathan Franzen has also commented on this, a wide gulf between what is read in the marketplace and what is read 'on campus'.

What are they reading over there? What would a syllabus of a course on contemporary literature look like?

> It's hard to tell ... I guess one thing that's done frequently is to organize a course along the lines of ethnicity, say, on fiction by 'women of color' – like Morrison, Jamaica Kincaid, Edwidge Danticat. Then there might be courses on the white male high-tech postmodern guys like Pynchon, DeLillo, Powers .... And of course there are classes designed to reflect a more complete picture.

I suspect that from an academic point of view the gulf might be wider than from me. Many of those people you named I reviewed, except Pynchon's *Mason & Dixon*, which I couldn't bear.

I feel like part of my job is to work as liaison between the guy in the bookstore trying to decide whether this is a dog Roth novel and the woman working on her dissertation on post-war American intellectuals. Because I bring, I hope, a certain kind of intelligence to bear that evokes a dialogue with either one of those readers. It's what I'm supposed to do as a critic for a mass newspaper. I think that the scholarly journal on DeLillo and post-apocalyptic thought and the modern novel is not going to be as useful to the person who wants to know ultimately whether or not I loved this novel. So I'd like to think that it's part of my job to fall somewhere in-between. That's also maybe why I wound up walking out of the academe and wanting to write for a broader world.

> If we move away from academic readers, then, one thing quite obvious about literary culture these days is the growing number of reading groups. Are you aware of the fact that more and more readers are not solitary anymore and instead form these circles? Does it play a role for your work at all?

I certainly know it's a phenomenon. It has no bearing on what I do. I don't think I ever would have been somebody who wanted to be in a book group. I think of reading as a hugely private experience.

> Wouldn't it be nice, though, to read and then share your thoughts in such a group?

It's funny, it holds no interest for me. And maybe it's just because I'm bossy. I can image teaching a novel or writing about it. But I don't think I want to sit around and go: "What, you didn't like that novel? Why not?"

It's probably an effect of your job, or? Does it sometimes occur to you that you cannot really participate in normal conversations about novels anymore?

You know it's strange because I do wish that I could have a normal conversation about favorite novels. I find myself saying things that are so qualified. People will go like "Oooh – did you love *Middlesex*?" and I'll say: "Well, I admired it deeply." It's not even the critic's language as much as it is a huge variety of emotional and personal and critical and psychological reactions to a book that are more belabored than they would be were I just reading for my own pleasure.[1]

Though the job of the critic and the pleasures of reading overlap so much: what can we expect from the book you are working on? Is it going to be a critic's memoir or the memoir of a reader?

More of a reader. It began as an idea. I had been approached for a long time to write a book and I had been really reluctant to do so for, I think, good reasons. I said to a literary agent years ago: "I'm like the person who works in a chicken factory all day long and then I come home and somebody wants me to make Chicken Kiev for dinner." And I'm like: "No!" I mean: how many books shouldn't get published – horrifyingly. Which is to say the lion's share of them.

I never wanted to write one of those books. I never wanted to write a book that didn't matter and that didn't have my full heart and attention and I never wanted to be a fiction writer. I'm like the housing inspector who wants to look at the bricks and the pipes and was not the architect. I wanted to write essays and autobiography. And so I had actually had the idea that I might write about a life that was really shaped by fiction because that had been the scaffolding of my own life for many, many years. A lot of it is a story about my father and me and about Texas and about growing up in the middle of a wheat field. But it really is an introvert's memoir because that was a life shaped by fiction. It's about a lot of things and it's been a good process for me to undertake.

So was it your father, then, who introduced you to fiction?

No, not at all, not at all. I think it was a classic, old Cordelia/Lear struggle. My dad died last year, so some of this is greatly poignant. I was in the middle of the book and I lost him at age 89. We were hugely close when I was young. We were in adversarial, but loving positions for about fifteen years, like a lot of kids in America. Most of it happened around the time of the Vietnam War. He was a Master Sergeant in World War II and I was his beatnik daughter who just came home going "Hell no, we won't go!" and he and I fought for a long, long, long time and then reconnected probably after I became a writer, after I moved to Cambridge. I shouldn't say reconnected ... The estrangement became a thing of the past. So in many ways it's probably a cultural memoir for that reason. And it's been good for me to find my narrative truth in that book.

Who was it then that made you want to read books instead of run around in the wheat field?

Oh, it's probably the wheat field that made me want to read books. It's that wonderful fact that nature abhors a vacuum and I grew up in one. My sister taught me to read when I was four. My mother was a great reader. I think that we were a kind of happy family of ... I was telling a friend of mine a story about me and my dad and she said: "Well, let's face it, you were a couple of oddballs!" And I thought that I would have never used that description in my life but I think that's what we were: a fairly benign family of introverts in the middle of the Texas Panhandle. So we all had our ways of going off and doing things. My dad took me hunting when I was little. He had two girls and I was kind of his scout – you know: *To Kill a Mockingbird* ... My mother was a great reader. She was not a reader of great literature, but she loved to read. I think I always had this idea that this [opens her hands, palms upward, as if holding a book] was a prayer. My sister was an artist and very good at it and would sit and draw for hours and I would sit and read for hours. It was a different time. I grew up in 1950s America in the middle of somewhat small-town Texas and there were not a lot of choices. So the idea to be somebody who kind of had an active inner life to begin with was what you did, what there was to do. I think I was shaped as a reader by default almost. And certainly that was true rather than having any kind of intellectual tradition or guidance.

Do you believe in the theory that people who come from small towns and boring places are just going to be more fascinated by art and culture and urbanity than people who grow up, say, in Manhattan and are taking it all for granted?

I think that's true. It's certainly been my experience since I moved here. I came up against all the people who were graduates of prep schools and Ivy League colleges and had grown up with these traditions that they utterly took for granted. And I think I had this profound hunger, and in some sense this complete innocence ... I wonder if that shaped my sensibility. I don't know how it couldn't. I think it was probably so informing that I don't even know it.

> *It would also be possible to entertain the notion that a novel about some place in Texas might be just more interesting than a novel about New York, which has been written about so much. But you probably feel that if it's good, it's good, if it's bad, it's bad, no matter where a novel is set.*

I hope that last part is true. But I do think that experiential things matter. I think one of the reasons people love Jhumpa Lahiri's stories is that she is so exquisitely careful in capturing this bicultural experience of assimilation and immigration. My guess would be that she is not as deliberately conscious of this as she is in just telling the truth that she knows. This is one of the advantages of a lot that has been published in the last fifteen years. I think we have a broader spectrum of that experience. If it was Roth and Malamud and Bellows after the war, the Jewish introvert in the cities, then we've got a different kind of experience to bear on today.

> *Who else would you cite, apart from Lahiri?*

There's Chang-Rae Lee, who I love. I loved *A Gesture Life*. That was a beautiful novel. There are many others. There's Louise Erdrich, who is a personal friend of mine. So I qualify that – but I love her work. She's been in that tradition of Toni Morrison, an heiress to the oral tradition and the magical phenomenon. Those are people who have given us a whole new world of what we now consider contemporary American fiction. Whereas Updike's North Shore is still very true. There are just more trailers in the park now, sharing the space.

> *Speaking of traditions: As you work on this autobiographical book, is there a model you have in mind? A kind of memoir you don't want to write?*

There are a lot of memoirs I don't want to write. In fact one of the reasons I was reluctant is that I think that the memoir which I love as a genre – or used to love as a genre – has been turned into the confessional and I knew I didn't want to write that. That I was not interested in pathography or any of what had been this kind of: "And then and then and then I ..." These are such narcissistic stories. I mean, we've all got life stories. I had such a desire to write something that would resonate with people about their own experiences. And one of the reasons I love being a book critic is that I felt like: for the rest of my life I would be able to write about something grander and higher and more exalted that my own measly existence on the planet. You know, that's the beautiful thing about being a critic of the arts. We want a great wall to bounce off of. Some kind of celestial subject.

I knew that I didn't want to write one of those low-ceilinged little stories about my life and the hard things in it and blah blah blah. And I think that's one of the reasons I started thinking about it in terms of the literary imprints. I started thinking about all the people like Anna Karenina and the women I grew up with, the fictional ideals and tragic paths to avoid and I thought: "This is the kind of book I can write."

So it's very much a kind of reader's memoir. I reread some things, interestingly, that I thought were in my mind, like *How I Grew* by Mary McCarthy, and my memory of it was kinder than my second return to it. At first I thought that was the model and then I went back to it and thought: "No, not really ..." And so in fact I've been happy to see that everything I looked at taught me maybe where I didn't want to go. It was more like: "No ... There's no memoir so far about wheat fields and Vietnam."

Note

1   In spite of this disclaimer, Caldwell is in many cases wonderfully unable to qualify her enthusiasm. When the critic says that she loves a book, 'I love' sounds like a soft 'I loooove'. By the same token, extreme disappointment with a novel sounds like a – not quite so soft – 'I looooathe that book'. After the 'official part' of this interview was over, Caldwell expressed her admiration for Carolyn Cooke's *The Bostons*, a 2001 short story collection, lauded *Oxygen* (2001), British author Andrew Miller's novel, and extolled American writer Julia Glass's National Book Award winning *Three Junes* (2002) ("especially the first part"). Finally, she talked about Ian McEwan's *Atonement* (2001) as a work whose sheer excellence, she said, created problems of its own, since the novel seemed to overshadow its contemporary peers completely. "I've had friends", Caldwell said, "who asked me: What should I read after *Atonement*? And I said: There's nothing to read. It's just too good. Go read *To the Lighthouse* or *Middlemarch*."

Greta Olson, Freiburg

Introducing Alice Sebold's *The Lovely Bones*

Like Holden Caufield, Susie Salmon, the fourteen-year-old narrator of Alice Sebold's *The Lovely Bones* (2002), touches the reader with her youthfulness, direct manner of address, and interest in subverting audience expectations. Witness her comment to the reader in the third paragraph of the book: "I wasn't killed by Mr. Botte, by the way. Don't think every person you're going to meet here is suspect. That's the problem."[1] The clarity and emotional vigour of Susie Salmon's voice as well as her liberal use of seventies teenage American's colloquialisms account in part for the enormous critical and commercial success of Sebold's best-selling début novel. Another cause for the novel's positive reception is its emotionally resonant exploration of experiences of trauma, loss and transformation. In this essay I discuss several interrelated issues that strike me as central to an introduction to the text: the narrative's premise and the resultant liminal state of its narrator, the title, the issues of rape and recovery. All of these elements contribute to the novel's exploration of rites of passage, the movement from life into death and from tragic loss to gradual recovery. I also want to voice a criticism about the novel's occasional fairy-tale sentimentality and end with a discussion of the centrality of the family to the story.

1. The Premise

The Lovely Bones is at once a crime story, a criminal's and a survivor's biography, a novel about a family, and finally a meditation on passages. The narrator Susie Salmon allows the reader to get the worst over with right off the bat. She begins her story with a detailed account of how she was raped and murdered by her malignant and eerily sane-seeming neighbour, the middle-aged bachelor and dollhouse builder Mr. Harvey. The narrative premise then is that the dismembered Susie has escaped from the world and her hideous death to a "perfect world" (preface, 140), an "Inbetween" (79), where she works on "fitting her limbs together" (8) and hovering over the remains of her devastated family. The threshold quality of this in-between site is illustrated by a picture, which is repeatedly referred to, that Susie's little brother Buckley made shortly before her death:

> Hours before I died, my mother hung on the refrigerator a picture that Buckley had drawn. In the drawing a thick blue line separated the air and ground. In the days that followed I watched my family walk back and forth past that drawing and I became convinced that the thick blue line was a real place – an Inbetween, where heaven's horizon met Earth's. I wanted to go there into the cornflower blue of Crayola, the royal, the turquoise, the sky. (34)

This picture reflects Susie's sense of being on the other side of a barrier that separates her from her family members. Unseeing, they walk by the picture that would give them a clue as to where Susie can now be found. And Susie, imprisoned on the other side of the "thick blue line", is fated to watch her family's movements without being able to actively communicate with them. Hence the novel is a vision of what it means to be in a state of transition, neither here nor there, but in the middle.

Susie is not the first narrator to tell her story from beyond the borders of life. Remember Laurence Sterne's *The Life and Opinions of Tristram Shandy* (1759-1767), in which Tristram begins his story truly *ab ovo* by narrating the events of the evening when his parents "begot" him.[2] Calculating his father's extremely regular, if reluctant, fulfilment of marital duties on the same evening that he wound the clock, Tristram tells his audience precisely when he was conceived and how his mother's conflation of clock-winding and sex contributed to his own temperamental peculiarities.[3] Whereas Tristram tells the story of his life from just before the moment of his conception, Susie begins her story from just before she died. She works forwards and backwards in time simultaneously, to tell her audience of her painful attempts to find peace in her in-between heaven and her family's mostly disastrous efforts to carry on with their lives after her death.

The liminality of this in-between narrator position highlights the novel's major theme: How does a lovable family, each member of which is both frail and human, all too human in her or his frailty, move on after one of its members has been brutally ripped out of its midst? And how does an individual who has experienced severe trauma go on, even in death? The answer is that the victim and the victim's family cannot go on, at least initially, but are caught in a state of transition, of not really being anywhere, for some time. Susie has been torn apart with sexual violence and then again with a knife. Scattered, she is unable to pursue her eventual destiny in death, to go to the "wide, wide Heaven" where her beloved grandfather resides. This is a heaven of "cakes and pillows and colors galore" (325). Susie remains trapped in a "small-heaven" (325) that is more closely attached to earthly doings, and her family remains stuck in a state of profound inability to continue in a life that no longer makes any sense to them.

The in-between place Susie finds herself in after death is in part heavenly. Here many of the dreams of a fourteen-year-old girl are in fact fulfilled. In this Inbetween she discovers a new best friend and the high school she never got to attend. This school is identical to the 'real' Fairfax High except that it has comfortable swing sets, is free from teachers, requires its students to attend nothing but art classes, and gives them women's magazines to read instead of textbooks. Susie lives with her new friend in a much nicer house than the one she once lived in, a duplex that borders on a wood full of animals. And she has no end of dogs to make up for the one she has left behind, the beloved Holiday. Susie even has a kind of guardian in her small-heaven, the middle-aged Franny, who also met a violent death. Although Franny gives no-nonsense advice and tells Susie and her friend how to navigate the geography of heaven, she cannot replace Susie's mother, the ambiguous, beautiful, unhappy and passionate Abigail Salmon.

Not only does Susie desperately miss her family but she is frustrated by her inability to pursue her aims on earth. She wants to make the police see what becomes obvious to her father, that their neighbour is not just her murderer and rapist, but the destroyer of many girls and women. She wishes to find out what would have happened between her and Ray Singh, the smart, exotic boy on whom she had a crush and who kissed her shortly before her life ended. In short she wants to live and grow up; this she cannot have.

Worse still, she cannot protect her family from the pain they must endure after her death. "[T]rapped in a perfect world" (preface, 140), she is unable to act with agency on earth. She frantically wishes to stop her mother and father from making fatal mistakes that bring them new pain. She even fears that her desire to protect her sister Lindsey, who turns into a one-girl avenger on Mr. Harvey, will cause her harm.

The anthropologist Victor Turner defines the liminal as part of all rites of passage. Liminality describes the threshold area that an individual in transition occupies while he or she is no longer one thing and not yet another. A liminal persona is, for example, a neophyte during an initiation ritual when she is considered no longer a child but not yet an adult. In this state the individual is "neither living nor dead from one aspect, and both living and dead from another. [This] condition is one of ambiguity and paradox, a confusion of all customary categories".[4] To become something new the liminal subject must detach herself from ties to her community and be in an ambiguous transitional state before emerging as someone else with a new social role.

In her liminal state Susie is alternately a witness to and a participant in her story. Sometimes she tells her story as a first-hand participant in the flashbacks to her former life, when she briefly returns to earth, and during her stay in the Inbetween. Otherwise, she hovers over the lives of those she is now separated from. In this mode Susie displays third-person omniscience typical of an authorial narrator who looks onto scenes as they transpire. This omniscience allows Susie to witness her sister's painful interview with the school principal shortly after her death, to watch her mother embark on a bleak affair, and even to return to scenes from Mr. Harvey's childhood.

One might examine Susie Salmon's position as a narrator who combines hetero- and homodiegetic qualities to demonstrate how telling a story from a given perspective affects the nature of what is told. An analysis of four select scenes shows how the narrator's varying level of participation in them alters the nature of the story. First, displaying a very low level of involvement, the narrator assumes an outsider's position to neutrally describe Ruana Singh's realization of how deep-felt her dissatisfaction in her marriage is. Susie in no sense participates as a character in this scene but is an omniscient non-present witness to it, who can tell the audience about Ruana's feelings via free-indirect thought: "She could not remember the last time she had gone to bed at the same time as her husband. He walked in the room like a ghost and like a ghost slipped in between the sheets, barely creasing them. [...] His cruelty was in his absence." (314) A scene that shows a greater degree of narrator involvement occurs when the dead Susie is forced to helplessly stand by and watch her father attack someone he thinks is Mr. Harvey in the field where she was killed. He is then beaten up with his own baseball bat. Here, Susie is a ghost witness who is present yet unable to participate: "I pushed and pushed against the unyielding borders of my heaven. I wanted to reach out and lift my father up, away to me." (139) And later: "But I had to turn my back in heaven. I could do nothing –" (139). She is allowed only the small grace of being able to blow out the candle next to the chair where her father was sitting before he went out to the field. Third, in the scene in which Susie returns to earth in Ruth's body to have sex with Ray, she is, of course, directly involved as a participant. Yet she also remains somewhat removed from events due to her awareness of her transitoriness and simultaneous consciousness of what is occurring in heaven during her absence: "My head throbbed then, with the thought of it, with me hiding inside Ruth in every way but this – that when Ray kissed me or as our hands met it was my desire, not Ruth's, it was me pushing out at the edges of her skin. I could see Holly [in heaven]. She was laughing" (304). Fourth, the scene in which Susie is raped shows the narrator as sole protagonist who is entirely involved in the action. Here, the reader learns about what happens solely on the basis of Susie's reported sensations: "I felt huge and bloated. I felt like a sea in which he stood and pissed and shat. I felt the corners of my body were turning in on themselves and out [...]." (14) The narrator's relative level of participation in these scenes reflects Susie's changing level of distance from the events she describes. This distance translates into textual signs about how emotionally involved the reader should be in each scene.

Analysing these scenes from a narratological perspective may help readers to grasp the confluence in the novel between form and content. One might also want to note that the time arrangements in the narrative vary greatly. The year following Susie's death is presented in slow scenic descriptions of events, interrupted by flashbacks to Susie's and Mr. Harvey's past; then the story time speeds up, and the reader is given a summary of several years, before returning to more slowly-told scenes at the end of the novel. Noting these formal qualities of the text as well as the several-line breaks within chapters to denote changes of subject will help the reader to register nuances in content.[5] One might want to ask students why two of the chapters have names whereas the others are numbered, or how the use of three asterisks between paragraphs signifies something other than the several-line breaks.[6]

2. Why Are the Bones Lovely?

Readers may puzzle over the novel's odd-sounding title. Like the image of the Inbetween in Buckley's crayon picture, the novel's title provides a salient visual image that is reflected on and reverberates in a number of different ways throughout the narrative. Why then are the bones lovely?

First, they represent Mr. Harveys's fetishizing of the physical remains of his many victims. The lovely bones are analogous with the tokens from his victims that he keeps and treasures and worries over like rosary beads. With her omniscient, if powerless, vision, Susie looks into the thoughts, the house, and even the past of Mr. Harvey. In so doing she helps to make his viciousness explicable to herself and her reader, while never condoning or justifying it. After Susie's murder Mr. Harvey begins to kill neighbourhood pets and put lime on their bodies in order to be able to enjoy their bare bones more rapidly. This self-prescribed form of therapy helps him to stave off his desire to rape girls and further possess them by cutting up their bodies and returning to their graves to be with their bones:

No one could imagine an appetite like the one in the green house.

> Someone who would spread quicklime on the bodies of cats and dogs, the sooner for him to have nothing left but their bones. By counting the bones and staying away from the sealed letter, the wedding ring, the bottle of perfume [talismans of his victims], he tried to stay away from what he wanted most – from going upstairs in the dark to sit in the straight chair and look out toward the high school, from imagining the bodies that matched the cheerleaders' voices, which pulsated in waves on fall days during football games, or from watching the buses from the grammar school unload two houses down. [...] What I think was hardest for me to realize was that he had tried each time to stop himself. He had killed animals, taking lesser lives to keep from killing a child. (131)

One of the novel's strengths is that while it examines someone whose actions can only be characterized as evil, it does not equate Mr. Harvey with an animal or monster or suggest that he is wholly without human feeling.

Second, the bones represent the healed soul of the dismembered Susie and her wounded family's growth into something new, several years after her death:

> These were the lovely bones that had grown around my absence: the connection – sometimes tenuous, sometimes made at great cost, but often magnificent – that happened after I was gone. [...] The events that my death wrought were merely the bones of a body that would become whole at some unpredictable time in the future. The price of what I came to see as this miraculous body had been my life. (320)

The dismembered body has grown into something new. Susie's loss can never be made into something good. Yet the horrible pain that her family members feel after her death slowly and incrementally gives way to their learning how to live in acceptance of her death and the necessity of their continuing to live and love without her. Likewise, Susie learns to accept the relationships that grow and change between her loved ones after her death.

Third, the lovely bones are part of a song about everyday things one misses that Susie's father – much the more easy parent to comprehend and idealize – sings to his daughters to put them to sleep. Susie then whispers this song to her parents during their reunion after a long and painful separation (144, 278). In this context the image of the lovely bones reminds the reader that the prosaic elements of life, the stones and bones, need to be treasured.

The repeated mention of the bones in several variations and from several perspectives exemplifies the use of imagery throughout the novel. A single image is introduced somewhat nonchalantly; the same image is brought up again and played with in another context. The resultant blend of images and connotations is finally brought to some form of closure. This is the case, for example, with the family name. Like the eponymous fish that swims against the current or 'goes the hard way', all members of the Salmon family have to undertake difficult emotional journeys before they can come to some sort of rest at the end of the novel. Similarly, images of the Inbetween, bones, the bracelet Susie wore when she was murdered, yellow flowers, the lip of the grave, and icicles are played with throughout the narrative.

3. Rape and Transformation

A brutal rape marks the beginning of this narrative. Rape and violence towards women and girls become central interests for Susie, her friend Ruth Connors, and Len Fenerman, the sympathetic cop whose own human frailty contributes to Mr. Harvey's avoiding arrest. Because rape figures so prominently in the novel as well as in Sebold's memoir *Lucky* (1999) the topic needs to be addressed when reading and teaching *The Lovely Bones*.

In a recent interview Sebold has said that she wrote *Lucky* after she had already done a significant amount of work on her novel. When she found that her own experience as a rape victim kept interrupting her telling of Susie's life, she decided to take a break to write her memoir. Later she went back to writing the novel.[7]

Lucky details a chapter of Sebold's life. As a student at Syracuse University, she was raped at the end of her freshman year, chose to return in the fall, then recognized her rapist on a street near the university campus, and saw her case go to trial and her assailant convicted. After the rape the police told Sebold that she had been "lucky" – hence the title – since another girl had been raped and dismembered in the same underground entrance to an amphitheatre where she had been violated. During the rape Sebold observes "among the leaves and glass [a] pink hair tie" and reports that she "will always think of her [the murdered girl] when I think of the pink hair tie. I will think of a girl in the last moments of her life."[8] Perhaps then *The Lovely Bones* is a telling of what could have been that murdered girl's life, an attempt to give this lost soul a voice.

One of the themes of Sebold's memoir is that rape never stops. She was a 'successful' rape victim, one of the few who actually go on to see her attacker put in jail. However, witnessing her assailant being incarcerated in no way sets her free. After a period of seeming recovery,

Sebold drops out of graduate school, lives in New York tenements, and snorts heroin as a way "to reach oblivion".[9] Some measure of recovery does not occur until years and years after the rape, after Sebold has come to realize just how deep the trauma of her rape has gone.[10]

The Lovely Bones transforms events that are told differently in Lucky. Both the novel and the memoir feature an act of traumatic violence against a woman and portray the effects of this violence on the victim and her family. Mirroring the insights of system therapy, both texts show that the wounding that is done to one family member inalterably changes the dynamics of the emotional system she moves in. Both narratives begin with detailed portrayals of rape, then move slowly forwards in time, and in the last chapter provide an overview of the years following the crime. Both works detail how trauma can lead to transformation – good and bad. It will be interesting to see how Sebold's future work translates the experience of life-altering trauma into new forms.

4. *Women's Fiction?*

If the novel has a fault it is its moments of dreams-come-true wish fulfilment. I fear that these moments give *The Lovely Bones* a mass-market, gendered quality. John Unsworth has written that the American literary marketplace is a binary one. The unwritten rule of this marketplace says that white, male academics write 'literate', emotionally detached form-heavy books for a few other white men with lots of academic credentials. By contrast, the bulk of book buying and reading is done by women, who want to read realistic, emotionally moving and spiritual narratives.[11] I wonder if Sebold caters to a mass constituency or to the norms of a 'women's fiction' that borders on sentimental kitsch in her portrayal of the following novelistic events: Mr. Harvey finally 'gets it' in the manner Susie would have chosen if she could have participated in a contest to commit the perfect murder. He is impaled by an icicle just after he has unsuccessfully tried to lure another girl to a brutally violent death. His use of his penis as a weapon against many girls and women is symbolically repaid by fate with a natural projectile whose form resembles a phallus. Ten years after her death a new Susie is born to Lindsey and her heroically faithful boyfriend, friend, and later husband Samuel. Finally, and most fantastically, Susie is granted her most urgent wish to return to earth and complete her adolescent discovery of what might have happened after her first kiss. She briefly trades bodies with Ruth Connors and comes back to earth to have sex with Ray (chapter 22).[12]

Susie is such an engaging and sympathetic character that one wants to see her happy. The pain she experiences is so profound and her love for her wounded family so palpable that one may wish to let this character-narrator have the fairy-tale ending she longs for. Yet Susie's reappearance among the living contradicts the logic of the novel's fictional premise. Caught in the Inbetween Susie can fulfil some adolescent fantasies in which her own agency is not involved, like living in a house nicer than the Salmon's. Yet she cannot interact with those she loves on earth directly or grow up and, for this reason, fails to let go of the earth. Susie's return to the living weakens the fabric of the narrative and has a clichéd woman-finds-happiness-in-emotionally-fulfilling-sex quality that typifies much fiction that is marketed to women.

5. Family

Strikingly, several currently acclaimed American best-sellers take families' confrontations with death as their subject matter. I am thinking of Jonathan Franzen's *The Corrections* (2001) and Paul Auster's *The Book of Illusions* (2002) amongst others. Surely these novels speak to the concerns of members of an ageing population, many of whom are watching parents die, themselves age, and their own nuclear families dissolve in divorce.

The portrait *The Lovely Bones* offers of the family is an overwhelmingly positive one. All of Susie's family members go through a liminal period that mirrors her own before they can learn to live with her death. Like Susie with her scattered pieces, each member of the Salmon family enters an inchoate state after Susie's death. Initially, Abigail and Jack refuse to believe that Susie is dead – there is no body – despite mounting evidence: an elbow is found by a neighbourhood dog; there is too much blood in the cornfield; saliva on the hat found after Susie's disappearance shows that her rapist gagged her with it. First bingeing on food and withdrawing from her family, Abigail then responds to Susie's murder by having an affair and leaving her family for several years. Lindsey attempts to become a superhuman with a limitless capacity to hide pain and deal with the stigmatization that attends being "the dead girl's sister" (30). Both surviving children try to parent their parents by trying to become perfect children themselves.

As the narrator exclaims with a bit of disappointment towards the end of the novel: "It was no longer a Susie-fest on Earth." (236) Every member of the family has – like a salmon – to take a hard path through enormous pain before finding a way to live again. Hence they also enter a threshold state after her death. As Turner writes of these moments of passage: "Liminality is the realm of primitive hypothesis, where there is a certain freedom to juggle with the factors of existence." After their forced separations from life as they have known it, the Salmons emerge in new forms. Lindsey no longer needs to always play the figure of Amazonian strength. Abigail and Jack Salmon take up their marriage on a new basis. Gone now is the fiction that having a garden and being a mom was all that Abigail ever dreamed of or that anything can make up for the loss of a loved child. Buckley perhaps finds solace for his decimated childhood in his drums and his marvellous garden.

The end of the novel comprises a second rite of passage. Having managed at last to let go of her former life, Susie travels from small heaven to "wide wide Heaven" (325). This event and the simultaneous uncovering of another 'lovely bone', another reminder of Susie's truncated life, remind us as readers to value what is transitory and small in our own passages.

Notes

1   Sebold (2002: 6). Further references to this edition will be included in the text. – Compare this to how Salinger's Holden opens *The Catcher in the Rye*: "If you really want to hear about it, the first thing you'll probably want to know is where I was born, and what my lousy childhood was like, and how my parents were occupied and all before they had me, and all that David Copperfield kind of crap, but I don't feel like going into it, if you want to know the truth" (1).
2   Sterne (1983: 5).
3   Tristram reflects on his father's meticulous regularity as follows: "[…] he had made it a rule for many years of his life, – on the first Sunday night of every month throughout the whole year, – as certain as ever the Sunday night came, to wind up a large house-clock which we had standing upon the backstairs head, with his own hands: – And being somewhere between fifty and sixty years of age, at the time I have been speaking of, – he had likewise, gradually brought some other little family concernments to the same period, in order, as he would often say to my uncle Toby, to get them all out of the way at one time, and be no more plagued and pester'd with them the rest of the month." (8)
4   Turner (1972: 340).
5   For a brief overview of narratological concepts and models, I recommend Nünning (1994).
6   Explaining her practice of numbering and not numbering some chapters, Sebold has said: The chapters that are numbered are chapters I consider moving forward in the narrative – they're driving the basic narrative forward. There are two chapters that aren't numbered: 'Snapshots' and 'Bones'. 'Snapshots' covers a larger period of time and moves more quickly. It's called 'Snapshots' to work with the idea of Susie as a wildlife photographer

following her family and the community. 'Bones' is the conclusion and is meant to underline the idea of the lovely bones formed after Susie's loss (n.d.).
7 Sebold (2003: 139).
8 Sebold (1999: 11).
9 *Ibid.*, 243.
10 Sebold's memoir makes transparent some ugly truths about how rape is prosecuted and handled: The officer who takes her statement does not initially believe her and suggests that her case be dropped; Sebold's father cannot comprehend how she could have been raped if the assailant was not holding his knife in his hands when coitus took place. Both of these men's reactions highlight a central factor in rape cases: victims are often disbelieved and they alone among crime victims have the burden of proving that they resisted the crime that was committed against them to the utmost. Hence judgements about the victim's character become central to prosecution. The fact that Sebold was a virgin at the time of her rape, that she was quite severely beaten, and that she was wearing frumpy clothes when she was attacked all helped to lead to her assailant's conviction.
11 Unsworth (1991: 693).
12 This scene is a central cause for Philip Hensher's highly negative review of the book in *The Observer* as "mawkish".

Bibliography

Hensher, Philip: "An Eternity of Sweet Nothings", *The Observer*, 11 August 2002.
Nünning, Ansgar: "A Survey of Narratological Models", *Literatur in Wissenschaft und Unterricht* 27, 1994, 283-303.
Salinger, J.D.: *The Catcher in the Rye*, Harmondsworth, 1994 [first published 1951].
Sebold, Alice: *Lucky*, New York, 1999.
–: *The Lovely Bones*, Boston, 2002.
–: "Ask the Author. Q & A with Alice Sebold", http://abcnews.go.com/sections/community/GoodMorningAmerica/lovelybones_email.html (accessed 15 November 2002).
–: "Ein solches Verbrechen kann dein Leben verändern", interview with Anja Jardine, *Brigitte* 4, 2003, 138-142.
Sterne, Laurence: *The Life and Opinions of Tristram Shandy*, Oxford, 1983 [first published 1759-1767].
Turner, Victor W.: "Betwixt and Between. The Liminal Period in *Rites of Passage*". – In William A. Lessa & Evon Z. Vogt (Eds.): *Reader in Comparative Religion. An Anthropological Approach*, New York, 1972, pp. 338-347.
Unsworth, John M.: "The Book Marketplace II". – In Emory Elliott (Ed.): *The Columbia History of the American Novel*, New York, 1991, pp. 697-725.

Claus-Ulrich Viol, Bochum

Golden Years or Dark Ages?
Cultural Memories of the 1970s in Recent British Fiction

> It's the end, the end of the Seventies
> It's the end, the end of the century
> (The Ramones, "Do You Remember Rock 'n' Roll Radio", 1979)

1. Four (Popular) Views of the 1970s

For once, the Ramones were wrong. Singing in 1979, they hailed both the end of the 1970s and that of the century. Yet, while the century came to an end four years ago, there still seems to be no end to the 1970s. The decade – in its various and ever new guises – appears to be as alive as ever. In recent years, the time has come to exert a particularly strong grip on the popular imagination. In Britain, there has been a flood of archival television programmes exploiting 1970s footage and trivia, a spate of re-releases of 1970s films and TV series, popular music has seen the rise of the 'easy listening' scene and glam rock quotations, popular culture the rehabilitation of the lava lamp, crushed velvet, and flares. In addition, there has been a reopening of the debate about the political legacy of the 1970s – not only, by the way, in Britain, but also in Germany and Italy – which until recently had been dominated by a rather one-sided condemning of the decade's record. What is more, and what will concern us in this paper, there have been new literary representations of the 1970s that engage in the new debate. These seek to change previous conceptions of the decade. As contemporary constructions of the past they might tell us more about the present than about the times they deal with. As pieces of popular literature they are expressive of current cultural climates, reflecting on and shaping the collective memories that exist at the time of their writing. Umberto Eco has pointed out that our thinking in decades (or centuries and millennia), though irrational and imprecise – as if decennial calendar periods coincided with meaningful cultural paradigms and developmental stages –, has considerable symbolic power and cultural use value.[1] Engrained in the popular imagination, these constructed decades acquire a reality of their own, they shape our perceptions of the past and, by doing so, the perception of ourselves and the present. How, then, do the 1970s speak to the readers of popular fiction after the turn of the century?

Before we turn to a reading of three recent British 1970s fictions, it seems useful to address the existing popular narratives about the decade, as it is these narratives that provide the context for the fictions, that the latter try to react to, modify, comment on. By and large, there are four main contemporary ways of conceiving of the 1970s in Britain. They may be summarised under the following headings:

(I) *social crisis and division*: the 1970s in Britain are often remembered as "a dark decade marked by social division, strikes, high inflation, unemployment and political violence", as a decade in which "the lights went out", both literally – because of the series of powercuts and strikes – and metaphorically speaking – because of the growing sense of desperation that, as some commentators have made out, spread among the population towards the end of the decade.[2] This is probably the most powerful conception of the 1970s today, which is also borne out by the headings devoted to the period by cultural histories as diverse as Arthur Marwick's *Culture in Britain Since 1945* ("The End of Consensus"), Bill Osgerby's *Youth in Britain Since 1945* ("The Mid-Seventies. A Context of Crisis"), David Childs's *Britain Since 1939* ("Trouble and Strife"), and David Christopher's *British Culture* ("Anger and Division").[3] To a degree this foregrounding of strife runs the danger of continuing all too easily with "the rhetoric of crisis which had filled the airwaves and editorials throughout the period".[4] After all, Thatcher herself famously declared that when she took over the government in 1979, she found "a nation disillusioned and dispirited". Looking back on the so-called 'winter of discontent' she was convinced that British society was "sick – morally, socially and economically. Children were locked out of school; patients were prevented from having hospital treatment; the old were left unattended in their wheelchairs; the dead were not buried".[5] Equally famously, Thatcher identified the ideas of the permissive society that had taken shape a decade earlier as the root cause for Britain's demise: "We are reaping what was sown in the Sixties [... when] fashionable theories and permissive claptrap set the scene for a society in which the old virtues of discipline and restraint were denigrated."[6] For Thatcher and other conservative contemporaries, the 1970s must have appeared as a time of undisciplined dissipation, self-indulgent pleasure-seeking, and political anomie. In popular and simplistic accounts like Christopher's *British Culture* this is taken up. For him, Britain in the 1970s "appeared to be descending into anarchy", as evidenced by the growing "racial tension" in the cities, the beginning of the IRA bombing campaign, the emergence of the National Front on the right and numerous Marxist and anarchist groups on the left, as well as the peaking support for Irish, Scottish and Welsh nationalism.[7] Christopher's over-emphasis of the "political and social fragmentation across

Britain" even leads him to excuse the tough turn British policing had taken, while perversely stating that Linton Kwesi Johnson's poems, which were to a large part a reaction to these law-and-order methods, "are often dark and violent".[8] On the whole, Christopher's own account of the decade differs only marginally from the "sensational stories of social problems and crimes, such as racial violence, robbery, football hooliganism, pornography and rape" that he identifies as having dominated the tabloids of the time.[9] Other commentators are more careful about their choice of words when describing the 1970s, differentiating between the crisis-ridden discourse of the decade and their own descriptive approach to both the decade *and* its discourse. Osgerby, for one, holds that the air of crisis and social polarisation that hung over British society also "manifested itself at a symbolic level in the youth styles and subcultures of the period".[10] Of course, it is punk in particular that seems to have appropriated and parodied the rhetoric of crisis (cf. John Lydon's stage name 'Rotten' and his diabolic "I am an anti-Christ / I am an anarchist"). The Sex Pistols especially were soon cast – and also cast themselves – as "immoral degenerates, a baleful influence on British youngsters and stark testimony to the nation's cultural debasement".[11] It is one thing to state that many people in 1970s Britain believed to have been in the midst of chaos and crisis (and that punk played on this perception), but quite another to suggest that 1970s Britain *was* in a state of chaos and crisis (and that the 'filthy' punks were a direct indicator of this). Both views, however, associate crisis and division with the decade, one holding it at arm's length as a discursive construction, the other accepting it as a historical 'truth';[12]

(II) *economic failure and depression*: a second approach to the 1970s focuses on Britain's economic problems in that period, eschewing questions of moral degeneracy and concentrating on the 'material' developments underlying the perceived socio-cultural disorder. These accounts usually stress that Britain's economy had been underperforming in comparison with international competitors for the whole post-war period, but that its structural weaknesses were bitterly exposed when the international boom period came to an end and, as oil prices went up, recession set in in the early seventies. What has come to be known as the English disease, i.e. low productivity, slow economic growth, a balance of trade deficit, stagflation, and poor industrial relations, seemed to many to have taken an all but fatal turn. Mostly, it has been noted, the unions were held responsible for this, and from the beginning of the 1970s measures were taken to weaken their influence. To this they responded by an increasing number of strikes, which, for instance, amounted to a figure of about 2,200 in 1971, bringing about a state of national emergency and, exacerbated by the oil crisis, the three-day week in early 1974. Both Conservative and Labour governments introduced public expenditure cuts and wage restraints in an attempt to secure the balance of payments and fight inflation, which had reached the record level of 23 per cent by the middle of the decade. Unemployment figures passed the two million mark in 1975, kept on rising until 1977, and only receded slightly in the last two years of the decade to a still high 5.9 per cent in 1979. This signalled the end of the full employment policy, one of the buttresses of the post-war consensus. Another buttress of that consensus was effectively destroyed when, after 1976, the Labour government could no longer keep up their spending on social welfare, which was meant to alleviate the strains created by rising unemployment and the rigid incomes policy. In return for vital loans from American and European banks and the IMF, the British government was made to impose severe limits on its budget. This is what leads many commentators to suggest that it was actually in 1976 – i.e. three years before Thatcher – that monetarism began.

It seems that this economic conception of the 1970s is much more factual than the moral one mentioned earlier. Despite its being backed by statistical data, however, there is nothing that warrants an unqualified and exclusive identification of the decade with 'economic failure'. Especially not if our understanding of economic success is not a myopic economist one but includes the global, the human costs and gains of economic performance. Compared to later unemployment figures, which took off astronomically in the early 1980s to reach 13.4 per cent in 1982 and which levelled off at around ten per cent in the early 1990s, the 1970s figures seem fairly low. Industrial relations, if anything, further deteriorated in the early and mid 1980s, manufacturing production declined by more than fifteen per cent between 1979 and 1983, and even the rate of inflation was up at 18.4 per cent at the beginning of the 1980s. Seen from today's perspective, the rapidly declining health of the 'English patient' in the 1970s extended way into the social desert of the 1980s and beyond, with the most severe bouts of illness (and wrongly applied medicine) coming after 1979.

Apart from these rather negative conceptions of the decade, there are modern accounts that see the 1970s in a more positive light, most notably championed by youth and subaltern interests:

(III) *pluralism and social advance*: what to some observers appear(ed) to be the symptoms of crisis and division will be seen by others as indicators of beneficial social change and progress. The 1970s were the time when the social effect of the permissive legislative reforms of the 1960s was widely felt, when the legalisation of homosexuality, abortion, birth control and divorce reform had an impact on the everyday lives of countless individuals.[13] In addition, the period saw the formation of social movements that pressed for further social change and acted as agents for creating self-awareness and positive identities among their constituencies. Especially important in this respect are the movements for women's liberation, gay liberation, and black rights. 1970 saw the first Women's Day and Gay Rights Marches and the Equal Pay Act, while throughout the decade there was an increasing amount of protest action – not just, as Arthur Marwick put it, "by gilded youth, but by ordinary, underprivileged working-class women"[14] and by immigrants and the immigrant-descended population, who for the first time rebelled and organised against the discriminatory treatment their parent generation had still had to put up with for lack of lobbies and resources. In the urban areas of Britain a lively gay and lesbian subculture began to flourish. Sex Discrimination and Race Relations Acts, from the middle of the decade, gave protection against the worst forms of discrimination, and civil rights campaigners and anti-Nazi activists managed to secure more platforms for their issues, not least through a new kind of underground journalism and the alternative political 'fringe' theatre. It is this historical conception of the 1970s as the founding period of the notion of Britain as a pluralist society, a community of communities, that is, for instance, promoted in the lyrics of British Asian consciousness rappers ADF and the poems of Linton Kwesi Johnson or represented in Hanif Kureishi's novel *The Buddha of Suburbia*, which stresses the liberating power of the period's social and intellectual climate, while also mildly satirising its excesses and inherent contradictions. It is this conception of a pluralist 1970s that seems to hold lasting appeal and offer new possibilities for the future of British society, now that Thatcher's negative concept of society, a market of individuals, has seen its day and Blair's rhetorically embellished variety of it, the stakeholder society, is coming in for more and more criticism;[15]

(IV) *fashion and style reservoir*: recently, and especially in popular youth culture and the media, the 1970s have been celebrated for their perceived flamboyant fashion styles, ranging from the bright colours of the clothes, wide collars, plateau soles, whiskers, bell bottoms, embroidered shirts, tank tops, hot pants, and 1970s sports bags to the synthetic forms, oppressively patterned wallpapers, and glitterball images of interior design. Probably more than that of any other decade, the style of the period has of late been used as a reservoir for postmodern eclectic revivalism, by whose carefully ironic detachment it is treated as a tacky – though far from uncool – joke. From a modern point of view, the 1970s are often seen as the decade that style/taste forgot. Thus, the styles of flower power, punk, and disco have all had their tongue-in-cheek, ephemeral, and – if meant seriously – largely epigonic revivals. Leon Hunt has pointed out that the underlying motive of such a treatment of the 1970s is essentially an affirmation of the present as it is about discovering a past that makes the present more tolerable, about laughing at the period's love of kitsch to celebrate the present and its cultural achievements. The past, according to this view, becomes a "cartoonish masquerade" that contrasts with contemporary progress and enlightenment.[16] It must also be noted that this approach to the 1970s is not endemic to Britain but rather a trend of internationalised youth culture. Also, it seems to be more popular with the older and more middle-class segment of youth. In Germany, for instance, the revival of 1970s style has led to a rediscovery of long-forgotten brands associated with the period, such as Jägermeister and Afri Cola, and fashion companies running photo ads that sell, with consummate irony, their product as the latest in Baader-Meinhof terrorist chic.

2. New (Fictional) Views of the 1970s and the Nostalgic Mind

While these seem to be the most powerful popular views of the 1970s, recent British fiction has brought forth a new way of constructing the decade. This is a construction that is both serious and positive at the same time, its main characteristic being a nostalgic turn that has its roots in a critical approach to the present. This nostalgia has a number of structural features: it focuses on a specific part of the decade, which is largely pre-punk, pre-jubilee, pre-winter of discontent, with the latter events already marking the transition points to constructions of the 1980s; it is based on a past-present relation that is one of plenitude and lack, as nostalgia – according to Stuart Tannock – "invokes a positively evaluated past world in a response to a deficient present world. The nostalgic subject turns to the past to find/construct sources of identity, agency or community that are felt to be lacking, blocked, subverted or threatened in the present".[17] More specifically, and in line with Tannock's findings about the "periodising emotion"[18] central to popular nostalgia, the imagined time configuration of these 1970s memories consists of three distinct motifs: a prelapsarian world, a lapse (a cut or catastrophe), and the present, postlapsarian world, which is felt in some way to be lacking or oppressive.

Jonathan Coe's 1970s novel *The Rotters' Club* (2001), my first example, is a case in point. The structure of the book reflects that central, nostalgic past-present relation. There is a frame story that introduces two young characters in their late teens, Sophie and Patrick, who at a chance meeting in Berlin in the year 2003 while away their time by recounting to each other the history of their parents and uncle. It is the frame story that keeps the text from functioning as a historical novel, i.e. a form of fictional narrative which reconstructs history and re-creates it imaginatively, and turns it into a kind of memory novel, i.e. a story that foregrounds the present processes of how that history is imaginatively (re-)created. The book is about a version of the 1970s, an after-the-event construction of the decade, pieced together by two youths who were only born in the mid 1980s and who have to rely for their material on hearsay, circumstantial evidence, and the allegedly "perfect recall" of one of the contemporary witnesses.[19] As a result, the narration remains tentative, searching (cf. Sophie's initial speech markers "I suppose", "probably", "maybe", "I think" or her meta-narratorial exclamation "I'm doing my best, Patrick. [...] But it's not an easy one to tell, the story of my family", 9-10). By introducing the frame story, the novel makes transparent the past-present relation of nostalgia, and, by doing so, becomes, in its turn, a piece of qualified or critical nostalgia. It is clear that the present informs the view of the past. Here, especially the description of the frame's setting presents an important foil for the depiction of the world of the 1970s:

> Sophie and Patrick watched as the vast, brightly lit glass-and-concrete extravagance of the new Reichstag came into view. The restaurant they had chosen, at the top of the Fernsehturm above Alexanderplatz, revolved rather more quickly than either of them had been expecting. Apparently the speed had been doubled since reunification. [...] As the crane-filled skyline, the ever-changing work-in-progress that was the Berlin cityscape unfurled behind her, Patrick looked at Sophie's face [...]. (1-3)

The present is characterised by movement, change, and restlessness. This is further reinforced by the characters' remarks at the end of the book, when, as the frame narrator tells us, the restaurant "continued to revolve" and the youngsters wonder why "the world [is] so restless with itself, these days" (401). Berlin, like London, is one big building site for them, constantly obscured by scaffolding, in a messed-up state. It seems the city remains beyond their grasp, their understanding, although they are at its very centre. The frequent mentioning of contemporary disorder reveals the characters' longing for a sense of order, security, and belonging. It is of course no coincidence that the narrative frame is set in Berlin. The city seems to embody the post-1989 world here, in which global factors have increasingly come to affect personal lives, leading, as some have argued, to cultural, economic, and political denationalisation, to social disorientation and instability. In this situation, Sophie and Patrick think back to a past England that is parochial and cut off from the rest of the world.

Another significant past-present contrast manifests itself in the darkness/light binary. As in the conservative popular conceptions, in Sophie's account the 1970s are a dark decade indeed. But the readers soon find out that for her this darkness holds some mysterious appeal and carries connotations of cosiness, rather than symbolising desperation and bleakness. Thus, she begins her story on a Thursday evening in "[m]id-November, the dark promise of an English winter" (10), finding the Trotter family gathered in the living room, "drizzle whispering against the window-panes" (9). There is a "weak light" from a pair of lamps, a coal-effect fire that hisses, and a long period of silence as the family members quietly pursue their individual tasks and hobbies (9). An overwhelming part of the book is set in winter; the dominating colours are grey and brown, there are references galore to inhospitable weather conditions ("the day was darkening already, and getting cold. This had been a bitter winter", 33; "The night wind rattled against the window-panes", 139; "the icy rain of that October night", 165; "It's [...] getting wintry out there", 167; "It was another grey, rainswept Friday afternoon", 196; "It was a wintry December evening", 270; "that bitterly cold January", 291). When Benjamin looks out of the school window at the rooftops "glistening silver with rainwater", he perceives "a blur of slate grey and chocolate brown and pastel green" (198). London, too, is described as grey, brown and rainy, "with almost every other colour [...] bleached out of the city's palette" (155). There is reference to the "sewagebrown" and "snotgreen" of the Thames (*ibid.*).

The interiors of rooms, especially those of pubs and restaurants, are done in shades of brown, from the tables to the walls, ceilings, and carpets (cf. 15). In the restaurant where Bill and Miriam have their secret tryst, there is a "funereal darkness that surrounded them" (81). Sophie's construction of the atmosphere, of place and time, shows that her image of the 1970s is highly subjective and selective; at no time does the narrative convincingly suggest that her account is factual or completely 'realistic', despite the inclusion of various 'authenticating' documents like letters, school paper issues etc. At the same time, her subjectivity taps into (and negotiates) the larger collective memories of the 1970s; she takes the common perception of the decade as the dark ages (cf. her statement that "these were brown times" [15], the crisis views of the popular imagination or, for instance, other literary representations like Rick Moody's *The Ice Storm* [1994], in which the narrator speaks of "those dark ages"[20]) and re-evaluates them. Winter (usually associated with death or endings) becomes the time of beginnings; lack (of colour, warmth, technical gadgets, media overkill) becomes enriching, enabling people to concentrate on life's essentials (the 1970s' plenitude, ironically, seems to be their lack, the present's lack its excess). In addition, her approach betrays the functional mechanisms behind the workings of the nostalgic mind; Sophie is clearly looking for something in the 1970s that is absent from her contemporary world. Hence, the dark of the 1970s contrasts with the "brightly lit" night scene in Berlin (1), representing the spurious dazzle of modern life. There is a comparable contrast with respect to the feeling of happiness. Looking around the restaurant, Sophie observes sad looks on the faces of the other customers, many of whom are dining by themselves. This contrasts with the relative happiness felt by the characters in her account, especially that of her uncle Benjamin in the last, stream-of-consciousness part of the narration. There is a similar contrastive approach in other recent books that deal with memories of the 1970s: the past-present relation of these memories is made explicit in John King's *Human Punk* (2001) by juxtaposing a first part, set in the 1970s, with two other parts that show the protagonist and narrator's life in the 1980s and the present respectively, or by introducing the 1970s as a striking reference point for all characters, also by way of personification and symbolism, in a narrative that is firmly set in the present, as rendered in Hanif Kureishi's *Gabriel's Gift* (2001). In narrating (and going back to) the 1970s the characters in these books try to unearth and recover a number of lost qualities, most notably (leisure) time, a sense of belonging, and personal freedom. Let us now look in detail at how these texts construct the decade, what their common features and differences are, and what the functions of these constructions may be.

3. *The Recovery of Slowness and Quiet*

All in all, the pace of life in Sophie's 1970s is remarkably slow. It takes the characters a lot of time to perform their actions and realise their plans. Readers thus learn that a "slow awareness" had been growing inside Lois about the existence of exciting life outside the confines of Longbridge. While Lois has enough time to daydream (cf. 13), members of the older generation find plenty of leisure to pursue their extramarital affairs. Much of what the characters do not only takes long, but, in addition, remains inconclusive, precarious or even futile. Two examples are especially striking: one is Benjamin's at first unrequited love for Cicely, which takes almost six years to come to fruition, and thus stretches over the entire length of the book. And even when the two do come together in the end, Sophie's allusions suggest that this is to be not more than a short and fleeting moment of twosomeness. The other is Benjamin and Philip's ambitious prog-rock band project, Gandalf's Pikestaff, which takes them about three years to put together only to disperse after their first rehearsal in 1976, when three out of the five band members spontaneously decide to set up as a punk outfit instead. In general there is a lack of efficiency and purpose about the characters' actions (Bill Anderton's activism comes to nothing, Barbara Chase's affair with her son's arts teacher is never consummated, Claire and Doug call it a day after three or four dates, etc.). Often the slow pace of life grinds down to a complete halt, and, like slowness, stagnancy is presented in a rather favourable light. Thus, in Sophie's narrative even the total breakdown of production – so central to the crisis views of the 1970s – acquires a positive meaning. Focalising on Irene Anderton, the proud wife of committed shop steward Bill Anderton, she gives a rather appealing account of the quiet and emptiness of Longbridge brought about by a workers' strike and the standstill of the assembly line: "Irene Anderton savoured the strange tranquillity as she walked back from the shops [...]. It was a long walk but sometimes she didn't feel like taking the bus, and today it was nicer than usual, with this silence hanging snugly over the whole area." (33) It is important to note that this is Sophie's representation of Britain in the early months of 1974, the time that saw the three-day week and, as a result, is usually considered to be the worst symptom of the country's decline and sickness before the so-called winter of discontent. It is also important to note that in the only other passage set at the Longbridge plant, again, the track has been stopped, this time for technical reasons. As in the previous scene (and in all other accounts of strike actions), Sophie's narrative foregrounds the notion that the stop of production gives most of the persons involved a well-deserved rest and reassuring calm. Although there are hints of acceleration towards the end of the book, the sense of sweet sluggishness continues well into the summer of 1977, which "had been a stagnant summer. Issues were left unresolved, narratives failed to reach their conclusion" (258-259).

Frequently, characters experience moments of silence and solitude. The quiet that dominates the family life of the Trotters has already been mentioned; in the second chapter of the book, which follows the introductory family scene, there is only subdued conversation and long gaps of silence in the informal pub meeting between the Longbridge management and workers' representatives; Claire comes home after school to a house that is "wonderfully quiet and still" (28), which provides her with the welcome opportunity of reading her sister's diary; Benjamin finds himself in "absolute" silence in the locker room, where he settles in for "a long *dark* fifteen minutes of the soul" (70; my emphasis) to contemplate the plight of his forgotten swimming trunks, and later in the school newspaper's editorial office, after everyone else has left, he sits on in silence, relishing this "strangely comfortable [...] listlessness, this solitude" (199). Then there is the idyllic scene that shows Benjamin and his school mate Philip lost in the "gently undulating countryside, with its indolent, nodding herds and tidy hedgerows" (210). For several minutes both are surrounded by an undisturbed "pastoral stillness" before this is crudely shattered by Benjamin's brother Paul, who comes cycling along the way, "pedalling furiously" and singing at the top of his voice "I am an anti-CHRIST / I am an anar-CHIST" (213). This passage is highly emblematic of the book's construction of the 1970s as a 'golden age' that is brought to its downfall by the sinister forces of dynamism and movement. We see two representatives of the old order, Benjamin and Philip, who still have time to compose extended rock symphonies and philosophise about the naked girls they have not yet seen, in a prelapsarian idyll (marked by childhood, the country, innocence). Benjamin's precocious and cynical brother and proto-Thatcherite campaigner, Paul, is the representative of the new order (or rather disorder). Characterised throughout the book as disruptive, spiteful and evil, he in this passage additionally stands for speed/movement and noise. Ironically, his penchant for speed and change, which is symbolic of the imminent Thatcherite revolution or 'lapse', is expressed in terms of burgeoning punk rock, as if the two shared some underlying qualities. Paul, indeed, seems to embrace the music playfully for some of its values (its irreverent destruction of the traditional, its tendency towards polarisation, its perceived anti-social stance, maybe even its DIY spirit). The passage's position in the book represents a turning point, a crucial moment in the development of the decade as constructed by the narrative: from then on there is an intensifying rivalry between different students in the run-up to their A-level exams (most notably between Culpepper and Steve Richards) and an increasing political polarisation among the characters, as expressed mainly in the contributions to the school newspaper.

As in *The Rotters' Club*, the 1970s constructed in the first part of John King's *Human Punk* are idyllic and innocent. While it must be said that there is also a lot of violence (the traditional end-of-term punch-up with the boys from another school, an instance of so-called queer-bashing, club brawls), a lot of noise (at punk gigs and blaring out of cassette players and transistors), and a lot of speed (joyriding, chases, dancing at gigs, and speed-taking, the excitement of which is usually conveyed in long rambling paragraphs without full stops), it is clear that we are being told about a world that is virtually free from cares. The protagonist and first-person narrator, Joe Martin, and his three closest friends are innocents. With their chopped hair, sleeper earrings and cap-sleeve T-shirts, the boys try hard to look the act of being experienced and tough, pretending to "love the horrible taste of alcohol".[21] Joe does not have any responsibilities, his actions have no serious consequences.

His life is running on sweetly. This is not least because the story starts on the first day of the boys' summer holiday: "it's a beautiful day and [...] I tell the others to have a look at the sky, how it looks as if it goes on for ever. Time doesn't matter. It's good to be alive." (7-8) The atmosphere evoked in the first part of the book is one of timeless happiness and seemingly endless optimism. There is an even more direct association of the 1970s with a prelapsarian pastoral than in *The Rotters' Club*. The narrator repeatedly escapes to the country, where he does a summer job picking cherries in an orchard:

> There's a place at the end of the fence where the grass is long and seeding, a good place to doss. [...] And I lay down and look at the sky, make shapes out of the clouds as they float along, imagine them as mountains, then cars, Ford Cortinas and Aston Martins. Winter goes on for most of the year so you have to make the most of the summer while you can, and I hope I don't end up stuck indoors all my life, when I leave school, working nine-to-five, under control. I'm not stupid, know that things are going to change when I leave, that I won't be able to come down here and do my own thing. (87)

While working in the orchard, Joe makes friends with a gypsy, Roy, whom he likes because the latter always has time to talk, does not pigeonhole people in the usual fashion, and lives a free life. Joe usually withdraws to some remote part of the orchard in order to be on his own, to find some peace and quiet. In search for the good life away from the trouble and pressures of the adult world, he opts for the paradisiacal garden complete with ripe cherries, carefree shepherd/gypsy, and dreams of sexual fulfilment. What he wants to get away from in particular is the negative, almost hysterical, constructions of the 1970s spread by the authorities and the media about crime threatening society, the need for law and order, the country being on the verge of anarchy etc. (cf. 43, 53, 117). These provide a constant backdrop to the narrative, be it in the form of broken sentences on police radios, TV news or newspaper headlines. Joe does not have a problem with life as it is, but with what he sees as a hypocritical and patronising attitude towards working-class youths. Being one of the media stereotypes himself, he feels misunderstood, sure that "[i]t's nothing to do with me" (43). The orchard, Joe's good place, is the perfect embodiment of what, to him, is the 'true' spirit of the times. The only thing that really acts as a check on his feelings of happiness is the sense of an imminent loss of that paradise, which is in keeping with the pastoral genre. Joe realises that his happy days are numbered, that he will be forced to trade in his timeless idyll for a nine-to-five schedule and that in view of his current state of bliss things can only get worse in the future. As he comments after an uplifting punk gig: "this is one of the best days of my life, I want it to go on for ever, know it's never going to get any better than this" (76-77). As in *The Rotters' Club*, too, there is a moment of lapse destroying the idyll. Yet, this is not the inevitable routine of life after school feared by Joe, but a more senseless and violent rupture. One night after drinking in a club, Joe and his best friend Smiles are beaten up by a group of youths and thrown into a canal. Smiles almost drowns, is saved at the last moment, but falls into a coma. When he eventually comes to he is no longer the same person. Over the next ten years, as we learn in the second part of the book, Smiles will become increasingly paranoid. He develops persecution mania and finally takes his own life in 1988. For Joe and his friends the incident of the canal means the end of innocence. Joe immediately realises that "[t]his is the real world now, and things have changed" (102). After the event, the friendship of the four will never have the same innocent quality, as they increasingly drift apart from each other. Joe reaches a new level of reflection about teenage violence, his subordinate position in society, and his relationship with all forms of authority. He becomes more of an individualist (in the Asian part even a loner) and identifies and sympathises more and more with representatives of the parent generation (as, for instance, Smiles's father, who the youths before only ever referred to as Stalin).

4. The Recovery of Community and a Sense of Belonging

Although in *The Rotters' Club* the story's background is one of embittered industrial action and political controversy, the overall atmosphere created by the narrator is that of remarkable social cohesion and togetherness. It is true, there are characters like Paul, shop steward Bill Anderton, who keeps insisting that "the class war was alive and well [...] even in Ted Heath's egalitarian 1970s" or – much worse – his obnoxious colleague, Roy Slater, who turns out to be a member of the fascist Association of British People and believes that "[i]t's every man for himself, as far as I can see" (16; 19). Yet, Sophie's account stresses that there are a number of traditional ties and human values that well manage to counteract the tendencies towards social fragmentation and strife (at least until the very end of the book, when there is increasing polarisation and conflict). This works on a number of levels: first, families still seem to be functional. The book's central family, the Trotters, are exceptional, but the Chases and Andertons also never come close to breaking up, although there are unfaithful partners in both couples. Examples of failed marriages (as in the case of Harding's parents) or family life becoming an oppressive burden (as in the case of Miriam

Newman, who has apparently run away from home) are marginal. To most of the characters in Sophie's 1970s, the integrity of the family is sacrosanct; it provides shelter, security and comfort to its members, especially the children (as is particularly evident in Benjamin and Lois's case). In this context, Sophie also speaks of the "impenetrable privacy of the family tea table" (25) or the "relative certainties of family life" (271). Second, the way the city of Birmingham is constructed in the book suggests that we are dealing with a small and tight-knit community rather than the second largest city in Britain. Most of the characters do not seem to be aware, like Lois in the beginning, that there is a universe beyond Longbridge or Birmingham, not to mention England. Benjamin tellingly compares the surroundings of Longbridge to Tolkien's Bag End and Hobbiton-across-the-Water. Tolkien's evocation of "one morning 'long ago in the quiet of the world, when there was less noise and more green'" reminds him of the area where he himself grew up, where the "inhabitants themselves were hobbit-like, in their breezy indifference towards the wider world, their unchallenged certainty that they were living the best of all possible lives in the best of all possible locations" (134-135). The smallness of that constructed location, Birmingham, is underlined by the striking frequency with which characters run into each other in likely and unlikely places and by their being part of a closely tied web of relations and entanglements (take, for instance, Miriam, who has an affair with Bill Anderton, the father of her sister's friend, who is in turn the best friend of that sister's later husband etc.). The Birmingham of the book is a particularly small world in which characters seem to have intimate knowledge about the other characters and in which no secrets are safe, as conversations keep being overheard and letters intercepted. The representation of Birmingham is so restricted that significant parts, like the multi-ethnic suburb of Handsworth, are almost entirely excluded. Handsworth, in fact, only comes into view (and to Benjamin's conscious attention) towards the end of the book (and thus in the latter part of the 1970s, i.e. after the 'fall'), when the atmosphere is already characterised by growing racial and political tensions. London, too, is only introduced in the book's post-1977 phase, characterised as an inhospitable place, and associated with the adventurous exploits of Doug Anderton, a character who very much stands for the political activism and social unrest characteristic of the late 1970s and early 1980s (cf. the violent suppression of the Grunwick strike and the Southall demonstrations).

The peaceful homogeneity of pre-1977 Birmingham is additionally underscored by the fact that, despite the strike background, social relations are calm; cross-class interaction is friendly (probably best symbolised by the friendship between Benjamin, the son of a Leyland executive, and Doug, the son of a shop steward); racism, although in existence, is not a serious topic as the characters still seem too naive and innocent to realise that it could be a problem at all. Thus, in the informal meeting between management and workforce at the pub, "after drinking in unison [all present] let out a collective sigh" (14), and looks are exchanged "with something almost approaching warmth" (15). The only black youth in Benjamin's school, Steve Richards, is simply called 'Rastus' by everybody, while students split their sides over minstrel elements in their dramatisation of *To Kill a Mocking Bird*. However, in the first part of the book, Steve, a bright and popular student and good sportsmen, seems to cope well and appears to be an equal among equals. It is only, once more, towards the end of the book that his underprivileged position shows and he fails to receive the good marks he needs for university because of a racist plot against him. Even as late as 1977, introvert and politically naive Benjamin is still able to feel a moving moment of national unity when he watches the *Morecambe and Wise* Christmas show on his grandparents' television: "it came to him that he was only one person, and his family was only one family, out of millions of people and millions of families throughout the country, all sitting in front of their television sets, [...] and he felt an incredible sense of ... oneness" (274). As these passages show, young Sophie imagines the 1970s to be much more homelike and cosy than the regular crisis narratives suggest or the more dynamic progress narratives (of the type of *The Buddha of Suburbia*) imply.

In *Human Punk*, the feeling of a community that is lost after the 1970s is strong as well. The nostalgic narrator celebrates the male bonding of his working-class peers and the friendship he shares with his best mates Smiles, Dave and Chris. Although the narrator is conscious of internal tensions within these groups at an early stage (Dave, for instance, has leader ambitions, is envious and spiteful, while the good-natured Smiles is frequently victimised by the others), he experiences moments of complete unity with the others, something that is absent from the second part of the book, in which he is mostly on his own in his Chinese 'exile' and on the train to Russia, and the third part, in which he tries to connect to some of his old friends, who have, however, all gone on to lead their own individual lives. The feeling of community is especially strong in moments of imminent violence, or 'aggro', as in the confrontation between the Langley boys and the narrator's group on the last day of term, when a surge of adrenaline speeds up his narrative: "And we are feeling good [...], keeping up with the others, going with the flow, like you do [...], we're nothing special, nothing at all, just your everyday garden boot boys out on the prowl [...], us younger kids bouncing along feeling like nothing can touch us, floating on air" (11-

12). Even more so than by violence, the feeling of community is created by going to gigs or discos and listening to the same music. Punk rock is seen as the perfect medium to express the group experience of young working-class school boys from the satellite estates: "That's the thing about music, specially the new bands, because they are putting into words what we're thinking. It's like *The Clash* album. The songs on there sum up our lives. That LP was already inside us, waiting for someone to write it down" (17). Two things are important about this view: first, punk is here seen as a formative movement that inspires coherence rather than destroying it; second, the narrator believes in punk's authenticity. For him it is not about dressing up in bondage wear or other fancy clothes, but about the feeling of community it creates (and gives expression to) and the values it promotes (such as, for instance, equality and acceptance, anti-authoritarianism and liberation, anti-consumerism, individuality and self-empowerment). It is important to note that while the narrator's scepticism about the value of boyhood friendships and his criticism of group pressures only increase during the book – so much so that towards the end of the first part he has definitively learned that "you've got to work things out for yourself" (15) – he manages to retain his belief in music's power to forge spiritual bonds and loyalties. In his later job as a DJ he helps to restore to people that sense of their group and class identities by playing meaningful music with lyrical content, while the "ordinary person [in Blair's Britain] is isolated, told they've never had it so good", succumbing to the state's values and "classic divide-and-rule tactics" (258).

Another indicator that the 1970s world had its remnants of social intactness, amid all the fighting and fragmenting of the youth and political scene, can be seen in the character of the Major, a veritable character, the local loony and self-appointed neighbourhood vigilante, who patrols the streets from nine to five, "his face turning red at the latest crime[s] against the community" (16). The Major plays an essential part in the rescuing of Smiles and, although laughed at, he fulfils a function that in the 2000 part of the book has, for instance, been taken on by a "local security firm [that] at the same time deal a selection of Class A drugs around the M25" (230).

5. The Recovery of Personal Freedom and Creativity

The presence of the Major in *Human Punk*'s 1970s points to another significant feature of the decade's construction. The 1970s characters seem to have comparatively great individuality and potential for personal development. It is as if society's quiet and coherent structure enabled the individual characters to cultivate their idiosyncracies and quirks, to develop their creative urges. In *The Rotters' Club*, there is a character comparable to the Major, Harding, a highly original prankster and troublemaker, who does not play by the conventional rules, using every opportunity to provoke his teachers and fellow pupils. Moreover, creativity is flourishing: Benjamin nurtures a "creative obsession" (57), tries writing, composing, and performing. He writes a cycle of piano pieces, rock symphonies, poetry, does school journalism, starts on a comic novel, and eventually seems to plan to become a professional writer. There is a similar energy for creative self-fulfilment in Joe Martin, the hero of *Human Punk*. Joe does not want to become a cog in the wheel of the adult machine, but although he admires his gypsy friend for the free life that the latter leads he cannot imagine living a life constantly on the move himself. The synthesis of these two extremes is presented by punk music: it is in the 1970s that Joe's wish to live a free, quiet, and relatively sedate life takes shape, which is then in the third part realised by his becoming a DJ. In both novels, the 1970s are thus constructed not as the end point of something negative, but the start of something positive, the values of which are worth preserving. This element is in keeping with 1970s conceptions that view the decade as the beginning of alternative social progress, but it conflicts directly with both the negative crisis views and the ironic kitsch celebrations.

There is another recent piece of fiction that makes a similar point and treats the 1970s as a reservoir of creativity and artistic and social freedom, which – if properly understood and updated – can help rejuvenate and improve the present. Hanif Kureishi's *Gabriel's Gift* is not set in the 1970s but in the present. It charts the story of a fifteen-year-old North London school boy who is forced to come to terms with the crumbling relationship of his parents after his bitter dad, an unemployed rock musician, has been turned out by his mother, an overworked former fashion designer, who now has to wait tables and whose "whole life had become a 'looking for something else'".[22] The present is characterised by hopelessness, unsettling change for the worse, and the fact that his parents seem to have lost their bearings, depending somehow on the help and gift of their son. Their relationship has gone wrong, Gabriel's father's creative energies have dried up, while his own have not yet fully developed. The 1970s stand for a more glorious past, when his mum and dad were starting out, when both were active, happy and committed semi-artists in the entourage of dazzling pop icon Lester Jones. Most importantly, the 1970s stand for the spirit of creativity itself, personified by that luminous star, who has managed to retain and renew his popularity. Idolised by millions of fans world-wide, Lester, "like most pop heroes [...] contained the essential ingredients of both tenderness and violence, and was neither completely boy nor girl, changing continuously as he expressed and lost himself in various disguises" (38). He is a symbol of a time when "people did stranger things than they seemed to now" (*ibid.*). As always in Kureishi, the dressing-up or cross-dressing element of the 1970s and the protean hybridity of pop stars is writ large. However, there is more to the 1970s here than the glitter clothes and excessive make-up. At a chance meeting, Lester tells Gabriel to believe in his creative gift, encouraging him to pursue his drawing, develop his own style, and not to let himself be contained by the envy and opinions of others. It is Lester's influence on Gabriel that in the end, in fairy-tale fashion, leads to a new start for his parents, with both being happier as they overcome their frustrations and depressions. The picture Lester draws for Gabriel becomes an important instrument in uniting his parents and setting Gabriel up as a future film maker. Like an opera stage prop, it is the central object that helps Gabriel to instil in (or bring back to) his parents the 1970s values of self-expression and liberation from social and artistic constraints. The picture, or rather the inspired copies painted by Gabriel, are like mythical objects that spread the magic of the 1970s to all who behold it and propel the plot towards its happy conclusion. The recycling of mere style, on the other hand, is not what recurrence to the 1970s should be about. The fans, faithfully copying Lester, have got it wrong; they are "wearing the clothes Lester had sported more than twenty years before, as if God the cartoonist had had Lester followed, for life, by mocking imitations in order to constrain his pride" (46). Ossified and backward-looking, they are shown as engaging in a fake nostalgia. 1970s values, Kureishi's novel suggests, have to be renewed to retain their potency. The message of the book is not nostalgic, but rather forward-looking; still, the 1970s are conceived in the familiar style, the past-present relation is similar to that of the other books: we have the image of a golden age interrupted by a fall (strikingly, we have a very literal case of 'fall' as the crucial moment for Gabriel's father was when he fell from his superboots during a gig, an accident that put an end to his stardom and to which all his present worries go back, and more general references to the times "when the country decided it should become entrepreneurial" [5], pointing to the Thatcher period and the detrimental influence its commercialism had on people's imaginations and happiness); we also have a defective present in which the characters have to deal with the fall-out of the catastrophe.

6. Conclusion

All of the three novels discussed in this essay, construct the 1970s as a golden age. All of them construct the decade as the time of beginning and of innocence, of not knowing (when parents groped about, hunting for pleasures like their children, political correctness was not yet an issue, responsibilities were few etc.). Likewise, all novels identify a moment or time of fall that put an end to that innocence, which, broadly speaking, is or coincides with Thatcherism (cf., for instance, Joe Martin's 1980s exile from formerly 'paradisiacal' England or Smiles's growing paranoia and death in that decade). All depict a present that, although it has overcome the worst excesses of the fall, still needs to salvage valuable bits from the world of the 1970s. None of the novels, however, is all-out romantic about that past period. While Kureishi's *Gabriel's Gift* puts its emphasis on the renewal, rather than reconstruction, of 1970s ideas, *The Rotters' Club* manages to fuse elements of the 'dark decade' view with the pastoral atmosphere, arriving at the image of a precarious idyll that is never free from the danger of disruption (cf. the impact of the IRA bombing in the first part of the book). What is more, by highlighting the constructedness of the narrative, the latter text turns into an exploration of how cultural memory and nostalgia work. The narrative is not shaped by what the 1970s were really like, but rather by the contemporary needs and projections of the narrators, Sophie and Patrick. Even *Human Punk*, which in many respects is the most strongly romanticising account of the three, stresses the fact that the causes which brought about the fall were already present in the pre-fall world, like the social pressures, brittle friendship and senseless violence among the youths of Slough. At the same time, Joe seems to have managed to transfer some 1970s values to his present life, which shows in his life choices and attitudes in the last part of the book (where he embraces aspects of modern life – and also of modern music – as long as they are in keeping with the lessons he learned in 1977). The fact, however, that Joe and his old mate Dave revenge Smiles's death in the last part by killing the person who threw him into the canal puts paid to the idea of general personal or social progress over the decades. It raises doubts about the notion that Joe Martin has been able to preserve the good and discard the bad of the 1970s; the present, with its continuation of violence, still seems to be too closely bound to the past. While the present loses some of its optimism by the act, the fact that Dave and Joe act in collusion reinstates an unwarranted romanticism about their past friendship (a friendship that has been problematic and has been seen critically by the narrator throughout the novel). By ending on that romantic note, the book appears to praise and glorify the same past 'values' that were also the cause of the destruction of the past idyll – a circular movement that must be unsatisfactory, if not unconvincing, to the reader.

Most importantly, all narratives use a positive image of the 1970s to criticise the present. In all of them, it is the present, the post-1970s time, that is in crisis, that is inhuman, commercial, fragmented and suffers from a lack of ideological orientation, social coherence, creative freedom, and functioning interpersonal relations. The novels must thus be read as necessary and urgently needed correctives of the crisis and kitsch views, which are by implication affirmative of the present, in an ongoing discussion about what the 1970s could really mean to contemporary society, if only it took the time to bother.

Notes

1. Cf. Eco (2002: 91).
2. Christopher (1999: 9-10).
3. Marwick (1991: 135), Osgerby (1998: 104), Childs (2002: 184), Christopher (1999: 9).
4. Hebdige (1979: 87).
5. Thatcher (2001: 89).
6. Quoted in Marwick (1991: 67).
7. Christopher (1999: 121; 9-11).
8. *Ibid.*, 9, 121, 54.
9. *Ibid.*, 11.
10. Osgerby (1998: 104).
11. *Ibid.*, 106.
12. The actual dissatisfaction with the political and social situation in Britain may have been, in fact, less marked than the crisis view suggests. The Conservative victory by a margin of 44 seats (70 more than Labour) in 1979 was not a proper landslide, with the absolute number of votes showing an even more balanced distribution. Niedhart quotes an opinion poll of the late 1970s in which about 80 per cent of the respondents registered their general approval of the conditions in Britain (cf. Niedhart 1996: 197).
13. It is interesting that for some observers there is also a downside to this trickling down of permissiveness and the high styles of the 1960s into broader society and commodity culture. Leon Hunt, for instance, has argued that the latter effect turned the 1970s into a "particularly cruel parody of the 1960s", giving rise to a cornucopia of what he calls "low cultural production" such as the sexploitation films, the Benny Hill show, politically incorrect sitcoms, and horror movies (Hunt 1998: v, 2). He points out that in view of this, other commentators have considered the 1970s, in more evaluative terms, a time of crisis and regression in their grand narratives of cultural and artistic progress. Although progressive in outlook, these commentators thus share the 1970s as crisis views of the conservative social and economic analysts dis-

cussed under I) and II) and extend the verdict of decline to the field of culture.
14 Marwick (2000: 253).
15 Cf., for instance, Viol (2001).
16 Hunt (1998: 5-6).
17 Tannock (1995: 454).
18 *Ibid.*, 456.
19 Coe (2001: 2). Further references to this edition will be included in the text.
20 Moody (1994: 4).
21 King (2000: 23). Further references to this edition will be included in the text.
22 Kureishi (2001: 5). Further references to this edition will be included in the text.

Bibliography

Childs, David: *Britain Since 1939. Progress and Decline*, Basingstoke, 2002.
Christopher, David: *British Culture. An Introduction*, London, 1999.
Coe, Jonathan: *The Rotters' Club*, London, 2001.
Eco, Umberto: "Die achtziger Jahre waren grandios" (1997). – In U.E.: *Derrick oder die Leidenschaft für das Mittelmaß. Neue Streichholzbriefe*, München, 2002, pp. 91-94.
Hebdige, Dick: *Subculture. The Meaning of Style*, London, 1979.
Hunt, Leon: *British Low Culture. From Safari Suits to Sexploitation*, London, 1998.
King, John: *Human Punk*, London, 2000.
Kureishi, Hanif: *Gabriel's Gift*, London, 2001.
Marwick, Arthur: *Culture in Britain Since 1945*, Oxford, 1991.
–: *A History of the Modern British Isles, 1914-1999. Circumstances, Events and Outcomes*, Oxford, 2000.
Moody, Rick: *The Ice Storm*, Boston, New York, London, 1994.
Niedhart, Gottfried: *Geschichte Englands im 19. und 20. Jahrhundert*, München, 1996.
Osgerby, Bill: *Youth in Britain Since 1945*, Oxford, 1998.
Tannock, Stuart: "Nostalgia Critique", *Cultural Studies* 9, 1995, 453-464.
Thatcher, Margaret: "The Renewal of Britain". – In Merle Tönnies & Claus-Ulrich Viol (Eds.): *British Political Speeches. From Churchill to Blair*, Stuttgart, 2001, pp. 85-113.
Viol, Claus-Ulrich: "Br-Asian Overground. Marginal Mainstream, Mixing and the Role of Memory in British Asian Popular Music", *Journal for the Study of British Cultures* 8, 2001, 73-90.

Ralph J. Poole, München

"I am the worst thing since Elvis Presley". J T LeRoy, Eminem, and the Art of Hate Speech

> This is another public service announcement brought to you in part by Slim Shady. Slim Shady does not give a fuck what you think. If you don't like it, you can suck his fucking cock. Little did you know, upon purchasing this album you have just kissed his ass. Slim Shady is fed up with your shit. And he's going to kill you. – Anything else? – Yeah, sue me.[1]

The ancient art of hate speech has experienced an invigorating boost not only in the fierce political debates on campus speech codes in the 1990s, but also in recent artistic outputs of American popular culture. Eminem and J T LeRoy are both highly praised yet fervently discussed icons of current youth culture. Albeit belonging to different segments of popular culture – namely the musical hip hop-scene and the so-called pop-literature, respectively –, I have chosen to join them for the sake of arguing in favor of their mutual performance of hate speech. Both Eminem and LeRoy conspicuously use the rhetoric of invective language, but with differing means and to varying ends. What is at stake in both instances is the demarcation of the exact borderline between inveighing for art's sake and assaulting as a violation of human rights. To what extent can we consider the art of hate speech exclusively within the realm of cultural production, and at what point do we need to be concerned about real-life consequences? In order to broaden the realm of my topic, a reminder of the origins of hate speech seems a fitting starting point for a historical and conceptual reevaluation of the contemporary hype surrounding the issue of invective rhetoric.

1. Juvenal, Cicero, and the Roman Art of Inveighing

Generally, an invective is a text written in prose or verse that is aimed at politically, culturally, or literarily destroying the accused opponent by deliberately making use of abusive language and/or bitter sarcasm. The genre's history dates back to Greek-Roman antiquity and has since undergone various transformations: an invective may be a polemic pamphlet or an illustrative caricature, but it can also be an elaborate literary satire. The term invective derives from the Latin *invehere*, meaning literally to be carried in, hence, assail physically or verbally. In this form of speaking one articulates displeasure, resentment, abomination, disgust or the like, and it is usually directed towards – or rather against – certain persons or groups, institutions or events, or even life as such. Prominent and exemplary samples are Juvenal's satires; in his sixteen verse satires, the Roman inveigher raves against the vices of the imperial Roman lifestyle, for which he was consequently banned from his home country. Juvenal denounces just about everybody one might think of: the Greeks, the Jews, the Egyptians, as well as all other foreigners, the rich for being stingy, the poor for letting themselves be degraded and humiliated. But above all, it is women he directs his hate speech against: he censures female sophistication, which he compares to crimes like poisonous murder or sadistic cruelty, or, as in Satire VI, appropriately titled "The Ways of Women", in which he condemns their grooming habits:

> There is nothing that a woman will not permit herself to do, nothing that she deems shameful, when she encircles her neck with green emeralds, and fastens huge pearls to her elongated ears: there is nothing more intolerable than a wealthy woman. Meanwhile she ridiculously puffs out and disfigures her face with lumps of dough; she reeks of rich Poppaean unguents which stick to the lips of her unfortunate husband. Her lover she will meet with a clean-washed skin; but when does she ever care to look nice at home? It is for her lovers that she provides the spikenard, for them she buys all the scents which the slender Indians bring to us. In good time she discloses her face; she removes the first layer of plaster, and begins to be recognisable. She then laves herself with that milk for which she takes a herd of she-asses in her train if sent away to the Hyperborean pole. But when she has been coated over and treated with all those layers of medicaments, and had those lumps of moist dough applied to it, shall we call it a face or a sore?[2]

This fairly harmless invective – there is to be found a lot more and testier bawdy speech in Juvenal – wishes to hurt and harm. In his satires, Juvenal utilizes sardonic, sarcastic, but also obscene language to articulate misogyny as well as xenophobia. Since they are satires, however, we can never be quite sure whether he exactly means what he says, or rather to what degree we need to take his speech literally. Whereas in general the art of rhetoric invariably aims at functionalizing language to achieve the highest possible effort in persuasion, the instance of invective triggers the question whether the things or persons attacked are really the true targets of assault, or whether they are part of a linguistic performance and stylistic design aspiring to a higher purpose instead. In Juvenal's case, his attacks that are clad in misogynist and xenophobic attire are in truth tirades against a gruesome, tyrannical regime of terror (i.e. against the reign of Emperor Domitian). His satires thus denounce foreigners and women *not* in general, but as parabolic specimen of the decline of mores as the consequence of a particular political system.[3]

Apart from polemic language and satirical witticism, there is yet another feature essential to the (ancient) art of invective, namely literary imitation. Paradigmatically, it is the philippic, born of a specific literary historical constellation, that stands for this variant of inveighing. The term derives from Demosthenes, who in the fourth century BC wrote his *Philippic Orations* (*Logoi Philippikoi*). Demosthenes was a well-known Greek orator, a younger contemporary and pupil of Plato. Even though politically futile, his fervent diatribes against King Philipp II of Macedonia, who threatened Athens' freedom, were held as literary highlights of the Greek art of rhetoric. And yet – the most important and consequential examples of literary history are Cicero's philippics written three centuries later. Turning to his literary predecessor, Cicero 'used' Demosthenes' originals as a model for his own 'philippic orations' and thus caused a first climax of Roman literature. One could say that this epochal switch from the literary and philosophical dominance of Greece to that of Rome was brought forth with these Ciceronian orations. And it is remarkable that whereas for centuries prior to Cicero Roman literature was considered a minor imitation of a Greek original, the paradigmatic shift was engendered precisely by the strategic act of literary imitation.

Cicero's success formula relies on a fundamentally altered notion of imitation, for his orations are far from simply being copies of Demosthenes' orations. Granting that like those of Demosthenes his speeches are politically motivated and serve to contest state enemies, Cicero nevertheless differs from his Greek predecessor in his transformation of style and content. In explicit reference to the original, Cicero's speeches are entitled *Philippic Orations* (*Orationes Philippicae*) and openly exhibit their citational stance, accordingly.[4] Cicero fights for a free and independent Roman republic, especially in his notorious, best-known second philippic against Marcus Antonius. The satirist Juvenal has called this oration 'divina Philippica', and it provides the prototype of what today is being considered a philippic in the sense of hate speech, even though this particular oration was never spoken to anyone in a literal sense, but distributed and circulated as a political pamphlet instead.[5] The essential difference to Demosthenes' original lies in investing the politically motivated invective, i.e. assaulting the state enemy, with a personal interest, namely the defense of one's own lifestyle and politics. The opening of the second philippic reads as follows:

> To what destiny of mine, O conscript fathers, shall I say that it is owing, that none for the last twenty years has been an enemy to the republic without at the same time declaring war against me? Nor is there any necessity for naming any particular person; you yourselves recollect instances in proof of my statement. They have all hitherto suffered severer punishments than I could have wished for them; but I marvel that you, O Antonius, do not fear the end of these men whose conduct you are imitating. And in others I was less surprised at this. None of those men of former times was a voluntary enemy to me; all of them were attacked by me for the sake of the republic. But you, who have never been injured by me, not even by a word, in order to appear more audacious than Catiline, more frantic than Clodius, have of your own accord attacked me with abuse, and have considered that your alienation from me would be a recommendation of you to impious citizens.
>
> What am I to think? that I have been despised? I see nothing either in my life, or in my influence in the city, or in my exploits, or even in the moderate abilities with which I am endowed, which Antonius can despise. Did he think that it was easiest to disparage me in the senate? a body which has borne its testimony in favour of many most illustrious Citizens that they governed the republic well, but in favour of me alone, of all men, that I preserved it. Or did he wish to contend with me in a rivalry of eloquence? This, indeed, is an act of generosity; for what could be a more fertile or richer subject for me, than to have to speak in defence of myself and against Antonius? This, in fact, is the truth. He thought it impossible to prove to the satisfaction of those men who resembled himself, that he was an enemy to his country, if he was not also an enemy to me. And before I make him any reply on the other topics of his speech, I will say a few words respecting the friendship formerly subsisting between us, which he has accused me of violating, – for that I consider a most serious charge.[6]

In what follows, Cicero offers both an utterly damnable portrait of his former friend Antonius and a zealous performance of his very own polemic-satirical art of rhetoric, marking the departure from the originator Demosthenes' sole purpose of political agitation: Cicero's speech figures as political invective *and* literary self-fashioning. There are two aspects, however, that further the importance of Cicero's philippic with regard to today's usage of hate speech: firstly, it stems from the context of a speech controversy, i.e. it is the response to a prior insult coming from Antonius and it calls for yet another counterclaim on behalf of the assailant. And for this purpose, secondly, Cicero uses not only pure verbal offence, but in his vicious and vituperative portraying of Antonius, the rhetoric of pointed denunciation commonly used at the time for dealing with political adversaries.

These examples of invective show the significance and indeed possible consequences of claiming the right to free speech when turning towards articulating dislike, contempt, or hate: Juvenal was banned, Demosthenes and Cicero were murdered. Hate speech is by definition located on the borderline of politics and art, or to put it differently, the art of invective is an art that reaches into the realm of politics, imitating political action with rhetorical means. This is also to imply that the spheres of politics and art do not seamlessly merge but always leave a gap in between, a space of difference. In the tumultuous history of hate speech there have been numerous efforts, however, to close this gap or to ignore it altogether. The American hate speech debates of the 1990s mark just another culmination of these antagonistic forces between the unrestrained will to claim the right to free speech and the determination to restrict this right on behalf of those who might suffer from unwanted or perhaps called for consequences.

2. Artless Art: Hate Speech and the First Amendment

The term 'hate speech' now commonly used derives in part from the tradition of invective rhetoric used by Juvenal and Cicero. Nevertheless, hate speech has gained a specific significance that evolved from American jurisdiction. Hate speech may be called the inversion of the constitutional right to free speech as protected by the First Amendment of 1791, for freedom of speech includes the unspoken right to articulate inveighing language.[7] In contrast to almost all other democratic constitutions of the world, in the US one generally cannot be sued for assaulting other people through verbal or nonverbal articulation, i.e. via any form of communication.[8] Not even the civil rights movements and the feminism of the 1960s could change that, constitutional complaints have usually been discharged, accordingly.[9]

It was not until the so-called campus speech codes of the 1980s – a decidedly academic battle against denunciation – that a set of rules and regulations was drawn up.[10] Referring to the constitution's Fourteenth Amendment, a far-reaching and highly publicized warfare has demanded the protection of equal rights for ethnic, religious, and sexual minorities. This has invariably had consequences for the realm of art, which in turn is protected not only by the freedom of speech, but by the

First Amendment's unabridged freedom of press.[11] Now, in the course of contesting this right, texts and other works of art have once again been discussed as to their possible misuse in one or more categories like discrimination, obscenity, defamation, pornography, or blasphemy whenever words like 'nigger', 'cunt', and 'faggot' were mentioned. An especially striking example was the campaign against scandalizing art in the 1990s US National Endowment of the Arts controversy, centering on Robert Mapplethorpe's employing sexually explicit representations of black male bodies in his photographs, Karen Finley's provocative nude performances, and Andres Serrano's application of urine to his paintings like "Pisschrist".[12] In these discussions, art seems to be on its way to deliberately transgress the borderline into the sphere of politics, and the cry for censure has grown louder and louder especially from the politically conservative and religious camps, but also from the radical-feminists' side. Here the question of representation has had to do less with aesthetic criteria or with the exclusively protected space of art, but rather with conflicting interests among different segments of the public. Art has been pushed into the territory of the commonplace and has been made volatile and responsible, i.e. art has been held accountable.

What is of interest is the specific rhetoric applied for accusing an art that has lost its claim to be art. Hate speech is being practiced to counter hate speech, thus pointedly exercising reduced and derogative tactics of inveighing. The assaulted artists, various groups or subcultures are labeled as threatening 'Others', as sick bodies endangering the welfare of American society. Patrick Buchanan puts it as follows: "A nation absorbs its values through its art. A corrupt culture will produce a corrupt people, and vice versa; between rotten art, films, plays, and books – and rotten behavior – the correlation is absolute."[13] This argument contrasts true and false art on the basis of morals and ethics: art is true and universal, because it is moral, and the tautological make-believe argument concludes logically that true art is moral, because it attests to universal truth. All of this inversely signifies, of course, that there is a kind of art that is unacceptable and false, illegitimate, abnormal, and perverse. This devalued anti-art may then be placed as misrepresentation in quarantined – censored – spaces out of reach for the public and the market.

It is a domain traditionally and auspiciously occupied by pornography. And indeed, the censorship debates of recent years have created a short cut between hate speech and sex speech; the reproaches against discriminatory and sexist speech acts tend to merge, the blame being that both acts have forsaken any intellectual and aesthetic value.[14] This short cut bears a historically reproducible logic as the rhetorical device of hate speech has always harbored a predilection for the obscene, i.e. in times of a repressive cultural climate pornography has been of use as a weapon against autocratic regimes. This was the case in Juvenal's epoch, it was true for the era of the French Revolution and its critic Marquis de Sade, and in the Victorian age it was Oscar Wilde who took to pornography as a means of inveighing against his bigoted society.

What lies behind the persecution of such writers is the question of defining pornography. Originally, the Greek term 'pornography' (*pornographos*) literally means the writing about prostitutes. Already this basic, preliminary definition constitutes a mediated act and any further possible definitions construct a relation between a sexual performance and its representation. Thus, pornography can never be a thing as such, for it is always embedded in a network of arguments and hence cannot be separated from rhetoric. Speaking about pornography invariably means taking on certain ideological, religious, or moral positions, or playing them off against another.

In my readings of J T LeRoy and Eminem the linkage between hate speech and sex speech plays a crucial role. Both artists have been accused of having forsaken the privileged cultural space of art by applying an artless language of abuse and insurgence. This on the artists' behalf seemingly willful transit from the legally highly protected realm of art to that disputably less protected terrain of politics makes them both prone to retaliations. For the sake of the argument, I shall provisionally play the *advocatus diaboli* and take on the role of a censor trying to prove why such a text as *The Heart Is Deceitful above All Things* by the young writer J T LeRoy is liable to be disapproved on the basis of obscenity. That is to say, I myself will use the rhetoric of hate speech to show that LeRoy's text is an artless art.

3. J T LeRoy's Sex Speech or the Art of Lamenting in Pop Literature

The Heart Is Deceitful above All Things (2001) is an episodic novel that in ten chapters recounts the childhood of Jeremiah. In the beginning, Jeremiah, then four years old, has been living with foster parents when his mother Sarah reclaims custody for him. Sarah, herself no older than eighteen, earns her living as a waitress and truck stop-hooker (i.e. lizard).[15] In what follows, Jeremiah is depicted in various situations of abuse, be it by Sarah herself, by several of her numerous customers, or even by Sarah's parents where Jeremiah is repeatedly deported to as consequence of the interventions by social workers. Without exaggeration, one could say that there is hardly an encounter that does not subject Jeremiah to sexual, physical, emotional, or economic mistreatment.

The last episode shows him as fifteen-year-old prostituting himself – mostly in female drag – together with his mother, performing as sisters. This white trash fate is every bit as desperate and bleak as it sounds, and the stylistically and rhetorically sensational text does not spare the reader any gory details. LeRoy's prose may be called naturalistic, not in the sense that proletarian literature purports in its depiction of poverty and misery, but by way of sexual explicitness instead. To give an example:

> The belt swings up and snaps down across Aaron's back, then across his ass. I know what that feels like. [...] The belt cracks hard against his ass. She holds me sometimes, her hand on my thing, and it's so nice. It slaps again on his ass. Sarah holds me while her boyfriend, any boyfriend, brings the belt down. Little flecks of saliva spray from Aaron's mouth. But her hand is beneath me, stroking me. [...] "You sinful, dirty fucker," [...] And it's hard, my thing, it's hard. [...] She holds me and it's hurting, but she holds me. And it feels like heaven. The beating has ended, and now I hope it's my turn, before he holds Aaron and forgets about me and my turn.[16]

A scenario of sado-masochistic pleasure, not only on behalf of the first-person narrator. The verbal simplicity and directness, and the scene's channeling via the focalizer of a sexually stimulated child protagonist may trigger the possible identification of a reader with similar sexual predilections. At first and without any contextual linkage, this scene stands for itself: an elderly man chastises a minor boy and lets another boy watch, who in turn is additionally stimulated by being reminded of similar situations where he himself was disciplined. The reader's potential pleasure may even be augmented by embedding this scene within the broader context: it is Jeremiah's grandfather who castigates his own son Aaron, and it is Jeremiah's mother who both manually stimulates and verbally abuses her son while he is being punished by one of her lovers. The passage's style and rhetoric suggest a sexual arousal of all participants, even while the restricted focus of narration does not state this explicitly.

This, unquestionably, is a scene of sexual inequality. Whereas, generally speaking, a sado-masochistic constellation invariably represents an inherent hierarchical order, in this case the binary hierarchy is further enhanced, since the adults take on the roles of the sadists and the minor boys are left with those of the masochists. What makes it still worse is the fact that it is within the realm of the legitimate parental authority where this sexually induced ritual takes place. That is to say parents here misuse their legal status for illegal purposes. A triple moral and legal breach of tabooed rules affirms the evidence of child pornography:

fornication with children, i.e. pedophilia; sexual performance with members of one's own family, i.e. incest; and sexual relationships between men and boys, i.e. pederasty or sodomy. The quoted passage is a rather subdued and harmless scene compared to many others, much more explicit ones throughout the novel, especially the portrayal of a sodomitic rape of the then only six-year-old Jeremiah, Jeremiah's minutely detailed seduction of his mother's lover while wearing her lingerie and thus imitating her role as prostitute, or the novel's end in which Jeremiah pays another hustler to perform as sadistic master to Jeremiah's by now frankly articulated masochistic lust.[17]

Following a widely held consensus that child pornography definitely figures as one of the speech situations not protected by the First Amendment, this novel would be in need of censoring.[18] Legally, the freedom of speech may be restricted with regard to sex speech, if there is proof of obscenity, i.e. if sexuality is represented in a repulsive manner, with the sole purpose of sexual arousal and without having a value of its own so that society's ethics are harmed. American constitutional law distinguishes pornography from obscenity. In contrast to obscenity, pornography includes material that may have serious artistic merit and is protected by the First Amendment, accordingly. This far from clearcut distinction makes it prone to viewpoint-arguments, or as Nicholas Wolfson puts it crudely but quite succinctly, "pornography is in the eye of the beholder. [...] Inevitably, when a court or other organ of the state labels a painting, book, or film as pornographic, it has made a fundamental, viewpoint-based judgment about speech".[19] If one follows, however, certain radical-feminist views on pornography like those purported by Andrea Dworkin and Catherine MacKinnon, the representation of sexuality on the principle of sexual inequality should in general be a criterion for censoring, because it symbolizes woman's subordination to man's hegemony. Hence, language is the tool by which powerful males dominate and construct reality. Pornography, then, is a political weapon in the hands of patriarchy, or as Andrea Dworkin says, "the way and means of pornography are the ways and means of male power". In this sense and according to MacKinnon, pornography is not *about* sex; it *is* sex: "Pornography is masturbation material. It is used as sex. It therefore is sex."[20] This argument asserts the primacy of language, since having control over language means having the power to exercise it. Real actions are viewed as secondary here, because they result only from the act of speaking. It is therefore language that must be regulated – i.e. censored – above all. A text like LeRoy's should underlie censure, precisely because its powerful language creates a reality that is strictly tabooed. LeRoy's sexually explicit material is hardcore pornography (meaning obscenity), since it is extremely graphic, patently offensive measured by contemporary community standard, and thus constitutionally proscribable.

It is about time to switch positions: LeRoy's novel has not been censored and for good reasons. Whereas in naming their adversaries MacKinnon and others have themselves unmistakably taken to the rhetoric of hate speech to promote their intention in the most pointed and strategic manner, there is yet another way of looking at a text like LeRoy's. His novel cannot only be situated in the long-standing literary tradition of the art of invective (especially in its sexually enticing variant), there is one further plausible claim to an aesthetic value way beyond the suspicion of the novel being nothing but artless art. Again, this aspect points toward a specific literary tradition operating on the basis of rhetoric.

The novel's title as well as the protagonist's name refers to the biblical Old Testament, namely the Prophet Jeremiah. The full quotation reads as follows: "The heart is deceitful above all things, and desperately wicked: who can know it? I the Lord search the heart, I try the reins, even to give every man according to his ways and according to the fruit of his doings."[21] There are two aspects worth noting. Firstly, the biblical Jeremiah's very own hate speeches (born of godly advice) are aimed against foreign peoples, against kings, priests, and other – false – prophets, even against his own family, and above all they are interrelated with a deeply felt self-examination, a search to inquire into the ways of his own deceitful heart.[22] Secondly, one of the most important Puritan literary genres grounds on the biblical elegy of Jeremiah, namely the Jeremiad. A Jeremiad like Michael Wigglesworth's notoriously famous *The Day of Doom* (1662) at first sight seems like a reprimanding sermon, a prolonged railing against the world, the times, the estate of man and God, proclaiming misery and suffering. Indeed, the Jeremiad invariably appeared whenever societal problems surfaced and the course of things would not go as one wished for. In this sense, the Jeremiad was set to regain control, to lead people back to regulated normalcy. It is the most politically motivated of all Puritan literary forms, a "political sermon", as Sacvan Bercovitch justly claimed.[23] Nevertheless, the New England Jeremiad is characterized not only by its rhetoric of decline and desolation, but by the visionary implication that God's wrath will not descend upon mankind with the purpose of destruction, but as an act of love and with the promise of a new and better community instead. Thus, quite paradoxically, the Jeremiad not only laments the state of arts, but also calls for a breach with old habits, and to accomplish this, sets off the writer's entire rhetorical armory.

With the Jeremiad, religion enters the discourse of hate speech, a scope not to be undervalued when regarding the history of the US.

Even though besides the guarantee of freedom of speech, the First Amendment vows that no law respecting the establishment of religion will be made, the Puritan theocratic reign has left noticeable, yet steadily contested traces on American cultural self-esteem. In this current culture of contention, LeRoy's novel may on the one hand easily be read as pornography, albeit in the most original and basic sense of a text about prostitutes. LeRoy's lending his text the rhetoric of a Jeremiad, on the other hand, recalls supposedly long-gone, but really ongoing religious pretensions. He thus reminds the reader of a rigidly religious heritage, but in his very manner of citation inverts its original meaning. He doubly perverts the religious context. His familial guardian figures, mother and grandfather, who rely on the rhetorical dogma of Puritan religion, act in stark opposition to ethical norms. They bodily castigate the children, especially Jeremiah, as a means of reprimanding false behavior. In truth, however, it is these actions that prove their parental inadequacy and lack of moral consensus. The act of religious education turns into an act of sexual perversion, and hence there appears the rhetorically crucial gap between word and action. Sarah's insult "You sinful, dirty fucker"[24] functions as a profane perversion of a Puritan invective, and in the same manner the citation of biblical Proverbs is perversely taken literally in the course of the grandfatherly ritual of castigation: "Withhold not correction from the child: for if thou beatest him with the rod, he shall not die."[25] Rhetoric being taken verbatim causes a satirical effect of inversion here: the literal enactment of the Proverbial speech on the novel's level of content unveils a metafictional counter-rhetoric. As a result, the hate speech does not reprimand the addressee (Jeremiah), but disavows the speaker (mother/grandfather) instead.

What is at stake here, as well as generally in the sex speech debate, is the crucial distinction between spoken language and accomplished performance. An argument like MacKinnon's that considers sex speech *as* hate speech relies on the simultaneity of word and action. By equating both, the cause and effect of wounding words become indistinguishable. John Austin has coined the linguistic term 'illocutionary speech acts', with which he defines speaking *as* acting.[26] The contrasting term would be the 'perlocutionary speech act', which harbors a temporal gap between the act of speaking and its actionable effect. As the radical-feminist stance makes clear, it is inevitable to avoid ideological, i.e. viewpoint-based positioning when tackling the right to freedom of speech, for only the illocutionary speech act as action-prone speaking may legally be requited by censoring measures.

A text like LeRoy's, however, evidently strives to exhibit the hiatus between speaking and acting by continually pointing towards its own rhetorical practice (citationality and self-reflectivity). Only with utter –

and politically biased – force can one arrive at the verdict of calling this novel artless art. On a much broader basis, this has nevertheless been the case ever since the debates on the aesthetic status of so-called pop literature emerged in the 1960s. Leslie Fiedler was the first to use the term in the context of literary studies, and he meant it as a sort of literature that deliberately jumps the borders distinguishing between high and low/popular culture.[27] This 'pop literature' absorbs and utilizes themes, styles, ways of writing and living taken from mass and everyday culture, and even back then Fiedler was acutely aware of the controversy to come. It is a dispute about aesthetic values that has reached a new climax in the 1990s, when a new wave of pop literature has achieved worldwide success with authors and novels like Nick Hornby's *High Fidelity*, Irvine Welsh's *Trainspotting*, José Angel Mañas' *Historias des Kronen*, Michel Houellebecq's *Les particules élémentaires*, Benjamin von Stuckrad-Barre's *Livealbum*, Bret Easton Ellis' *Glamorama*, or, for that matter, LeRoy's novels, to mention but a few.

Reproaches against such works blame this literature for being like a "super movie" (Maxim Biller), for enhancing the "destruction of literature" (Heinrich Vormweg), for exposing a literary program that is pleased with surface design only (Roger Willemsen),[28] and – most important for the issue at hand – for trusting in a literary quality that solely relies on the author's cultural standing and a provocative subject matter based on certain biographical incidents of marginalization.[29] Already Fiedler has stood against such an argument, speaking of a "revival of pornography" as that form of pop art which ever since Victorian times has been "the *essential* form of Pop Art, which is to say, the most unredeemable of all kinds of subliterature, understood as a sort of entertainment closer to the pole of Vice than that of Art".[30] Fiedler insists that pop artists not so much fear the compromise by the market place, but, quite on the contrary, that they expressly choose pornography as one of the genres most associated with exploitation by the mass media.

Today, art understood as pop has certainly changed since the first language destroyers of the twentieth century, namely the Dadaists, or since the anti-establishment movements of mid-century, especially the Beats. There may be no more scandalous performing acts like those of Elvis – the Pelvis – Presley or the Sex Pistols (an argument I shall contest myself in the following remarks on Eminem). But still, LeRoy's novel is on a par with the protest-sensibility of traditional pop-literature. When a six-year-old, who is totally unaware of the consequences he is about to face, is naïvely and exuberantly about to (mis)quote the lyrics of a Sex Pistols song as 'I am a Annie-christ' and mistakes it as a biblical Proverb, this alone is at once hilariously funny and ironically blasphemous. When, however, this boy has to drop his pants to receive a grandfatherly spanking for his false declamation, LeRoy subscribes to pop-literature's battle against bourgeois double standards and bigotry, applying the style of popular culture and the rhetoric of parodic imitation.[31] On the one hand, this coming-of-age novel is a tale of woe that performs the rhetoric of complaint known from the ancient invective and the biblical Jeremiad. In doing so, on the other hand, it recalls and imitates the inherent blasphemy and pornography of those literary genres, but not as an end in itself – as artless art –, but as rhetorical devices for the sake of an art of hate speech instead.

LeRoy's sex speech does not qualify as a masturbatory tool in MacKinnon's sense. In contrast, his representation of pornography makes use of the media (literature in this case) that are essential elements of public discourse. He thereby raises questions about the status and function of pornography up to the point of ridiculing common views on normative sexuality. In this sense, LeRoy partakes in an ongoing dispute about regulating and banning pornographic representations in which law professor Owen Fiss, for example, opposes MacKinnon's argument by saying: "Pornography is an expression of the creators and producers of the work and is most certainly part of the discourse by which the public understands itself and the world it confronts."[32]

Much as LeRoy's novel marks the point where sex speech figures as hate speech, Eminem, whose lyrics I will now explore, uses long-standing rhetorical standards of inveighing. His form of hate speech takes on a white-trash-performance of parodic self-castigation in order to insult and affront the bourgeois musical, political and cultural establishment. LeRoy himself denies any connection to Eminem claiming, "I'm not being like Eminem and saying my mother is like this and suing her and blah, blah, blah. I just write whatever I write and I think about it after."[33] Nevertheless, LeRoy has been read as an antidote to Eminem's music, as yet another horrifying side of white American culture.

4. Eminem. Hate Speech or Rap's Art of Boasting

In the case of the 2001 controversy surrounding Eminem, there is no need to play the devil's advocate, since others have done that for me. Marshall Bruce Mathers III alias Eminem, rapper of the white underclass, is the most successful hip hop-star to date.[34] He faces two serious reproaches. First of all, parts of the African American community blame him for making use of the tradition and repertoire of black music. His immense success grounds on the exploitation of a genuine black heritage, the argument goes. Statistics are cited to prove that no other rap artist, i.e. no *black* rap artist, has ever earned that kind of money, has been given that much public visibility, or has been played that much on radio and television.[35]

But even more, he is attacked by (white) religious-conservative, feminist and gay-and-lesbian spokespersons, an unlikely alliance claiming that Eminem subscribes to hate speech and thus to propaganda for the sake of discrimination and violence. Again, statistics are produced to help enforce the validity of the argument by counting, for example, how often Eminem uses the word 'faggot' in his songs and correlating the figures to the given number of violent attacks on gays. The cry for censure is evident in comments like Tyler Robin's: "Eminem's speech is not 'free' to those of us who've been brutalized, beaten, murdered, and raped. [...] The reason Hitler and his followers were able to kill millions of Jews, Gypsies, and Gays was that his rhythmically powerful hate speech had dehumanized these people."[36] Robin and others call upon the legal exception to the First Amendment rule of 1941 to censor speech that includes "fighting words".[37] Much like the instance of obscenity as artless art mentioned above, the usage of "fighting words" figures as a manner of speaking that exceeds the formally restricted framework of simple speech, because it openly calls for violence and thus bridges the crucial gap between word and action. Accordingly, "fighting words" are no longer to be protected by the right to freedom of speech. As Stanley Fish points out, the trouble with the 1941 court definition of "fighting words" as words "likely to provoke the average person to retaliation, and thereby cause a breach of the peace", is that it "distinguishes not between fighting words and words that remain safely and merely expressive but between words that are provocative to one group (the group that falls under the rubric 'average person') and words that might be provocative to other groups, groups of persons not now considered average."[38] The double reproach against Eminem's music and lyrics demands a closer look at his very own rhetoric of hate speech. In what ways does he situate himself and his art within the tradition of hip hop-culture? Does his rap differ in any knowledgeable manner from that of his African American colleagues?

Generally speaking, the cultural roots of rap reach back to the rhythms and vocal art of Western Africa, resurfacing within the modes of blues, jazz, and reggae of the Caribbean.[39] The street cultures of US metropolitan ghettos, suffering increasing impoverishment under Reagan era deindustrialization, took up this tradition. In the 1970s, these cultural practices and socio-political factors came to a climax in the New York Bronx where a hip hop-street culture emerged, consisting of graffiti-painting, break-dance, the rhythmically rhymed recitative of rap, and the Jamaican discjockey-technique of record-mixing. Block parties flowered as alternatives to the established scene of disco, since these parties had no cover charge and everybody could join in this form of popular party culture. At the same time, the music's cut'n'mix-principle of montage as well as the lyrics based on personal experience broke with the rules of copyright and the plagiarist system of covering in disco/pop-music. Rap-music could not be covered, because its primal asset was originality and authenticity that in turn could only be legitimized by the rapper's very own experience. With the support of the record industry and the mass-media distribution by MTV, hip hop reached a first peak as dance music in the early 1980s. At this time, the new, aggressive variant of 'Gangsta Rap' gained significance in Los Angeles and with it the black macho figure of the 'Gangsta' – most noticeably Ice T –, who raved about drugs, violence, and women. Shortly later New York's counter-movement of Agit-Prop hip hop bands like Public Enemy presented a politically induced form of rap that sounded just as aggressive, but in its lyrics explicitly dealt with the desolate social situation of the black population. In this last form, rap has shed all traces of the 'happy dance' feeling of earlier variants in favor of stressing word and rhythm as well as a newly arisen African American national self-confidence.[40] During the 1990s another shift occurred, bringing rap into the global sphere with the so-called 'Native Tongues'-school. Rap has not only gained worldwide significance for youth cultures as a favored political device, finally. It has also entered the globalized economics of youth and pop-culture. On the one hand, rap's musical and visual style has had a profound impact on all contemporary popular music with highly visible artists like Madonna wearing hip hop fashion and using hip hop dances in their stage shows and rap lyrics and slang words in their recordings. On the other hand, rap style's transmitting and disseminating has also remained black culture's at times very personal medium for alternative interpretations of key social issues like racial discrimination or censorship debates. In this sense, rap is dependent on technology and mass reproduction and distribution while relying on intimate messages. "Such tensions between rap's highly personal, conversational intimacy and the massive institutional and technological apparatuses upon which rap's global voice depends", says Patricia Rose, "are critical to hip hop, black culture and popular cultures around the wold in the late 20th century."[41]

Rap's rhetorical strategies are boasting and toasting, talking 'smart' and talking 'shit', dissing and menacing.[42] All of these may be called acts of 'signifyin(g)'.[43] This refers to a subversion of dominant modes of speaking through forms of linguistic role playing like innuendoes, ambiguities, metaphors, citations, implications, and, above all, code switching, i.e. the varying usage of standard American and vernacular or slang.

Most importantly, 'signifying' is a practice of citation: given words and their meaning are used – quoted – in bits and pieces, and put in a new context. Russel Potter and Judith Butler both speak here of a "repetition with a difference", which in the case of rap means that there is an interface between a genuinely African American cultural tradition and a postmodern textual strategy on the basis of resignification.[44] The constitutive citationality of rap does not consist in mere repetition, but in a self-referential recycling of language. What is being said and what is signified can be utterly opposed to one another. Rap's 'signifying' functions may therefore be called the perfect chiasmic trope, the simultaneity of opposites.

When one takes into account the actual practice, the signifying of rap gains an additional – performative – meaning. In alternating speaking contests, the speakers boast about their respective rhetorical faculties in the same manner that they shame themselves as well as their opponents. The hate speech thus articulated relies on a mutual understanding of signifying: the invective figures as strategic repetition of a prior wounding, i.e. the battle functions as a ritualized performance of a hurtful assault. Denunciations personally or collectively experienced are taken up as citations and directed – as counterspeech – against their originator. Two things happen at the same time in this speech performance: on the one hand, hate speech is directed against its original intention, causing a reversal effect. On the other hand, a consensus exists in the rap-community – a rhetorical behavior ritually bound – that guarantees the mutual interrelation of speech and counterspeech, including all kinds of bragging and denouncing verbal gestures.

This play of insult and respect can be decoded only within its special context; however, its multiplicity and situationality must not be restricted to African American rappers. White rappers like Eminem – and the Beastie Boys or Vanilla Ice before him – may very well participate in this rhetorical playfulness. The question remains whether Eminem simply copies black rap without altering its performative signification, or if he succeeds in claiming his very own act of copying as a "repetition with a difference". At first sight, as a white American, he stands on the side against which rap aims its polemics, especially in the politically charged version of rap. Therefore, Eminem cannot claim a minority identity, at least not to begin with. He may strive to construct and legitimate one, however. And that is exactly what he does in stylizing himself as ultra-white poor trash bad-boy. Taking on the pose of utter surprise as to his own success, he mimes that boasting with which (black) rappers have always praised their own rhetorical assets:

[...] who woulda thought, standing in this mirror bleachin my hair, with some peroxide, reaching for a t-shirt to wear / that I would catapult to the forefront of rap like this? How could I predict my words would have an impact like this / I must've struck a chord, with somebody up in the office, cuz Congress keeps telling me I ain't causin nuthin but problems / and now they're sayin I'm in trouble with the government, I'm lovin it, I shoveled shit all my life / and now I'm dumping it on White America! I could be one of your kids [...]"[45]

What distinguishes Eminem from his white rap predecessors is his own low-class background. Having spent his impoverished childhood in Detroit, Michigan, he was part of only about ten to twelve percent white population there. Carl Hancock Rux translates these facts into the basics of Eminem's cultural profile: "Eminem may have been born white but he was socialized as Black – in the proverbial hood – and the music of the hood for the last twenty five years has been rap music."[46] Eminem certainly does not hide his whiteness, nor does he attempt to imitate black rap style in a straightforward manner. On the contrary, with his platinum-blond dyed hair and his rather down-dressed street-clothes, he resembles much more hip hop's white adolescent audience than any glamorously clad, prominent black rapper. In this sense, one could say his "presentation is authentic, because he has lived in their [i.e. the 'Niggaz'] neighborhoods and listened to their music and learned their cadence – but he does not attempt to mimic them like his misdirected forefathers – those who came before him and poorly adapted the ideologies and style of the oppressed."[47] Eminem himself claims in his song "Who knew": "I don't do black music, I don't do white music / I make fight music."[48]

Eminem's fame thus highlights not only the issue of race in America, but also of class. His white trash background and stage performance demonstrates how class – this often ignored social marker in America's supposedly classless society – is speaking up and talking back.[49] 'White trash' seems very much like America's flip side to white supremacy. As a long-standing derogatory stereotype, white trash signifies a substandard whiteness that is unwanted and in need to get rid of. The clichés surrounding this culturally all but invisible – because overlooked – category include poverty, laziness, poor education, bad taste, and excessive behavior. And above all, applying the white trash stereotype means blaming the poor for being poor.[50] One reason why Eminem is so shocking to many is that he has made visible this abject 'un-white' category of whiteness. He crosses an imaginary boundary, not because of what he says, but because of whom he represents. Other rappers have used violent, sexist, and homophobic language – but they were mostly black and speaking of and to a basically black community. This sort of hate speech nobody really worries about – as long as it remains within black and/or low-class borders. With Eminem, however, a low-class white man brings all that black hip hop entails into white middle-class living rooms. To cross this distinctive border and to reach towards the white middle class sets off the censors' alarm. Part of why Eminem disturbs people is that he features – in Roseanne Barr's (from famous sitcom *Roseanne*) humorous self-description – America's worst nightmare: 'white trash with money'.

In a clever maneuver, Eminem in his lyrics adheres both to his participation in America's 'white' hegemony and his marginal position as underprivileged ghetto underdog. The programmatic song entitled "White America", quoted above, is an inveighing hymn on the freedom of speech. This rhetorical scheme helps Eminem to justify as well as denounce himself again and again, and at the same time he succeeds in a jocular feast by reclaiming and thus confirming the arguments of his opponents *and* using them as recycled verbal material for his own rhetorical art:

> So to the parents of America I am [...] [t]he ringleader of this circus of worthless pawns Sent to lead the march right up to the steps of Congress And piss on the lawns of the White House and to burn the casket and replace it with a Parental Advisory sticker to spit liquor in the face in this democracy of hyprocisy [*sic*] Fuck you Ms. Cheney! ~~ Fuck you Tipper Gore![51]

Passages like this resist categorization, since they evade clear-cut demarcations of what are reproofs brought forth against him and what are invectives he takes on himself. Rhetorically speaking, he herewith glides from the rap-mode of running down, which primarily aims at information, to the mode of putting down, i.e. openly aggressive speaking. This strategy of deception and cheating is an essential part of the role-playing of signifying. Eminem invents a persona, Slim Shady, that allows him to articulate the most vicious things, but in a third-person voice and thus to keep himself – as Eminem – clear of any reproachable speech. It is through his alter ego Slim Shady that Eminem exposes his modus operandi of self-shaming: he is not the great actor at all, but a low-grade imposter. Eminem's white signifying as chiasmic trope takes hold, because he remains within the black modes of rap-speech and signification *and* positions himself visibly outside of this black range at the same time:

> Look at these eyes, baby blue, baby just like yourself, if they were brown Shady lose, Shady sits on the shelf / but Shady's cute, Shady knew Shady's dimples would help, make ladies swoon baby, ooh

baby! Look at my sales / Let's do the math; If I was black I would've sold half [...]⁵²

The coda of "White America" condenses the technique of the treacherous double-voice: he rails against Al Gore's wife and her efforts to ban rap,⁵³ he scorns the freedom of speech – albeit using it exultingly and generously –, he shames himself, *and* he completely turns round once more with a mock reconciliatory gesture in the very last sentence by applying the skill of a code switch decoding his own rhetoric as 'playing'. In the rhetoric of rap, "playing" belongs to the above-mentioned mode of talking shit and functions as a code word meaning a speaking battle, i.e. a rhetorical contest between like-minded combatants: "Fuck you Tipper Gore! Fuck you with the freest of speech this divided states of embarassment [*sic*] will allow me to have, Fuck you! I'm just playing America, you know I love you."⁵⁴

Eminem and his alter ego Slim Shady embody signifying as rhetorical play and as self-fashionable identification. Eminem *is* white America attacking itself from within. He thus participates in an articulation of social crisis that has been part of rap's ethics from the very beginning. At the same time, Eminem embodies white-trash America, this contested cultural category that makes whiteness visible by pointing at its abjected – trash – existence. This articulated talking-shit as an art of ambiguous speech simultaneously cooperates with and denounces America's white linguistic supremacy. For this reason, Eminem accomplishes the art of cross-over, for his shit-talk is accepted by the community of black rappers as part of their own street language and thus part of their hip hop culture precisely because this language remains an artificial language for all others – namely, for "White America". For them, nothing in this codified and ritualized rhetoric of invective may be taken at face value.

Just as Cicero, who in his philippic orations 'recycled' the speeches of Demosthenes as a "repetition with a difference" by resignifying them as a rhetorical model of counterspeech, Eminem utilizes his cultural predecessors to perform similarity and difference.⁵⁵ Eminem does not shy away from comparisons. On the contrary, he parodies any kind of supposed original by infusing it with self-contempt and boasting. His hate speech is clad in utterly playful garb, making it difficult – and senseless – to try and strip him down. Like Eminem, Elvis Presley was alleged to have stolen his music from blacks and to have established his success under false pretences.⁵⁶ The black rappers of Public Enemy have denounced Elvis' stardom in their song "Fight the Power": "Elvis was a hero to most / But he never meant shit to me, you see / Straight up racist that sucker was simple and plain."⁵⁷ Eminem joins this iconological chain of citations. He does so in seeming self-degradation, yet actual rhetorical inversion, and thus boasts about reclaiming a renewed, even more powerful status of stardom for himself as the climactic merging of two traditions:

> But sometimes the shit it just seems, everybody only wants to discuss me / So this means I'm disgusting, but its just me I'm just obscene / Though I'm not the first king of controversy / I am the worst thing since Elvis Presley, to do Black Music so selfishly / and use it to get myself wealthy (Hey) [...][58]

5. J T LeRoy and Eminem. Pop Culture's Resurgence of the Homo Rhetoricus

Mark De'Rozario argues that pop has turned into a managed spectacle, and that "[p]erhaps the most shocking aspect of the recent furore over Eminem is the revelation that pop still has the capacity to disturb".[59] Much the same might be said about recent pop-literature's mainstream marketing strategies and J T LeRoy's rebellious outcast status within this development. Both are decidedly poor white trash 'boys' ranting on about their miserable lives, their destructive homes, their fear of and longing for love and understanding in a world that is likely not to acknowledge their respective quest. Artistically privileging the white underclass and its 'bad taste' aesthetics takes part in popular culture's effort to oppose highbrow attitudes, ever since Elvis shocked America's bourgeois decency by publicly displaying his sexual stamina. Elvis, quickly becoming the icon of white trash, is a figure of terror and grotesqueness to middle-class arbiters of 'good taste' precisely because with his spectacle of excess he unleashed subcultural forces hitherto restricted.[60] Elvis was charged with corrupting the American youth and, accordingly, American family ethics. And indeed, his art may justly be called provocative, exploitative, and offensive. Above all, however, it was intentional: Elvis performed the poor white trash boy for everyone to see and to listen.

Like Elvis, who by singing about being "In the Ghetto" triumphantly rose from low-class status to iconographic stardom, both LeRoy and Eminem rely on their mutual street and ghetto talk as artistic tool. Nevertheless, it is not any ordinary use of language, but an intentional imitation of it. And since it is 'bad language' they rely on, the artistic act will be one of 'bad style'. Whereas "good style", according to Richard A. Lanham, "will be the transparent style, the style which is looked through rather than noticed", "bad style" signifies the excessive style, "the style which shows".[61] Ever since Aristotle, rhetoric's practical purpose has always been to win, to persuade. The relation between reality and rhetoric is one of un-seriousness, therefore. Man given to rhetoric – *homo rhetoricus* – takes on a rhetorical view of life and as such his view rests on the centrality of language. In contrast to self-centered and self-reliant *homo seriosus* whose ideal of life is philosophical, because it is based on the knowledge of human nature and of what is best for it, the rhetorical man continually aims at reassuring his socially aligned identity.

This categorical dichotomy leads to interesting, far-reaching implications, relevant for discussing the current art of hate speech. In his conception of reality as fundamentally constructed, the rhetorical man views social situations as dramatic, very much like a stage play or a strictly regulated game. And it takes one who knows – and knows how to manipulate – the rules in order to master the game. *Homo rhetoricus* therefore "hits the street already street-wise".[62] Since language for him owes no transcendental loyalties, he is morally free to play with it at his own will, for his own advantage, and for his own pleasure, too. Rhetoric is hence stylizing purpose in order to enjoy it more, and the rhetorical man – not pledged to a single set of rules and values – cannot be serious, accordingly. One could say that *homo rhetoricus* is the prototypical actor, a satirical performer of commonplace ethics. And thus, suspects Lanham, rhetoric's real crime "is its candid acknowledgment of the rhetorical aspects of 'serious' life".[63]

LeRoy and Eminem trust in the logic of rhetoric understood in this sense. Their understanding and view of life as performed in their art indeed acknowledges 'serious' life, but in a wholly rhetorical fashion. Reveling in exposing any idealist, universal – serious – notion of reality, they radically reduce and abrogate the standard – white, middle-class – American value system. Like Cicero's, theirs is a vested interest: the politically motivated invective is invested with personal interests, namely defending one's lowbrow aesthetics *via* the inveighing mode of self-fashioning. Both have chosen the rhetoric of hateful speech in its ghetto-inflected street vernacular to publicly perform their agonistic view on reality. As such, they are tackling the borderlines between politics and arts, and between true art versus false art by intentionally playing these pairings off against each other.

Their practice of injurious speech underlies a redoubled exposure, since it both adheres to real street language and performs it as imitated representation. Here, speech has become citational, it is cited against its original purpose and thus performs a reversal of effect.[64] Whereas the original purpose of sexist or racist utterances aims at hurting specific groups of people (women, gays, blacks, etc.), the restaging of offensive utterance in rap music and pop literature seeks at once to expose and counter the offensive exercise of speech. It is important to take into account that hate speech uttered for the sole purpose of harming somebody is not the same as hate speech performed on stage or in print. Whereas some forms of hate speech (namely 'obscenity' and 'fighting words') may lead to the crucial collapse of speech into conduct that in turn leads to possible state intervention, there are other forms of hate speech that insist on and thus further the gap between speech and conduct. In this very manner – and by no means claiming that they are not to be taken seriously –, LeRoy's and Eminem's hate speeches are 'unserious' in that they are acted and performed, restaged and resignified speeches. Their mutual art of self-fashioned inveighing attests to twenty-first century pop culture's resurgence of the long-serving, but newly contested inventiveness of the *homo rhetoricus*.

Notes

1. Eminem (2000a).
2. Juvenal (2003).
3. For a discussion on women in Roman satires, specifically in Juvenal's sixth satire, see Braund (1992), Gold (1998), Richlin (1984), and Wyke (1994).
4. On Cicero's imitation of Demosthenes see Stroh (2000).
5. Strictly speaking, of the fourteen orations against Antonius, Cicero himself only entitled the last twelve 'philippic', excluding the first two. Paradoxically, today the term 'philippic' as hate speech does not apply to the originator Demosthenes, nor to the self-acknowledged Ciceronian philippics, but precisely to the second (un-acknowledged hate-)speech against Antonius. Ever since the Roman rhetoric scholar Quintilian, this philippic has served as a prime model of invective.
6. Cicero (2003).
7. See Whillock & Slayden (1995), Heyman (1996), Fish (1997), Downing (1999).
8. For various historically grounded definitions and terminologies of 'hate speech' like 'race hate' in the 1920s and 1930s, 'group libel' in the 1940s or 'racist speech' in the 1980s see Walker (1994). For hate speech regulation in other countries see Coliver (1992).
9. See Gates (1994). For the joint perspectives of critical legal scholarship and critical race theory see Matsuda (1993).
10. See Berman (1992), Walker (1994: 127-158), Anastaplo (1997), Weinstein (1999: 71-98).
11. See the website 'Maledicta Press' that specializes in uncensored language research protected by the First Amendment.
12. For this discussion on art see Slayden (1995).
13. Buchanan quoted in Bolton (1992: 33).
14. See Lederer & Delgado (1995), Delgado & Stefancic (1997), Maschke (1997), Zingo (1998).

15 Sarah's own career as teenage lizard features in LeRoy's first novel *Sarah* (2000).
16 LeRoy (2001: 73).
17 See the chapters "The Heart Is Deceitful above All", "Baby Doll", and "Natoma Street", respectively.
18 Historically, see for example the governmental attempts to outlaw works like James Joyce's *Ulysses* or Henry Miller's *Tropic of Cancer*, or the more recent pornography debates concerning Kathy Acker's or Bret Easton Ellis' novels, especially *Blood and Guts in High School* (1984) and *American Psycho* (1991), respectively. On the censorship of Acker's novel in Germany and especially with respect to child pornography, see Poole (1995).
19 Wolfson (1997: 107).
20 Dworkin (1981: 128), MacKinnon (1993: 17). For the proposal of an antipornography ordinance see Dworkin & MacKinnon (1988). The ordinance passed the Indianapolis Court, but was struck down by the Court of Appeals for the Seventh Circuit on First Amendment grounds. For a discussion of this feminist anti-porn debate in the context of queer fiction see Poole (1997).
21 Jeremiah 17.9-10. The verse's first part is quoted in LeRoy (2001: 44). For another novel that has chosen this verse as a motto for a gothic tale about adolescent and illicit sexuality see Truman Capote's *Other Voices, Other Rooms* (1948).
22 Like his Greek and Roman hate speech predecessors, Jeremiah's vision ends tragically. He is the prophet who won't be listened to, and whose religious *and* political agenda results in nothing but misfortune.
23 See Bercovitch (1978).
24 LeRoy (2001: 73).
25 Proverbs 23.13, quoted in LeRoy (2001: 70).
26 Austin (1962). Weinstein briefly mentions the possible application of Austin's to MacKinnon's terminology, and he quotes MacKinnon's own claim distancing her specific political argument from a broader philosophical one: "Austin is less an authority for my particular development of 'doing things with words' and more a foundational exploration of the view in language theory that some speech can be action." (Weinstein 1999: 237, fn. 37)
27 Fiedler (1971). For the ongoing effort to delineate a pop-aesthetic see Geuen & Rappe (2001), Baßler (2002), Schumacher (2003).
28 These quotes from German critics are cited in Ernst (2001: 67-69). See also Oberschelp (1991), Poschardt (1995), Kemper, Langhoff & Sonnenschein (1998).
29 Whereas LeRoy seems extremely shy to appear publicly, he nevertheless admits that his novels are based on his own childhood experience. The stories that make up *The Heart* were supposedly written as part of a therapy at age fifteen. There remains, however, a highly debated suspicion that J T LeRoy (who has also published under the street name 'Terminator') is really but a juvenile pen name for writer Dennis Cooper. See, for example, Meghan Austin's comment: "As the rumor goes, LeRoy is a boy impersonating a girl impersonating novelist Dennis Cooper . . ." (n.d.). LeRoy, on the other hand, names Cooper among his closest friends and mentors, whereas Cooper himself even chose LeRoy's picture on the cover of his novel *Period*

and based one of the characters, Dragger, on LeRoy. See also Press (2001), and for interviews, information, and a personal day-by-day diary LeRoy's web Site www.jtleroy.com.
30 Fiedler (1971: 475, emphasis in the text).
31 LeRoy (2001: 58-73).
32 Fiss (1996: 14).
33 Quoted in Austin (n.d.).
34 See the biography by Huxley (2000) and the documentary by Eminem (2000b).
35 In reference to Eminem's semi-autobiographical film *8 Mile* (dir. Curtis Hanson, USA, 2002) see Hartmann (2002). '8 Mile' is Detroit's racial and class crossroad, the borderline between black and white, as well as between city and suburbia.
36 Robin (2001: 12). See also Smith (2001), Grantham (2001), Renna (2001), Nyong'o Turkish (2001), Duralde (2001).
37 See Greenawalt (1995), Marcus (1996).
38 Fish (1992: 236). Fish's definition is a quote from *Chaplinsky v. New Hamphire* (1941).
39 For the historical roots and the emergence of hip hop culture see Toop (1984), Jacob (1993). For a discussion of rap in the context of black studies see Baker (1993).
40 At the time Chuck D, speaker of Public Enemy, called hip hop the "CNN of the black community" and claimed that "[r]ap and black are kind of synonymous. The people who have problems with rap usually have problems with black people, even if they are black themselves." (Chuck D, quoted in Karrer & Kerkhoff 1995: 187)
41 Rose (1993: 25). On the relationship between rap and black political ideology see also Dawson (1999).
42 'Boasting' is a fundamental attitude; self-experienced stories are told in an exaggerated, bragging manner. 'Toasting' raps are small narratives in the mode of trickster-stories, told in the first or second person and dealing with daily issues and experiences. 'Talking smart' and 'talking shit' are forms of aggressive, witty talking as performance, with 'talking smart' a more seriously performed dialogue and "talking shit" the more jokingly competitive variant. 'Dissing' and 'menacing' mean talking *dis*respectfully or threatening somebody while showing off and praising oneself.
43 See Gates (1988).
44 Potter (1995), Butler (1997). See also Menrath (2001).
45 Eminem (2002a).
46 Rux (2003).
47 *Ibid.*
48 Eminem (2000c).
49 On Eminem's white trash style and background see De'Rozario (2002) and Dirks (2002).
50 See Wray & Newitz (1997).
51 Eminem (2002a).
52 *Ibid.*
53 In 1985, Tipper Gore, wife of Bill Clinton's vice president Al Gore, together with other wives of politicians founded the Parents Music Resource Center

(PMRC). In her fight to ban many rappers, Gore called for self-restraint in the record industry by placing an advisory notice on all rap albums that the PMRC considered 'unbecoming to minors'.
54 Eminem (2002a).
55 For a comparison between Eminem and Juvenal see also Rosen & Baines (2002).
56 See Spencer (1997); for comparing Elvis and Eminem see Fields (2001), Derbyshire (2000).
57 Public Enemy, "Right the Power", quoted in Karrer & Kerkhoff (1995: 187).
58 Eminem (2002b).
59 De'Rozario (2002).
60 See Sweeney (1997).
61 Lanham (1976 :1).
62 *Ibid.*, 4.
63 *Ibid.*, 7.
64 Butler (1997: 14).

Bibliography

Austin, Meghan: "JT LeRoy", *Resonance* 27, n.d., http://www.insound.com/zinestand/resonance/feature.cfm?aid=6881 (accessed 20 July 2004).
Anastaplo, George: *Campus Hate Speech Codes and Twentieth Century Atrocities*, Lewiston, 1997.
Austin, J. L.: *How to Do Things With Words*, Cambridge, 1962.
Baker, Houston A., Jr.: *Black Studies, Rap, and the Academy*, Chicago, 1993.
Baßler, Moritz: *Der deutsche Pop-Roman. Die neuen Archivisten*, München, 2002.
Bercovitch, Sacvan: *The American Jeremiad*, Madison, 1978.
Berman, Paul (Ed.): *Debating P.C. The Controversy over Political Correctness on College Campuses*, New York, 1992.
Bolton, Richard (Ed.): *Culture Wars. Documents from the Recent Controversies in the Arts*, New York, 1992.
Braund, Susanna M.: "Juvenal – Misogynist or Misogamist?", *Journal of Roman Studies* 82, 1992, 71-86.
Butler, Judith: *Excitable Speech. A Politics of the Performative*, New York, 1997.
Cicero: "The Second Speech of M.T. Cicero Against Marcus Antonius, Called also the Second Philippic", trans. C.D. Yonge, http://www.perseus.tufts.edu/cgi-bin/ptext?lookup=Cic.+Phil.+2.1 (accessed 10 February 2003).
Coliver, Sandra (Ed.): *Striking a Balance. Hate Speech, Freedom of Expression and Non-discrimination*, London, 1992.
Dawson, Michael C.: "'dis beat disrupts'. Rap, Ideology, and Black Political Attitudes". – In Michèle Lamont (Ed.): *The Cultural Tradition of Race. Black and White Boundaries*, Chicago, 1999, pp. 318-342.
Delgado, Richard & Jean Stefancic: *Must We Defend Nazis? Hate Speech, Pornography and the New First Amendment*, New York, 1997.
Derbyshire, John: "First Amendment First. Why Hollywood Should Be Left Alone", *National Review*, 9 October 2000, http://www.findarticles.com.

De'Rozario, Mark: "The White Crap that Talks Back. Eminem 2001", http://www.hyperdub.com/softwar/eminem.cfm (accessed 20 July 2004).
Dirks, Doris: "Eminem's Message more than Stereotype", http://www.westernherald.com/vnews/display.v/ART/2002/12/03/3ded701e09e6f (accessed 3 December 2002).
Downing, John D.H.: "'Hate Speech' and 'First Amendment Absolutism' Discourses in the US", *Discourse & Society* 10, no. 2, 1999, 175-189.
Duralde, Alonso: "The Trouble With Eminem", *Advocate*, 27 February 2001.
Dworkin, Andrea: *Pornography. Men Possessing Women*, New York, 1981.
Dworkin, Andrea & Catherine A. MacKinnon, *Pornography and Civil Rights. A New Day for Women's Equality*, Minneapolis, 1988.
Eminem: "Public Service Announcement 2000". – In E.: *The Marshall Mathers LP*, Aftermath Ent. / Interscope Records, 2000a.
–: *Angry Blonde*, New York, 2000b.
–: "Who knew". – In E.: *The Marshall Mathers LP*, Aftermath Ent. / Interscope Records, 2000c.
–: "White America". – In E.: *The Eminem Show*, Aftermath Records, 2002a.
–: "Without Me". – In E.: *The Eminem Show*, Aftermath Records, 2002b.
Ernst, Thomas: *Popliteratur*, Hamburg, 2001.
Fiedler, Leslie: "Cross the Border – Close the Gap". – In L.F.: *The Collected Essays*, vol. II, New York, 1971, pp. 461-485.
Fields, Suzanne: "Bad Raps. Music Rebels Revel in Their Thug Life", *Insight on the News*, 21 May 2001.
Fish, Stanley: "There's no such Thing as Free Speech and It's a Good Thing, too". – In Paul Berman (Ed.): *Debating P.C. The Controversy over Political Correctness on College Campuses*, New York, 1992, pp. 231-245.
–: "Boutique Multiculturalism, or Why Liberals Are Incapable of Thinking about Hate Speech", *Critical Inquiry* 23, 1997, 378-395.
Fiss, Owen M.: *The Irony of Free Speech*, Cambridge, 1996.
Gates, Henry Louis: *The Signifyin(g) Monkey. A Theory of African-American Literary Criticism*, New York, 1988.
Gates, Henry Louis et al: *Speaking of Race, Speaking of Sex. Hate Speech, Civil Rights, and Civil Liberties*, New York, 1994.
Geuen, Heins & Michael Rappe (Eds.): *Pop & Mythos. Pop-Kultur, Pop-Ästhetik, Pop-Musik*, Schliengen, 2001.
Gold, Barbara K.: "'The House I Live in Is not My Own'. Women's Bodies in Juvenal's Satires", *Arethusa* 31, 1998, 369-386.
Grantham, Christian: "Why Artists Defend Eminem", *The Gay & Lesbian Review Worldwide* 8, no. 3, 2001, 18.
Greenawalt, Kent: *Fighting Words. Individual, Communities, and Liberties of Speech*, Princeton, 1995.
Hartmann, Andreas: "Niggers Like Us. Eminem will nicht Elvis sein", *Jungle World* 1/2, 24 December 2002, 31.
Heyman, Steven J. (Ed.): *Hate Speech and the Constitution*, New York, 1996, 2 vols.
Huxley, Martin: *Eminem. Crossing the Line*, New York, 2000.
Jacob, Günther: *Agit-Pop. Schwarze Musik und weiße Hörer. Texte zu Rassismus und Nationalismus, HipHop und Raggamuffin*, Berlin, 1993.

Juvenal: "Satire VI", trans. G.G. Ramsay. – In *Internet Ancient History Sourcebook*, http://www.fordham.edu/halsall/ancient/juvenal-satvi.html (accessed 6 February 2003).
Karrer, Wolfgang & Ingrid Kerkhoff (Eds.): *Rap*, Hamburg, 1995.
Kemper, Peter, Thomas Langhoff & Ulrich Sonnenschein (Eds.): *"but I like it". Jugendkultur und Popmusik*, Stuttgart, 1998.
Lanham, Richard A.: *The Motives of Eloquence. Literary Rhetoric in the Renaissance*, New Haven, 1976.
Lederer, Laura J. & Richard Delgado (Eds.): *The Price We Pay. The Case Against Racist Speech, Hate Progapanda, and Pornography*, New York, 1995.
LeRoy, J T: *The Heart Is Deceitful above All Things*, London, 2001.
MacKinnon, Catharine A.: *Only Words*, Cambridge, 1993.
'Maledicta Press': http://www.sonic.net/maledicta (accessed 20 July 2004).
Marcus, Lawrence R.: *Fighting Words. The Politics of Hateful Speech*. Westport, 1996.
Maschke, Karen J. (Ed.): *Pornography, Sex Work, and Hate Speech*, New York, 1997.
Matsuda, Mari J. et al. (Eds.): *Words that Wound. Critical Race Theory, Assaultive Speech and the First Amendment*, Boulder, 1993.
Menrath, Stefanie: *represent what... Performativität von Identitäten im HipHop*, Hamburg, 2001.
Nyong'o Turkish, Tavia: "Who's Afraid of Marshall Mathers?", *The Gay & Lesbian Review Worldwide* 8, no. 3, 2001, 14.
Oberschelp, Jürgen: *Das Verschwinden der Kunst in der „Kunst des Zitats". Versuch über Popästhetik in den 80er Jahren*, Bielefeld, 1991.
Poole, Ralph J.: „Sex-Text-Gewalt. Wen gefährden Kathy Ackers 'Harte Mädchen'?", *Frauen in der Literaturwissenschaft*, Rundbrief 44 („Zensur"), 1995, 13-16.
–: „Queer Porno? S/M-Fiktionen". – In Stefan Etgeton & Sabine Hark (Eds.): *Freundschaft unter Vorbehalt. Chancen und Grenzen lesbisch-schwuler Bündnisse*, Berlin, 1997, pp. 99-126.
Poschardt, Ulf: *DJ Culture*, Hamburg, 1995.
Potter, Russel A.: *Spectacular Vernacular. HipHop and the Politics of Postmodernism*, Albany, 1995.
Press, Joy: "The Cult of J.T. Leroy", *The Village Voice*, 13-19 June, 2001.
Renna, Cathy: "Own up to Your Own Words!", *The Gay & Lesbian Review Worldwide* 8, no. 3, 2001, 16.
Richlin, Amy: "Invective Against Women in Roman Satire", *Arethusa* 17, 1984, 67-80.
Robin, Tyler: „Eminem. Pied Piper of Hate", *The Gay & Lesbian Review Worldwide* 8, no. 3, 2001, 12.
Rose, Patricia Lorraine: *Black Noise. Rap Music and Black Culture in Contemporary America*, Ann Arbor, 1993.
Rosen, Ralph M. & Victoria Baines: "'I am Whatever You Say I Am ...'. Satiric Program in Juvenal and Eminem", *Classical and Modern Literature* 22, no. 2, 2002, 103-127.
Rux, Carl Hancock: "Eminem. The New White Negro", http://randomhouse.com/boldtype/0303/tate/essay.html, repr. in Greg Tate (Ed.): *Everything but*

the Burden. *What White People Are Taking from Black Culture*, New York, 2003.
Schumacher, Eckhard: *Gerade eben jetzt. Schreibweisen der Gegenwart*, Frankfurt a.M., 2003.
Slayden, David: "Holy Wars and Vile Bodies. The Politics of an American Iconography". – In Rita Kirk Whillock & David Slayden (Eds.): *Hate Speech*, Thousand Oaks, 1995, pp. 196-225.
Smith, Steve: "Not a Sweetie", *New Statesman*, 23 January 2001, 44.
Spencer, Jon Michael: "A Revolutionary Sexual Persona. Elvis Presley and the White Acquiescence of Black Rhythms". – In Vernon Chadwick (Ed.): *In Search of Elvis. Music, Race, Art, Religion*, Boulder, 1997, pp. 108-120.
Stroh, Wilfried: „Ciceros philippische Reden. Politischer Kampf und literarische Imitation". In Martin Hose (Ed.): *Meisterwerke der antiken Literatur. Von Homer bis Boethius*, München, 2000, pp. 76-102.
Sweeney, Gael: "The King of White Trash Culture. Elvis Presley and the Aesthetics of Excess". – In Matt Wray & Annellee Newitz (Eds.): *White Trash. Race and Class in America*, New York & London, 1997, pp. 249-266.
Toop, David: *Rap Attack. African Jive to New York HipHop*, Boston, 1984.
Walker, Samuel: *Hate Speech. The History of an American Controversy*, Lincoln, 1994.
Weinstein, James. *Hate Speech, Pornography, and the Radical Attack on Free Speech Doctrine*, Boulder, 1999.
Whillock, Rita Kirk & David Slayden (Eds.): *Hate Speech*, Thousand Oaks, 1995.
Wolfson, Nicholas: *Hate Speech, Sex Speech, Free Speech*, Westport, 1997.
Wray, Matt & Annalee Newitz (Eds.): *White Trash. Race and Class in America*, New York & London, 1997.
Wyke, Maria: "Woman in the Mirror. The Rhetoric of Adornment in the Roman World". – In Léonie J. Archer, Susan Fischler & Maria Wyke (Eds.): *Women in Ancient Societies. An Illusion of the Night*, Basingstoke, 1994, pp. 134-151.
Zingo, Martha T.: *Sex-Gender Outsiders, Hate Speech, and Freedom of Expression*, Westport, 1998.

Christoph Ribbat, Bonn

Nomadic with the Truth.
Holocaust Representations in Michael Chabon,
James McBride, and Jonathan Safran Foer

"We may read the Holocaust as the central event of this century", Irving Howe proclaimed in 1988, "but finally we must acknowledge that it leaves us intellectually disarmed."[1] There is no reason why today, at the beginning of the twenty-first century, Howe's statement should have lost its validity. The Holocaust still ranks both as the singular tragedy of modernity and as one of the central paradoxes of Euro-American literary criticism. All attempts to turn the catastrophe into a literary subject seem bound to fail. A "novel about Auschwitz", Holocaust survivor Elie Wiesel once stated, "is not a novel, or else it is not about Auschwitz".[2] Realist prose fiction especially, with its emphasis on authenticity, experience, and narrative directness, is bound to encounter the limits of representation. Framing the inconceivable as a story seems an impossible task. Since central elements of storytelling – personhood, individuality, motivation – were denied in the Holocaust,[3] the reflection of representational limits, as Geoffrey Hartman states, is always part of Holocaust literature, the notion that "there is something that cannot be presented".[4] The trio of twenty-first century novels discussed in the following pages – Michael Chabon's *The Amazing Adventures of Kavalier & Clay* (2000), James McBride's *Miracle at Sant'Anna* (2002), and Jonathan Safran Foer's *Everything Is Illuminated* (2002) – all explore atrocities committed by Germans in wartime Europe. They all have to be considered in the context of the debates on Holocaust representation.

1. Holocaust Memory in American Culture

Twenty-first century fiction on the Holocaust doubtlessly wrestles with a challenging subject. "To suppose that some redemptive salvage can be eked out of the Holocaust", Irving Howe writes, might be only human, yet nevertheless, to Howe, leads to "self-delusion".[5] Interested readers, many of them familiar with the representational problems, will be critical. Authors of Holocaust literature, Andrew Furman points out, "can expect their work to elicit a special kind of scrutiny".[6] Sara Horowitz has described audience response to Holocaust fiction in similar terms. Against the horrifying facts of history, she argues, readers perceive fictional versions of the catastrophe as a "weaker, softer kind of testimony", as "misleading", as a "dangerous confusion of verisimilitude with reality".[7]

A close look at the history of Holocaust representations and the debates on memory reveals that the sense of distance has always been predominant not only for readers, but for the storytellers themselves. In an essay on Jewish American Fiction, Andrew Furman has commented on the reluctance even of authors writing in the years immediately following World War II (such as Bellow and Malamud) to incorporate the events as dramatic elements in their fiction.[8] Against the background of survivors' accounts, representing the Holocaust in narratives based on second- or third-hand sources was a difficult matter. In fact, many Holocaust survivors themselves did not tell their stories at all. They belonged to a "community of silence", as Stéphane Gerson argues in an essay on the enormous problems survivors encounter when trying to present the traumatic experience in the framework of a story.[9] Elie Wiesel, the survivor and activist, talks about the "common obsession" to "tell all, to relate everything", to "fight against forgetting". Yet it might have been precisely the devotion to truthful representation which kept many Holocaust survivors from narrating their experiences: any story would have blocked something out, any story could have falsified or romanticized the facts.[10] To do justice to the enormous problem that "telling the story" causes for Holocaust survivors, literary critics have recently argued for new ways of reading survivor narratives. They call for readings that are just as attentive to the silences and the gaps as to the stories actually told. The problems of storytelling are just as important as the account itself. Only this, they explain, can preserve the particularity of the witness's voice. Listeners should be interested not so much in the "meaning" of a story, but in the "trauma that destroys it".[11]

This, then, is another paradox of Holocaust narratives: the greater the distance between author and events, the more critical the audience will be; the closer the author has been to the universe of horror, the more difficult the act of storytelling. The conventions of realism – of directness and 'authentic' experience – do not apply. As John Limon has argued in the related context of American war fiction, World War II as a whole seemed "too large" for realists and modernists alike. Any artistic representation of the catastrophe was bound to fail; even decades after the end of the war no 'neutral' territory existed from which an adequate story of the events could have been told. Only through the 'postmodernization' of the war, Limon demonstrates, only in novels such as Joseph Heller's *Catch-22* (1961) or Thomas Pynchon's *Gravity's*

Rainbow (1973), did American authors develop a literary idiom which made sense of the war precisely by refusing to make sense of it.[12] Instead of attempting to portray the violence of the conflict with as much authenticity as possible, the postmodernists focused on the way the twentieth-century watershed had transformed experience and the systems of representation themselves.

These issues are central for literary critics. A much different picture emerges, however, once we begin to investigate the popular response to the Holocaust in the United States. The three twenty-first century novels discussed below are all products of an extremely lively American interest in the catastrophic events of wartime Europe (cynical observers could add that their commercial success will surely profit from it). While the problematic aspects of representation may dominate academic discourse, it is quite obvious that the Holocaust has become one of the central narratives of American culture, and that both fictional and nonfictional accounts can count on an enormous audience. Hilene Flanzbaum, editor of the 1999 volume *The Americanization of the Holocaust*, has stated that those who "wished and worked for wide Holocaust remembrance" in the United States could feel as if their "prayers" have been "answered". Numerous memorials and museums have been constructed across America (most prominently, the U.S. Holocaust Museum in the heart of Washington, D.C. and thus in one of the symbolically most highly charged locations of American political culture). Steven Spielberg's *Schindler's List* was an enormous popular success in the 1990s. Courses on the history and representations of the Holocaust are constantly oversubscribed in American universities. The Holocaust, Flanzbaum concludes, has become "deeply embedded" in the American psyche and serves as "a measuring stick against which all oppression is measured".[13]

At the same time, popular Holocaust narratives, too, have always triggered critical comments, especially on the moral and aesthetic questions about the way directors such as Steven Spielberg appear to be "romancing the Holocaust".[14] Recently, however, a new direction in criticism can be observed. Prominent scholars have raised a set of issues which seem to question the centrality of Holocaust memory in contemporary American culture itself. In his 1999 volume *The Holocaust in American Life*, historian Peter Novick argues that the trope of the Holocaust's uniqueness has been instrumentalized in US culture. Novick explicitly compares the German and the American discourse. He observes that Germans who "insisted on the uniqueness of the Holocaust [...] did so to block what they correctly regarded as a move to evade confrontation with a painful national past". In the American context, however, Novick sees a much different process at work:

> The identical talk of uniqueness and incomparability surrounding the Holocaust in the United States performs the opposite function: it promotes *evasion* of moral and historical responsibility. [...] And whereas a serious and sustained encounter with the history of hundreds of years of enslavement and oppression of blacks might imply costly demands on Americans to redress the wrongs of the past, contemplating the Holocaust is virtually cost-free: a few cheap tears. [...] [T]he pretense that the Holocaust is an American memory [...] works to devalue the notion of historical responsibility.[15]

Novick's book points to one particular aspect that sets off American from German debates on memory. In the American context, questioning the uniqueness of the Holocaust does not necessarily have to be read as a rhetorical move performed by revisionist, right-wing *agents provocateurs*. In fact, precisely those cultural movements that helped establish the Holocaust as one of the central narratives of American culture are now, in the early twenty-first century, producing rival narratives competing for the same kind of attention in the cultural marketplace. First, in a postmodern process of dehierarchization, the Holocaust became part of popular culture. Most Americans, as Hilene Flanzbaum observes, "seem so well acquainted with at least some version of the Holocaust that they freely invoke it in metaphor" – frequently though, as Flanzbaum hastens to add, "with an inflammatory casualness".[16] Second, and more importantly, these references are inextricably tied to discourses on ethnicity. The new ethnic paradigm in American literature at first helped to develop a Jewish American tradition of writing and reading and thus also a tradition of American Holocaust fiction. However, it is precisely the 'ethnic turn' in American writing which also brings 'competition', as other groups claim their histories of trauma. As Asian American, Latino/a, African American, and Caribbean voices become much more central in the American literary canon, the Holocaust as a subject might lose its importance. The murder of the European Jews might become a marginal subject, eclipsed by various narratives of other events (colonial genocides, slavery, marginalization and domination of aboriginal peoples). Due to the growing attention to non-white, non-Western experiences, a curiosity that is an original product of the multicultural turn, many American writers and artists concerned with the trauma of history may now be more interested in exploring the "Black Atlantic" as a memory space than in investigating the European history of the Shoah.[17]

"There is enormous tension between blacks and Jews", Lawrence Mordekhai Thomas observes in a case study, "a competition, if you will, over who has suffered the most".[18] In light of the horrors of the Middle

Passage and centuries of slavery, African American historians and writers insist on using the term 'Holocaust' to describe the Black experience with as much symbolic weight as authors of narratives on Jewish history. In 1987 Toni Morrison dedicated her novel *Beloved* to "sixty million and more" – a direct, though uncommented reference to the victims of slavery and a highly significant gesture in opening up this new phase of the debates on memory.[19] What is at stake in these debates, according to Thomas, is a "hallowing of the group's suffering". Whose experience, minority intellectuals ask, is representative? Whose experience is allowed to serve as an icon? Which group's experience, as Thomas puts it, "would be enshrined in the American mind"?[20]

The debates on memory are not always so clear-cut. However, a brief look at two twenty-first century academic projects on the Holocaust reveals that Holocaust scholarship has truly entered a new phase. "We aim not to produce another book on the 'uniqueness of the Holocaust'", Gary Weissman states in a recent call for papers for a collection of original essays. The volume, co-edited by Weissman and Michael Rothberg, proposes to investigate how the Holocaust has served as a "screen memory for events closer to home than the Nazi genocide of the European Jews". Weissman refers to slavery, segregation, and to the genocide of Native Americans. Other histories, anxieties, and concerns, the two scholars argue, frequently hide behind Holocaust narratives. Such fears concern, for instance, the "disappearance of historical memory" or the "vanishing American Jewish identity and community".[21]

A second academic project currently in the works, *A Critical Holocaust Anthology*, is a little less cautious than Weissman and Rothberg's proposed volume. The two editors, Robert Soza and David Leonard, posted their call for papers on a major academic mailing list in late 2002. The joint proposal of the two scholars proclaimed that contemporary American "calls to consciousness" in the Holocaust memory discourse relied on "mystified and Eurocentric constructions of humanity and suffering".[22] Interviewed for an article about their project, David Leonard voiced his hopes to "strike a chord with those who are struck by the overwhelming focus given to the Jewish Holocaust". Leonard explained further that he and Soza saw "a lot of potential" for their project "with Ethnic Studies and from scholars of color, who know all too well the silencing of other historical narratives".[23] Inadvertently, the project raises an extremely important question for the future of Holocaust literature: will the multiculturalization of the Holocaust follow its Americanization? As narratives of trauma compete for attention, will the Jewish Holocaust be marked as a "white" experience and thus as too dominant? At the moment, it is difficult to determine whether such projects usher in a new phase in the debates on memory or whether it is simply an esoteric idea by junior academics with "a partisan agenda", as political scientist Richard Dougherty has stated.[24]

2. Two Novels of the 1990s. Bukiet's After *and* Begley's Wartime Lies

While novelists of the Holocaust do not necessarily have to deal with current scholarly debates on memory and representation, they will have to acknowledge the distance to the events created by the passing of time. In a 1997 study, Marianne Hirsch proposes the term "postmemory" to identify a form of recollection that is not directly linked to the past and is characterized instead by generational distance and the absence of a "deep personal connection". Hirsch states that she uses the prefix "post" with hesitation. Instead of suggesting that in the late twentieth century remembering the Holocaust might in some sense be "over", "postmemory" signifies a new stage in remembering the events. It "characterizes the experience of those", Hirsch writes, "who grow up dominated by narratives that preceded their birth". Stories told by these individuals are "belated" stories, in a sense. They have been "evacuated" by the stories of the previous generation, parental narratives "shaped by traumatic events that can be neither understood nor recreated".[25]

Contemporary American novelist Melvin Jules Bukiet has been identified by critic Ruth Klüger as a member of a literary generation of survivors' sons who have listened their entire lives to detailed descriptions of the Holocaust.[26] Representing the facts, however, is not what Bukiet is interested in. In the tradition of Pynchon and Heller, history and fiction are indistinguishable in his work. His novel *After* (1996), which explores the lives of Holocaust survivors in the immediate aftermath of World War II, makes no attempt to tell "the story" of genocide.[27] "They're gone" are the first words spoken in the book, by its main protagonist Isaac Kaufman, a camp prisoner (3). With this symbolic breaking of silence, Bukiet's novel begins a wild, boisterous game with representations that reflects a plethora of possible Holocaust stories, photographs, and memoirs. Trying to find an accurate manner in which to describe the horrors of the Holocaust seems like a perverse notion in this novel. Instead, *After* investigates how, in the aftermath of the events, human communication starts again, and in myriad ways transforms the reality of the events into stories. In the beginning of Thomas Pynchon's *Gravity's Rainbow*, "a screaming comes across the sky" of wartime London.[28] Bukiet's *After* refers directly to this phrase: not at the beginning of the narrative, but as it ends. It is not a "screaming" that can be heard in the Holocaust's immediate aftermath as described by

Bukiet. "One could hear a whisper", the narrative voice says, "and the whisper was sighing [...] that [...] age-old, heartfelt, eternal resolution: 'Again'." (383). Instead of emphasizing silence and fragmentation – the established responses to the Holocaust[29] – Bukiet's novel stresses that the human ability to tell stories has survived mass-murder. In an essay for *The Review of Contemporary Fiction*, Bukiet has commented on the literary strategies that inform his writing. One of the arguments the novelist makes in the piece is that in fiction – and perhaps only in fiction – "notions of regeneration"[30] can come out of the Holocaust, as it forces writers to take literature to another level: "into an orbit where the imagination changes the [...] ground rules of existence".[31]

As Susanne Rohr has observed in a reading of Bukiet's novel, *After*'s point of reference is the Holocaust as an Americanized imaginary space, a space dominated by the media and a reservoir of images. As a matter of course, contemporary American narratives explore Holocaust representations rather than its reality (unless they are survivors' accounts). Bukiet, however, accentuates the fact that his text is involved in representational games. He makes no claim to realism.[32] In some cases and to some observers, such narrative strategies produce banal versions of history. Some texts working in this vein, however, investigate the complexity of storytelling rather than the story itself. Most prominently, the cartoonist Art Spiegelman has explored the tension between trauma and pop culture images in his book-length cartoon *Maus*.[33] Bukiet's *After* makes a similar attempt to discuss the problems of memory, storytelling, and the media of representation. These problems, as his novel makes clear, cannot be separated from each other.

The fact should not be overlooked that even in the 1990s it was still possible for a Holocaust survivor to tell his or her story not as one level in a postmodern negotiation of the possibilities and failures of representation, but as a comparatively simple, realist text.[34] In 1991, Louis Begley published *Wartime Lies* – the story of a young Polish Jew and his aunt hiding in German-occupied Poland. Again and again, Begley, a Holocaust survivor, emphasized that the story of his own life should not be confused with the story his novel tells. And again and again, his readers did link the two tales, in spite of the author's warning. The enormous success of *Wartime Lies* proved that more than half a century after the end of World War II, two modes of representing the Holocaust in literary form continued to exist. Postmodern metafiction still has a counterpart: the 'authentic' story could still be told. *Wartime Lies*, however, makes the survivor's story seem far more complicated than Begley's fairly straightforward narrative suggests. Two inserted chapters present the boy survivor as a grown man in contemporary America. Nevertheless, they do not establish an 'organic' connection between the boy and the man. The controlled voice of the narrative does not belong to the child; it belongs to the narrator who "has no childhood he can bear to remember; he has had to invent one".[35] The direct links between the events of the Holocaust and contemporary American culture are thus interwoven only on the surface. *Wartime Lies* avoids the elaborate games played in Bukiet's high postmodernist *After*. Nevertheless, Begley's novel also focuses on a protagonist whose memory is crowded in by texts: most prominently, the *Aeneid*.

3. Popular Culture and the Holocaust. Michael Chabon and James McBride

While the discussion of 1990s Holocaust novels attends to the postmodern discourse on history and fiction, twenty-first century debates cannot ignore the firmly established tradition of Holocaust representations in popular culture. From the 1970s TV series *Holocaust* to Art Spiegelman's *Maus* to Roberto Benigni's and Steven Spielberg's films, it seems as if any popular genre could fashion its own version of the Holocaust: melodrama, comedy, the comic strip.[36] Will this lead to a trivialization of Holocaust memory? Or will these popular genres open the discourse on memory by making it more democratic and more accessible? Definite answers to these questions will always depend on the individual text and its ability to incorporate and reflect the complexity of the events. The only certain result of these cultural transformations is that literary representations will respond to them. In fiction, too, World War II and the Holocaust have long ceased to be territories commanding novelists to silence and fragmentation. Three developments have intersected in this transformation: the postmodernist insistence on the past as text and on the constructedness of memory, the ever more intimate linkage between American literature and popular culture, and, finally the passing away of many Holocaust survivors whose voices have thus ceased to speak in a discourse marked by authentic trauma. Hence, fragmented narratives – with their gaps, silences, and ruptures caused by pain – are rapidly receding into the past. In their place, the historical novel seems to be usurping the subject.

Michael Chabon's *Amazing Adventures of Kavalier & Clay* and James McBride's *Miracle at Sant'Anna* serve as characteristic examples of this transformation. *Kavalier & Clay* makes one meta-fictional reference to the adaptation of the Holocaust by popular culture – more precisely, to Spiegelman's *Maus*. In Chabon's post-war America, a boy regularly stops by 'Spiegelman's Drugstore' to examine the comic books on the store's racks. Yet any resemblance between Chabon's novel and

Spiegelman's postmodern cartoon ends with their interest in the comic book genre. Whereas *Maus* presents its story in several layers and thus frequently calls into question the very possibility of telling the story, Chabon's novel unfolds a unified, coherent tale of two young Jewish comic book artists, Josef Kavalier and Sam Clay. Their friendship, their business partnership, and their lives supply a firm and solid narrative frame. One of the two protagonists, Josef Kavalier, has escaped from Prague at the last minute in 1939, while his family remained in Eastern Europe. Despite all his efforts, they cannot be saved. In an attempt to battle against Nazi Germany with their own means, he and his partner design a comic strip series in which, again and again, a super-hero fights and wins against Nazi opponents.

Chabon's novel is a sprawling tale that covers the period between 1939 and the 1950s and encompasses American neighborhoods as diverse as ethnic, working-class Brooklyn and the planned, suburban environment of the fictional community 'Bloomtown'. The work cannot be classified as a Holocaust novel proper. Rather, the narrative concentrates on the figure of the popular artist. Kavalier & Clay, as comic-book creators, work in the pre-Television 'Golden Age' of the comic strip. And Chabon's novel describes the history of the pop culture medium with much more interest and energy than it invests in the story of World War II, raging at the same time. Even Joe Kavalier's escape from wartime Europe, conveyed in a chapter titled "The Escape Artist", is described as an ingenious feat by a young man whose spectacular ability to escape Houdini-style literally saves his life.

A decade earlier, Louis Begley's *Wartime Lies* invented two distinctly different voices to reflect the unbridgeable distance between Holocaust Europe and the safety of contemporary American life. There is no sense of such disconnection in Chabon. The novelist is careful not to turn the story of the Holocaust into just another episode of the American Dream. Kavalier is not successful in saving his family: the story of his failed attempts to do so is intertwined with his success story as a celebrated comic book artist. Chabon's novel certainly demonstrates, however, that the ruptures, fragmentations, and silences of earlier Holocaust texts do not play an influential role in its narrative strategies. The novel attempts to convince its readers that the cartoon, the moving picture, and the popular novel itself are indeed able to represent the Holocaust, which for so many decades was perceived as a subject that prohibits coherence, entertainment, and popularization and should be located in a tightly defined high art context. In *Kavalier & Clay*, popular culture is open to all subjects, even to genocide and war. The events themselves call for the most basic forms of narrative: "They were children. We were wolves", the novel quotes the German submarine officer responsible for sinking a ship evacuating Jewish children – among them, Joe Cavalier's brother – to America.[37] While the surreal dimensions of World War II forced previous generations of novelists to limit their own narratives,[38] Chabon feels encouraged to link the enormity of these events with the history of the comic book, a popular genre that thrives on enormity, on supernatural strength and size, and on the ever-ranging battle between good and evil. In turn, the history of this art form is used to tell the story of Jewish Americans in the mid-twentieth century, a story which is just as informed by the American metropolis and its highly modern and diversified popular culture as by knowledge of the destruction of the European Jews.

In James McBride's *Miracle at Sant'Anna*, a much different version of World War II is presented. While Chabon's Jewish American protagonists perceive the conflict as a series of heroic battles, a campaign that directly links them to the suffering European Jews, James Mc Bride's African American heroes – four soldiers in 1944 Italy – perceive the campaign as a meaningless event. To emphasize their mode of experience, McBride's focus is much narrower than Chabon's. McBride tells one episode of the war, an episode related to a mass shooting of civilians committed by German soldiers in an Italian village church.[39] After the shooting, late in 1944, the four black soldiers find refuge in this Italian village. While he focuses on the experiences of this quartet, McBride does provide the historical context by outlining the background of the atrocity, the history of wartime Italy, the conflicting biographies of the villagers, episodes from the history of the Partisan movement. More important than these narrative strands, however, are the histories of his four protagonists: the African American soldiers taking part in a war so meaningful to Jewish Americans, yet so foreign and meaningless to them.

The Italian campaign in which many black soldiers were involved was "fought out of the public eye", as McBride states, "in cold, chaotic blackness".[40] The African American GIs in *Miracle at Sant'Anna* are just as terrified by the dangers of the mountain battles as they are frustrated by the racism they encounter in the US armed forces. Only one of the four soldiers survives: in the novel's opening, this man commits a murder in late-twentieth century New York City that is directly linked to the episode in the village. In this fashion, McBride establishes a connection between wartime Italy and contemporary America. He thus also reconnects to his original territory as a writer: *Miracle at Sant'Anna* (2002) marks the novelistic debut for an author whose first book, the memoir *The Color of Water* (1996), spent two years on international bestseller lists, selling more than 1.3 million copies.[41] In this autobiographical success, McBride, the son of a Jewish mother and an African

American father, pays tribute to his white mother who had crossed over into Black America. *Miracle at Sant'Anna* also crosses over: it presents the story of World War II – frequently told from the European and/or the White American angle – from the perspective of the so-called 'Buffalo Soldiers', the members of the African American 92nd Division of the US Army involved in the liberation of Italy.

The myth of the 'Good War' – the victory of a multiracial, multiethnic nation against fascism and racism in World War II – falls apart in McBride's narrative which stresses the rifts created by racism in the American military. Seen from the perspective of the black soldiers, the mass shooting of civilians by the Germans is not unique. It ranks as just another horrible event in an absurd conflict. In the great scheme of things, the Holocaust as such is perceived as an almost secondary occurrence. One of the protagonists reflects on genocide against the background of institutionalized American racism. "In America", Second Lieutenant Aubrey Stamps thinks, "Germans could eat first class, go where he couldn't go, live where he couldn't live, get jobs where he couldn't, and over here in Europe they were killing Jews like it was lunch." (174) Stamps also places reports from the first liberated concentration camps in the context of African American identity:

> He'd read all about it in the Negro press. How the first American troops were finding giant camps full of dead Jews, burned to death, cities in Poland with human ash falling like snow from the smokestacks when they were burning children, entire families. What Negro would do that? A Negro couldn't even think up enough hate to do that. A Negro was trying to make rent, save up enough to buy milk for his kids, survive this fucked-up war, and, still, when the war was over, when all the fighting was done and all the people made up, a German could go to America and live well, start a factory, work in business, run a bank, while Stamps would still be ... a nigger. He'd be lucky to get a job delivering their mail. (174)

Obviously, the "buffalo soldiers"[42] feel no personal connection to the European conflict. In spite of this surface jadedness, however, *Miracle at Sant'Anna* does evolve into a moral tale in which the sacrifice of these African Americans helps to create a new world. A lost child the soldiers save embodies an innocence that transcends the violence of war. This, in fact, is the "miracle" the title announces. A child that is all by itself and a group of American soldiers who unselfishly care for it: this also becomes a symbolic episode within the narrative, as it signifies relief to the Italian civilians. This "child of innocence", an Italian villager reflects, had brought the Americans to them: "The war was going to end, and they all would be free soon." (249)

In the end, racial lines are crossed, yet in unfamiliar ways. In light of the success of McBride's exploration of Black-Jewish relations in *The Color of Water*, it is interesting that the author establishes a connection between black soldiers and Catholic Italians here and only touches on the subject of the Jewish Holocaust. The black and white coalition that develops in this episode of war is not the alliance between African Americans and Jews, both groups the most prominent victims of racism in the twentieth century (though lately also competitors for the public's attention to their collective suffering). Instead, a bond is formed between Black GI's and Italians. Like the earlier coalition of African and Jewish Americans, it is read, among other things, as a bond created by similar pain and marginalization: "The Italians were like the colored", one of the soldiers thinks, "they know what it's like to be on the outside looking in." (174) But the similarities extend beyond these group's shared victimhood. McBride's protagonist discovers similar mentalities as he reflects on Italian culture: "They got it, he thought. They understood it. Love. Food. Passion. Life's short. Pass me a cigarette. Gimme that grappa. Live a little. They were like coloreds without the jook joints" (175). The novel ends with the embrace of the only two survivors – Hector, the black Puerto Rican veteran, and the Italian man who once, as a child, was saved by a group of black GIs.

In the acknowledgments that close the book, McBride extends this image of coming together: "I am thankful", he states, "to the survivors of the so-called Good War." Then, he lists the three groups of survivors he interviewed while researching his novel: "the veterans of the 92nd Infantry Division who fought in Italy [i.e. the African American soldiers], the Italians who fought with them, and the Germans who fought against them – they were victims all" (274). One of the reasons why the author seems to count the perpetrators of the atrocities with the group of victims might be, quite simply, the passing of time. All the survivors – German, Italian, or American – are now, McBride writes, "in their twilight years" (274).

Italian prosecutors think differently, however. Three German SS members, suspected of being among those men who committed the Sant'Anna atrocities, were brought to trial in April 2004. While the fact that these men are now in their eighties makes a prison sentence unlikely,[43] their prosecution shows that the lines between perpetrators and victims that seem so blurred in McBride's paratext to his novel are still very present in the actual historical case his fictional text refers to. Why does the gap between SS men and Italian civilians close so smoothly in McBride's novel? One of the answers could be that the atrocities of World War II only serve as a background to the story the author is really interested in telling. To McBride, the European events pale in significance next to the story of African American courage. And this, in turn, is connected to the author's family history. "He spoke with such pride. He was so proud of what he'd done" (274), McBride remarks on the war stories told by his Uncle Henry; this man's pride, he states, was his incentive to write the novel.

There is a prominent difference between the 1990s novels by Begley and Bukiet and the twenty-first century works by Chabon and McBride. Neither Begley nor Bukiet presents families – and the central experience of the Holocaust survivor was to have lost his or her family connections. Thus, and this probably in an attempt to realistically represent the impact of the events on storytelling and community, Begley's and Bukiet's protagonists are described as solitary figures whose only intimate relationship seems to be with texts. Chabon and McBride, in contrast, interweave the history of war and atrocity with family stories and tales. This makes it possible to construct an unbroken future-oriented narrative. By connecting the catastrophic events of World War II and the Holocaust to contemporary America via family ties, their novels make the events seem less apocalyptic. The atrocities do not stand alone, nor do they erase all possibilities of storytelling. They can be worked, these novelists seem to suggest, into the larger narrative of American history, both public and private. Does this approach trivialize the catastrophic events? Do the novels by Chabon and McBride construct the Holocaust as a morality tale, thereby covering up trauma that cannot be covered up? Or is this the only way to remind twenty-first century readers of the events, by representing the Holocaust in gripping, coherent novels whose narrative energy profits from their closeness to popular culture? Again, these questions are open to debate in each special case. How they are answered will probably depend less on the position of critics in the discourse on Holocaust memory than on the attitudes of individual readers toward literature's involvement with popular culture.

4. Nomadic with the Truth.
Jonathan Safran Foer's Everything Is Illuminated (2002)

This essay can only investigate a small segment of the multiple ways in which the American Holocaust novel has crossed the distance between contemporary America and traumatic European history. It leaves unexplored highly influential late twentieth-century texts – Cynthia Ozick's stories "Rosa" and "The Shawl" could be cited as examples.[44] Another significant phenomenon can also only be touched on: two postmodern *Künstlerromane* of the twenty-first century – Richard Powers's *The Time of Our Singing* and Siri Hustvedt's *What I Loved* – have Holocaust survivors who have lost their families as protagonists. These characters' memories, however, are marginalized by the events in their families' contemporary American lives.[45] In a more detailed exploration of this subject, it would be productive to ask whether both of these novels employ the survivor figure – rootless, disconnected from family and history – as a symbolic counterpoint to the narrative richness of the present that the novelists are truly interested in.

The last novel discussed here is singled out because it looks at the Holocaust from a point of view that at first glance seems thoroughly detached. In Jonathan Safran Foer's *Everything Is Illuminated* (2002), partly set in the 1990s, the main protagonists are not much older than teenagers: the Jewish American protagonist (eponymous with the author) and the Ukrainian Alexander Perchov, who claims to have never seen a Jew in his entire life. In a second narrative strand, the novel tells the story of an Eastern European Jewish shtetl – this tale begins in 1791. Whereas Art Spiegelman, in *Maus*, explores the issue of memory once removed with his survivor father, Foer's contemporary American protagonist – frequently and self-consciously referred to as 'the hero' – is twice removed from events. In the late twentieth century, he travels to the Ukraine to find the woman said to have saved his grandfather from the Nazis during World War II. The novel travels with him. This is where *Everything Is Illuminated* parts company with most American novels on the Holocaust: in spite of its protagonists' youth, contemporary America only plays a marginal role in Foer's novel. It only exists as a phantom, a cliché in the dreams of Alex, Jonathan's guide and translator with 'Heritage Tours'. "I dig American movies", Alex states early in the novel, "I dig Negroes, particularly Michael Jackson. I dig to disseminate very much currency at famous nightclubs in Odessa".[46]

In enthusiastic reviews of Foer's novel, such passages, with their English always slightly wrong and slightly 'too much', have received extraordinary praise. The hero, semi-accidentally named Jonathan Safran Foer, is not given a voice by his author. Instead, the journey the two young men embark on is told from Alex's point of view, in his highly creative English. Sleeping protagonists "manufacture Z's" (passim); joking protagonists "manufacture funnies" (5); a disappointed Alex is "underwhelmed to the maximum" (32), while his erotic successes in Odessa nightlife are summed up in the brief statement: "Many girls want to be carnal with me in many good arrangements." (2) The comedy of Alex's monologues has an important effect. The world *Everything Is Illuminated* investigates is not America. It is extremely difficult, if not impossible, to read the novel as the story of a hero's quest to find his roots and perhaps succeed in connecting his American self to his European past. Rather, the novel switches perspectives. The American is perceived as Other, as the stranger who has come to explore events that are ignored in post-communist Eastern Europe, largely because of the troubles of the present.

There is no coming to terms with the past in Foer's novel – and very little linkage to contemporary America. The only direct encounter with history is experienced by a local. Alex's grandfather, who also accompanies the 'hero' on his 'heritage tour', is confronted with his own role in the Holocaust and kills himself in desperation. Early in the novel, the Ukrainian family running the travel agency 'Heritage Touring' with the help of a dog – a 'seeing-eye bitch' named Sammy Davis Jr Jr – provides slapstick humor. In the end, though, the family of men (Alex, the grandfather, Alex, the father, Alex, the older son) falls apart. The mission of 'Heritage Touring' was to guide American Jews on emotional journeys into the stories of their past. On this specific trip, however, the tour guides encounter their own heritage. And at this point the farce ends, the comedy implodes. In the grandfather's narrative of the Holocaust, which he, as a non-Jew, survived by pointing out a Jew to the Germans, words are pulled together, all punctuation disappears. Instead of silence, Foer presents a breathless monologue:

> and then the General shothiminthehead and said I am becoming tired of this and he went to the next man in line and that was me who is a Jew he asked and I felt Herschel's hand again and I know that his hand was saying pleaseplease Eli please I do not want to die please do not point at me you know what is going to happen to me if you point at me do not point at me I am afraid of dying I am so afraid of dying I am soafraidofdying Iamsoafraidofdying who is a Jew the General asked me again and I felt on my other hand the hand of Grandmother and I knew that she was holding your father and that he was holding you and that you were holding your children I am so afraid of dying I am soafraidofdying Iamsoafraidofdying Iamsoafraidofdying and I said he is a Jew. (250)

Finally, the trauma of history is unearthed. A young Jewish American who knows only 'post-postmemory' (because that is all there is too know) witnesses the destructive force of a much more painful, much more direct form of memory as it destroys another person. As the non-Jewish Ukrainians of the late twentieth century discover what is hidden underneath the post-communist present, the impossibility of a sane, harmonious learning process remains. This reading, however, only points at one of the functions of the grandfather's monologue. The story he tells ends both Heritage Touring's trip into the past and the second strand of *Everything Is Illuminated*: Foer's generous, highly imaginative narrative of the Shetl Trachimbrod. As the grandfather recalls the mass shooting, two narratives come to a conclusion: the comedy of the present and Foer's surreal tale of the functioning, vibrant Jewish community that reached deep into the past. Also, the breathless narrative, a modernist stream of consciousness, serves as a fulcrum between the magic realism Foer employs to tell the history of Trachimbrod and the postmodern globalized pseudo-English that Alex's letters to 'the hero' employ.

With its pastiche of styles, Jonathan Safran Foer's novel serves as a proof that these aesthetic strategies can indeed coexist. Thus, two years into the twenty-first century, the novel by the young American author might have opened a new chapter of Holocaust representation and of literary debates on storytelling and history. It reflects an approach frequently sketched by literary critics. As outlined above in the brief overview of the scholarly discourse, Holocaust representation seems too large for realist depiction. The aesthetics of immediacy and authenticity do not seem adequate to describe what cannot be described. Realism, a product of middle-class values, and of the bourgeois individual and family, is seen as an unsuitable mode to conjure up events which question all of these values. At the same time, both modernism's fragmentary aesthetics and postmodernism's irony do not seem to be adequate either: after all, there are facts to be related. The trauma of history cannot be described by a Joycean monologue, nor can the facts of the Shoah be treated as just another text in a world made of paper. In a recent book on the demands of Holocaust representations, Michael Rothberg has argued that the three '-isms' – realism, modernism, postmodernism – should not be seen as mutually exclusive aesthetic programs or styles, but as continual frameworks and answers to the challenges of history.[47] Realist strategies of depicting the world, modernist questionings of history's transparency, postmodern negotiations on the dissemination of texts – these aspects, according to Rothberg, do in fact coexist in narratives and thus enable writers of fiction to respond to events that at first glance only seem to call for silence.

While Foer's novel succeeds in combining these frameworks in a truly innovative fashion, one of the central notions of the memory discourse remains. Even in the richest literary collage, a sense of insecurity refuses to disappear. Foer's hero, Alex from Odessa, coins a dictum that sums up contemporary debates on mediated memory and popular culture and links them to earlier debates on Holocaust representation. "We are being very nomadic with the truth, yes?" Alex asks in his idiosyncratic English as he considers the textual versions of the past that he and his friend, 'the author', produce. And he adds another question, a question that will always be central to any debate on Holocaust literature: "Do you think that this is acceptable when we are writing about things that occurred?" (179).

Notes

1 Howe (1988: 175).
2 Quoted in Schöpp (1990: 144).
3 Lang (1992: 316).
4 Hartman (1992: 321).
5 Howe (1988: 198).
6 Furman (1999: 84).
7 Horowitz (1997: 1).
8 Furman (1999).
9 Gerson (1997: 103).
10 *Ibid.*, 113-114.
11 Bernard-Donals & Gleizer (2000: 18-19).
12 Limon (1994: 128-135).
13 Flanzbaum (1999: 7, 13).
14 Leventhal (1995).
15 Novick (1999: 14-15, emphasis in the text).
16 Flanzbaum (1999: 7).
17 Cf. Gilroy (1993).
18 Thomas (1999).
19 Morrison (1987).
20 Thomas (1999: 207).
21 Rothberg & Weissman (2003).
22 Leonard & Soza, (2001). Asked to comment on the details of the anthology project, editor David Leonard declined to answer questions (e-mail correspondence with the author).
23 Makson (2003).
24 *Ibid.*
25 Hirsch (1997: 22).
26 Klüger (1997: 64).
27 Bukiet (1996a). Further references to this edition will be included in the text. See also Ribbat (1999: 331-341).
28 Pynchon (1973: 3).
29 Horowitz (1997); Patterson (1992).
30 Bukiet (1996b: 22).
31 *Ibid.*, 14.
32 Rohr (2002: 549-551).
33 Spiegelman (1992); see extended discussions in Liss (1998: 52-69) and Hirsch (1997: 25-40).
34 See, however, the case of the 'Holocaust impostor' Binjamin Wilkomirski (Eskin 2002).
35 Begley (1991: 196).

36 On cinematic and televised versions of the Holocaust (before *Schindler's List*) see Insdorf (1989) and Shandler (1999).
37 Chabon (2000: 401).
38 Hartman (1992: 321).
39 The massacre took place on 12 August 1944. More than 560 villagers were shot by SS men fighting partisans. Perpetrators were not prosecuted until the early twenty-first century (see: Levy 2004).
40 McBride (2002: 33). Further references to this edition will be included in the text.
41 Figures according to McBride's website (www.jamesmcbride.com).
42 For historical background see for instance Arnold (1990).
43 Levy (2004).
44 Ozick (1988).
45 Powers (2003); Hustvedt (2003).
46 Foer (2002: 2). Further references to this edition will be included in the text.
47 Rothberg (2000: 9).

Bibliography

Arnold, Thomas St. John: *Buffalo Soldiers. The 92nd Infantry Division and Reinforcement in World War II*, 1942-1945, Manhattan, KS, 1990.
Begley, Louis: *Wartime Lies*, New York, 1996.
Bukiet, Melvin Jules: *After*, New York, 1996a.
–: "Crackpot Realism", *The Review of Contemporary Fiction* 16, no. 1, 1996b, 13-22.
Chabon, Michael: *The Amazing Adventures of Kavalier & Clay*, New York, 2000.
Bernard-Donals, Michael & Richard Gleizer: "Between Witness and Testimony. Survivor Narratives and the Shoah", *College Literature* 27, 2000, 1-20.
Eskin, Blake: *A Life in Pieces. The Making and Unmaking of Binjamin Wilkomirski*, New York, 2002.
Flanzbaum, Hilene: "Introduction". – In H.F. (Ed.): *The Americanization of the Holocaust*, Baltimore, 1999, pp. 1-17.
Furman, Andrew: "Inheriting the Holocaust. Jewish American Fiction and the Double Bind of the Second-Generation Survivor". – In Hilene Flanzbaum (Ed.): *The Americanization of the Holocaust*, Baltimore, 1999, pp. 83-101.
Gerson, Stéphane: "Silent Tales. Survivors as Storytellers", *Response. A Contemporary Jewish Review* 68, 1997, 102-116.
Gilroy, Paul: *The Black Atlantic. Modernity and Double Consciousness*, Cambridge, 1993.
Hartman, Geoffrey: "The Book of the Destruction". – In Saul Friedlander (Ed.): *Probing the Limits of Representation. Nazism and the 'Final Solution'*, Cambridge, 1992, pp. 318-334.
Hirsch, Marianne: *Family Frames. Photography, Narrative, and Postmemory*, Cambridge, 1997.
Horowitz, Sara: *Voicing the Void. Muteness and Memory in Holocaust Fiction*, Albany, 1997.

Howe, Irving: "Writing and the Holocaust". – In Berel Lang (Ed.): *Writing and the Holocaust*, New York, 1988.
Hustvedt, Siri: *What I Loved*, New York, 2003.
Insdorf, Annette: *Indelible Shadows. Film and the Holocaust*, Cambridge, 1989.
Klüger, Ruth: "Was ist wahr?", *Die Zeit*, 12 September 1997, 64.
Lang, Berel: "The Representation of Limits". – In Saul Friedlander (Ed.): *Probing the Limits of Representation. Nazism and the 'Final Solution'*, Cambridge, 1992, pp. 300-317.
Leonard, David & Robert Soza: "PNASA Call for Papers", http://maillist.isu.edu/pipermail/pnasa/2002q4/000020.html (accessed 1 March 2003).
Leventhal, Robert: "Romancing the Holocaust, or Hollywood and Horror. Steven Spielberg's Schindler's List", 1995, http://www.iath.Virginia.edu/holocaust/schinlist.html (accessed 20 July 2004).
Levy, Clifford J.: "Italian Town, Lost in History, Now Fears Memories of Nazis", *New York Times*, 18 April 2004, 4.
Limon, John: *Writing after War. American War Fiction from Realism to Postmodernism*, New York, 1994.
Liss, Andrea: *Trespassing through Shadows. Memory, Photography, and the Holocaust*, Minneapolis, 1998.
Makson, Lisa: "Did Uncle Sam Play the Role of Hitler in Killing Blacks and Indians?", *History News Network*, 2003, http://hnn.us/articles/1231.html (accessed 20 July 2004).
McBride, James: *Miracle at Sant'Anna*, New York, 2002.
Morrison, Toni, *Beloved*, New York, 1987.
Novick, Peter: *The Holocaust in American Life*, Boston, 1999.
Ozick, Cynthia: *The Shawl*, New York, 1988.
Patterson, David: *The Shriek of Silence. A Phenomenology of the Holocaust Novel*, Lexington, 1992.
Powers, Richard: *The Time of Our Singing*, New York, 2003.
Pynchon, Thomas: *Gravity's Rainbow*, New York, 1973.
Ribbat, Christoph: "Shiny Silk Blouses. Luxury and Memory in the Novels of Louis Begley", *ZAA* 46, no. 2, 1998, 243-252.
–: "After Reading After. Melvin Jules Bukiet's Novel and the Limits of Representation". – In Ralph Dietl & Franz Knipping (Eds.): *Begegnung zweier Kontinente. Die Vereinigten Staaten und Europa seit dem Ersten Weltkrieg*, Trier, 1999, pp. 331-341.
Rohr, Susanne: "'Playing Nazis,' 'mirroring evil'. Die Amerikanisierung des Holocausts und neue Formen seiner Repräsentation", *Amerikastudien / American Studies* 47, no. 4, 2002, 539-553.
Rothberg, Michael: *Traumatic Realism. The Demands of Holocaust Representation*, Minneapolis, 2000.
Rothberg, Michael & Gary Weissman: "Call for Papers. The Holocaust as Screen Memory", 30 September 2003, http://mailman.acomp.usf.edu/pipermail/cultstud-1/2003-September/006744.html (accessed 15 January 2004).
Schöpp, Joseph C.: *Ausbruch aus der Mimesis. Der amerikanische Roman im Zeichen der Postmoderne*, München, 1990.
Shandler, Jeffrey: *While America Watches. Televising the Holocaust*, New York, 1999.
Spiegelman, Art: *Maus. A Survivor's Tale, Vol. I & II*, New York, 1992.

Thomas, Lawrence Mordekhai: "Suffering as a Moral Beacon. Blacks and Jews". – In Hilene Flanzbaum (Ed.): *The Americanization of the Holocaust*, Baltimore, 1999, pp. 198-210.

Contributors' Addresses

Dr. Astrid Böger, Amerikanistik, Heinrich-Heine-Universität Düsseldorf, Universitätsstr. 1, D-40225 Düsseldorf.

Dr. Fiona Mills, Department of English, Curry College, 1071 Blue Hill Avenue, Milton, MA 02186 (USA).

Dr. Greta Olson, Englisches Seminar, Albert-Ludwigs-Universität Freiburg, D-70985 Freiburg.

PD Dr. Ralph J. Poole, Department of American Studies, Fatih University, Büyükcekmece, Istanbul 34900 (Turkey).

PD Dr. Christoph Ribbat, Nordamerikastudienprogramm/Englisches Seminar, Universität Bonn, Regina-Pacis-Weg 5, D-53113 Bonn.

Dr. Nicole Schröder, Amerikanistik, Heinrich-Heine-Universität Düsseldorf, Universitätsstr. 1, D-40225 Düsseldorf.

PD Dr. Merle Tönnies, Englisches Seminar, Ruhr-Universität Bochum, D-44780 Bochum.

Dr. Claus-Ulrich Viol, Englisches Seminar, Ruhr-Universität Bochum, D-44780 Bochum.